KU-709-783

THE PARADOX
OF DEBT

THE PARADOX OF DEBT

OF DEBT

A New Path to Prosperity
Without Crisis

RICHARD VAGUE

FORUM

FORUM

First published in Great Britain by Forum, an imprint of Swift Press 2023

Copyright © Richard Vague 2023

The right of Richard Vague to be identified as the Author of this Work has been asserted in accordance with the Copyright, Designs and Patents Act 1988.

Typesetting and text design by Tetragon, London
Printed and bound in Great Britain by CPI Group (UK) Ltd, Croydon, CRO 4YY

A CIP catalogue record for this book is available from the British Library

ISBN: 9781800752184
eISBN: 9781800752191

MIX
Paper | Supporting
responsible forestry
FSC
www.fsc.org
FSC® C171272

CONTENTS

List of Figures

Essentially, all models are wrong, but some are useful.

GEORGE E. P. BOX AND NORMAN R. DRAPER, 1987

INTRODUCTION

In 2020, during the darkest hours of the global coronavirus pandemic, the US government spent $3 trillion to help rescue the country's – and, to some extent, the world's – economy. This infusion of cash increased US government debt and thus reduced US government wealth by almost the entirety of that frighteningly large amount – the largest drop in US government wealth since the nation's founding. Surely something this unfavorable to the government's 'balance sheet' would have broad, adverse financial consequences.

So what happened to household wealth during that same year? It rose. And it improved by not just the $3 trillion injected into the economy by the government but by a whopping $14.5 trillion, the largest recorded increase in household wealth in history. As a whole, the wealth of the country – its households, businesses, and the government added together – increased by $11 trillion, so this improvement in wealth was contained largely to households.

How and why did such an extraordinary increase occur?

To understand this paradox, we need to seek answers to some of the most fundamental questions in economics: What is money? What is debt? What brings about increases in wealth? Often the most basic questions can be the most challenging to answer. They appear deceptively simple but they are complex and vitally important.

To address these questions, in this book I share a new approach to analyzing US economic data. I then set this data in the context of total global money and debt, comparing the US to the six other largest economies in the world: the UK, China, France, Germany, India, and Japan. This provides crucial insights into how the US economy operates while also offering a generalized model of how most economies work, even as some details vary from country to country. In so doing, we learn not only what precipitated the increase in household wealth in 2020 but also build a much deeper understanding of global economic trends and their policy implications.

THE STATE OF DEBT TODAY

Even the casual observer is likely to be aware that debt has grown rapidly in the US and other major, developed countries over the past half century. This is true of both government debt, which has been closely studied by a broad range of economists and policymakers, and private sector debt, which has been analyzed to a lesser degree but is integral to the growth and health of an economy. Private sector debt includes everything from secured real estate debt, such as home mortgages and commercial real estate loans, to personal debt such as credit card balances, student loans, and healthcare expenses being paid off over time.

Nor is the trend of debt growth unique to the US. From 2001 to 2021, when global gross domestic product (GDP) more than doubled, global debt tripled, to $230 trillion. Of that total, more than 60 percent – $145 trillion – was private sector debt, while $85 trillion was government debt.

In fact, over the past fifty years, the quantity of total debt as a percentage of GDP has grown substantially in every one of the world's seven largest economies. Together, these seven countries represent 62 percent, or nearly two thirds, of global GDP and 75 percent of global debt. For convenience, I refer to them as the Big 7.

Figure 0.1 shows the ratio of total debt to GDP for the Big 7 from 1970 to 2021. GDP is national income and spending, so the ratio of debt to GDP is, in effect, the ratio of a country's debt to its income. Just as a high ratio of debt to income would be concerning to a household, a high ratio of debt to GDP, especially of private sector debt to GDP, is concerning for an economy. The striking feature of the past fifty years is the inexorable rise in debt in relation to the GDP of all of the Big 7 economies.

Global debt is concentrated in just two countries: the US and China. The private sector portion of that debt is largely comprised of real estate debt. Figure 0.2 shows the relative amounts of total debt among the Big 7, along with the relative types of debt – that is, government debt as compared to the key private sector categories of business and household debt.[1]

FIGURE 0.1. Total debt of the Big 7 economies, 1970–2021

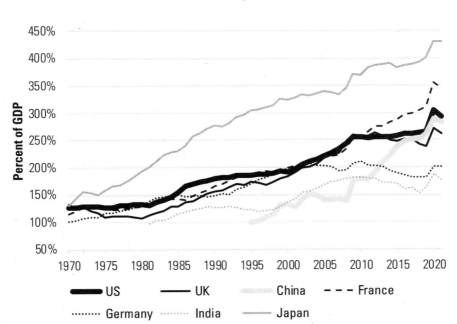

FIGURE 0.2. Total debt by country and by type, 2021, in billions of US dollars

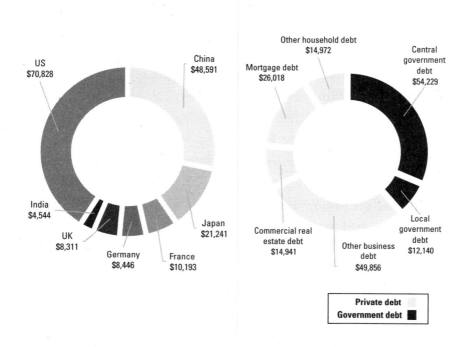

These economic trends are clearly significant, but most economists – and the most prominent books explaining economics – pay
little attention to total debt. Politicians and the financial media also
give total debt short shrift. Either the role of debt in the economy is
set to the side in favor of focusing on spending and growth, or the discussion of debt is directed more narrowly on government debt alone,
ignoring both the size and the weight of private sector debt. Yet there
is far more private debt than government debt, and so private debt
should be of much greater economic concern. Studying government
debt without understanding private debt is like studying the heart
without understanding the circulatory system: it is helpful for fixing
problems with the heart, but if there are wider problems of circulation,
it will not heal the patient, or help them to survive.

A RECKONING FOR DEBT

In this book, I look at the causes and consequences of increases in total debt – public debt integrated and analyzed in tandem with private debt – and likewise combine the study of liabilities with the study of assets, which are largely comprised of debt, both what is owing and what is owed. This involves applying basic financial and business accounting rules to the Big 7 economies. While such an approach is uncommon in the field of economics, it yields powerful insights into the complex interactions underlying an economy.

In the business world, debt numbers are important, but they are only one set of numbers in a company's *statement of condition*, a financial report that is usually, and more casually, referred to as the 'balance sheet'.[2] The statement of condition compiles the business's assets and liabilities to show net worth or wealth; to gain a full picture of financial standing, assets and debt must be weighed against each other. In this context it is perhaps not surprising that money and debt have grown at a stratospheric pace in recent decades, with the global money supply of $16 trillion in 2001 rising to $82 trillion in 2021. Wealth has generally grown faster than both money and debt over the same period.

The balance sheet is accompanied by an equally important financial report called the *income statement*, which records the income and expenses of the business for a given time period. Income statements and balance sheets are typically published at least annually and are connected, given that increased net income adds to wealth.

I have taken economic data[3] for the US in the form of income statements and balance sheets and analyzed them for the US economy as a whole and for each of its major subsets or 'macrosectors' – namely, households, non-financial businesses, financial institutions, governments, and that sector of the economy that represents financial transactions with the 'rest of the world', or ROW.

The economic statistics of a country are, in essence, simply all the financial information of the country's individuals, businesses, and institutions added together. Since those entities manage their records, formally or informally, as income statements and balance sheets, it follows that considering these number in the aggregate is an appropriate and straightforward way to analyze the economic status of countries and the world as a whole. Some of the data we seek is easy to obtain and other data not so much, partly due to more limited interest in documenting phenomena related to private sector debt. Nevertheless, I'm grateful for the data that is available. It is due to the considerable efforts of the US Federal Reserve Bank, the World Bank, the Organisation for Economic Cooperation and Development (OECD), the Bank of International Settlements (BIS), and others that my colleagues and I have been able to undertake the analysis in this book, which would have been painstaking if not impossible a generation ago.

As we take this unique economic journey together, it will become clear that debt, especially private debt, represents an overlooked and misunderstood but powerful economic force – so much so that the methods and analysis in this book might be considered the debut of a new discipline, *debt economics*, that could help us to better manage economies in the future. As we as a society come to better understand debt, it will become possible to more accurately forecast economic trends, predict financial crises, shape policy decisions, and understand how national wealth grows, and thus how to address inequality.

A NEW UNDERSTANDING OF DEBT

When you set aside the specialized tools of economists and instead use the conventional and familiar methods of financial analysts and accountants, several things come into view:

- The ratio of debt to income in economies almost always rises, with profound consequences, both good and bad.
- Money is itself created by debt.
- New money, and therefore new debt, is required for economic growth.
- Rising total debt brings an increase in household and national wealth or capital. Most wealth is only possible if other people or entities have debt. As wealth grows, so too must debt.
- At the same time, debt growth brings greater inequality, in part because middle- to lower-income households carry a disproportionate relative share of household debt burden. In fact, in economic systems based on debt – which is the world as it operates now – rising inequality is inevitable, absent some significant countervailing change such as a major change in a nation's tax policy.
- A current account and trade deficit contributes to private sector debt burdens.
- The overall increase in debt, especially private debt, eventually slows economic growth and can bring economic calamity.

While economists often assume a tendency towards a natural point of equilibrium for economies, the lens of debt economics shows us that there is no stasis, no natural level of equilibrium, for debt, money, or wealth. Our system of money, debt, and wealth requires and provokes constant change. This has implications for how we devise monetary and economic policies.

For example, how do we deal with the dark side of debt, the destruction that debt can bring? The 1990s financial crisis in Japan and the Global Financial Crisis of 2008 are prime cases; these crises were the product of long-term debt cycles. Typically, these cycles make a permanent mark on an economy, with each cycle lifting an economy to a higher plateau of total debt – creating, in effect, a *debt staircase*. To better understand the aggregate effect of such debt staircases, I review four long-term debt cycles in US history and the lessons that can be drawn from them.

Given the inevitability of rising levels of debt, I examine why the conventionally cited strategies for deleveraging usually do not succeed. This underscores the need for new approaches to deleveraging and the development of debt forgiveness and restructuring strategies under the umbrella term of *debt jubilees*. Surely debt growth does have a limit, and we must create a set of tools to ensure that we do not reach it.

With a view on the creative and destructive aspects of debt informed by income statements and balance sheets, we can decisively consider policy ideas that constructively address the dynamics of debt economics. I discuss ways that we can monitor debt growth to prevent excess or, where prevention fails, remediate excessive debt that has accumulated. I review how we might overcome growing trade deficits, phenomena which create higher private sector debt burdens, and design debt jubilee programs that are both productive and fair. Together such strategies could mitigate rising inequality, which is integrally linked to rising levels of total debt, as well as to strategies that could boost the incomes and net worth of the average working family.

In this policy discussion I also look at strategies that could help to alleviate or prevent high levels of inflation, which was a great concern in many Big 7 economies in 2022, and will likely continue to be a pressing problem as economies continue to recover from the pandemic. Because high oil and natural gas prices have often been the source of high inflation, and because households often rely on debt to cope with this inflation, I ask if there is a way to reduce, if not end, fossil fuel dependence.

Finally, I consider whether economic growth is possible without overreliance on debt growth. While economies cannot function without debt, its overuse can bring harm and disaster. The ratio of debt to income almost always rises, with the only exceptions coming from a small number of economically painful, calamity-induced contractions. These disasters interrupt, but do not stop, the upwards march of debt. The inexorable march of debt may well be the most important economic fact of our lifetime.

Debt is a paradox. It creates and destroys. Even short of those extremes, it distorts, as we'll often see in the pages of this book. The goal of debt economics is to discover new and better ways of employing and controlling debt and its consequences.

1

WHY DEBT GROWS

In essence, all growth in GDP stems from growth in debt. Or, more accurately, almost all growth in GDP comes from the creation of new money, and almost all new money is created by debt – which is why GDP growth comes from growth in debt.

HOW WEALTH IS CREATED

In every country, most individuals and businesses persistently attempt to grow their incomes and wealth. If enough of them succeed, more money is spent and economic growth – an increase in GDP – occurs. National GDP figures are calculated by adding together several specific spending totals. These include:

- personal consumption spending (labeled C by economists), such as your supermarket shopping or your dinner out at a restaurant;
- fixed investment spending (I), such as a business building a new headquarters or factory;
- government spending (G), such as the army buying uniforms for personnel; and

- net exports (X – M), the spending of foreign people or entities on a country's goods and services (X) – which count as an increase in GDP – minus imports (M), the spending of a country's people or entities on foreign goods and services.

The formula for GDP, then, is:

$$C + I + G + (X - M)$$

Critically, other types of spending are *not* counted towards GDP. A major category of 'non-GDP' spending is the purchase of existing assets, such as homes or businesses. If, for example, you buy a house that is ten years old, that purchase does not get added to GDP, because the value of the house was added to GDP back when the house was originally built.

Increasing any of the spending in the formula for GDP increases GDP, regardless of whether the spending in question brings more economic productivity or efficiency. For example, an increase in spending on computer microchips is an addition to GDP, even if those new chips are no faster than the old ones. Of course, if the new chips are faster, it may mean that you get more wonderful features from a new computer with them – which may motivate you to buy a new computer sooner, and that spending would be added to GDP. But it is important to keep in mind that increased nominal GDP depends simply on more spending and has nothing to do with the quality or increased efficiency of the things you buy.

While in theory a population could at some point decide en masse to stop trying to grow their businesses and their wealth and be content with their status quo financial position (and proponents of a nascent 'no growth' movement argue for exactly that), no such country exists among the forty-seven largest economies in the world, which together constitute 91 percent of global GDP. Economies almost always grow. As it stands, if over a certain period of time, economic growth fails to occur or, worse, if GDP contracts, then widespread harm or discontent typically follows. A recession is one of the surest predictors of economic duress for a country's citizens and residents, as well as trouble for its incumbent government.

But here's the key point: almost all the spending in that C + I + G + (X – M) formula is dependent on the creation of new money. And the creation of new money is dependent on new debt.

MONEY IS CREATED BY DEBT

We can best see why this is so – and illustrate why money, and thus new debt, is required for growth – if we imagine an economy that has only ten people in it. Let's call it LoanLand. One person in LoanLand has a food store, another a bookstore, another apartments, and so forth. Despite this, no one starts with any savings or net worth. Precisely because this model begins with all citizens at a net worth of zero and no savings, it affords us a clear view of how money is created.

Now, each of the citizens of LoanLand spends and also makes $50,000 each year, which means the GDP of the total economy is $500,000. Now imagine that one of those people, Ruth, wants to spend more on food. She could do this by spending exactly that amount less on something else, for example, on books. In that case, LoanLand's GDP would remain at $500,000. If Ruth wants to spend more on food without having to spend less on books, she has to find *new* money somewhere. Since she has no savings, she can get that new money only by borrowing.

Let's say Ruth borrows $5,000 from a bank. Because Ruth borrowed the money for her extra food, she does not need to reduce her spending in some other area. This debt would prompt and encourage the production of additional food without a commensurate reduction in the production of books. The economy would have both more money and more production. GDP has increased to $505,000. An increase in debt supplies extra money that grows the economy. It's that simple.

I call this LoanLand model an *incremental transaction model*. In mathematics, 'incremental' denotes a small positive or negative change, and here it means that we build a model of a small economy, one transaction at a time. The value of the incremental transaction model is that if a transaction cannot happen a certain way in the incremental model, then it cannot happen that way in the economy as a whole; if a transaction can happen a certain way in the incremental model, then it's possible it can play out the same way in the economy as a whole. Only by understanding the changes and consequences of a single transaction of a given type can we begin to understand the changes and consequences of millions of transactions across an entire economy.[4]

It's worth noting that Ruth does not have to do the borrowing personally. It might be that she gets paid by a customer, an employer, or perhaps the LoanLand government, so that she makes $55,000 this year. But that extra earning could only happen if someone, or some entity, somewhere, had borrowed to inject the new money into the economy. (More on this later.) The bottom line is that borrowing leads to growth in GDP. More specifically, borrowing *for spending* leads to growth.

Why not circumvent borrowing altogether and simply put the extra money in Ruth's deposit account and let her spend that instead of borrowing? I could use my prerogative as arbiter of LoanLand to provide her with funds, leaving aside the question of how she got those funds. If I did, it would indeed be possible for GDP to rise without the need for a loan (though it would of course raise the question of where that deposit came from). However, unless I'm made of money, such a deposit of funds would only allow growth in the extra amount that Ruth spends. To grow the economy beyond that would require Ruth or another of LoanLand's citizens to take on debt.

In fact, looking at US data over the last several decades, there has never been enough money in total deposit accounts to fund but a few months of growth. If growth came from existing deposits, we would see overall deposits staying level – with money simply changing hands – and no growth in GDP from new borrowing for spending. Instead, both deposits and loans have grown markedly in the US.

We'll visit LoanLand again later in this chapter, but the discussion of its economy thus far makes a fundamental point: by definition, GDP can only grow if more money is spent (in one of the ways that counts towards GDP). The total supply of money therefore imposes a constraint on GDP. If more money is not created, not much if any increased spending can occur.

HOW WE 'MAKE' MONEY

Money is generally defined as a medium of economic exchange. In this book, I define 'money' more technically and specifically, using the approach taken by the US Federal Reserve Bank, in particular, the Federal Reserve's money supply measure called M2. M2 includes bank deposits, money market funds, and currency (those bills you have in your pocket). As of December 2021, M2 in the US totaled $21.5 trillion, comprised of $18.4 trillion in bank deposits, $1 trillion in money market funds, and $2.1 trillion in currency. In other words, the vast majority of what the Fed calls 'money' is bank deposit accounts (see Figure 1.1). For that reason, I use the terms 'money' and 'deposits' essentially interchangeably for the purposes of the analysis in this book.

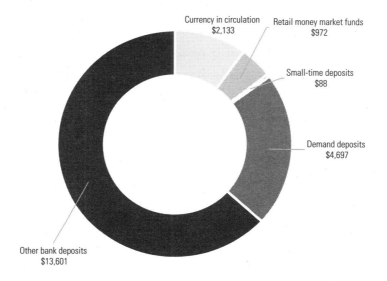

FIGURE 1.1. Components of M2 in the US, 2021

Total M2 $21,491
(billions of US dollars)

Currency in circulation
$2,133

Retail money market funds
$972

Small-time deposits
$88

Demand deposits
$4,697

Other bank deposits
$13,601

Money is not a perishable thing. It does not disappear once you spend it. Instead, it simply belongs to someone else. It stays in the system once it is created, and gets re-spent over time, sustaining GDP as that happens. It is a quantifiable and fixed amount unless augmented by the creation of money (a process I'll describe shortly).

In 1972, when US GDP was $1.3 trillion, the money supply was only $800 billion. Since then, GDP has increased by $21.8 trillion to $23.1 trillion, while M2 has increased by $20.8 trillion to $21.5 trillion. The money supply has had to grow to keep the wheels of commerce turning and enable GDP to grow. If the money supply does not grow, then nor does the economy, which would in fact grind to a halt.

It is *bank lending* – a bank extending a loan to a borrower like LoanLand's Ruth – that has been the predominant way to create a meaningful amount of money.

Suppose a bank makes a $100,000 loan. It does not get that money by nabbing someone else's deposits and moving them over to the new borrower's account, nor does it go down to the vault with a sack and gather up bills to place in the borrower's account. It creates the deposit with a computer entry that adds new money into the borrower's account.

Once this entry, as a function of the loan, is made, the new money shows up as an asset on the borrower's balance sheet – namely, the new money in the borrower's deposit account. As a result, the borrower has also assumed a new liability, the obligation to repay the loan. The assets and liabilities of the borrower therefore both go up by $100,000 while the borrower's net worth remains the same.

Corresponding changes occur on the bank's balance sheet. For the bank, the borrower's loan is an asset, while the additional money in the borrower's checking account is a liability (because if the borrower writes a check on the account, or goes to the bank and requests part or all of those funds, the bank is obligated to provide the money). The bank's assets and liabilities also each increase by $100,000, and so its net worth similarly remains constant.

In Figure 1.2, I show this with the balance sheets for a hypothetical bank loan. I have started both the bank, Bank X, and the borrower, John Doe, at zero, as I did in my LoanLand exercise, to make the balance sheet changes clearer.

Because the money supply of the entire US is simply the sum of all the individual deposits and currency that count as M2, the increase in John Doe's account increases the US money supply by $100,000. That in itself does not change US GDP. However, if John goes out and buys a new car with that $100,000, the additional money created by Bank X's loan ends up in the account of that car dealer. In this case John's purchase of a new car is a form of new spending that increases GDP. Similarly, if a company were the borrower and received a loan to retool a factory, then the loan would create new money and then the company would increase GDP by spending it on that retooling.

FIGURE 1.2. Sample bank loan deposit creation

BEFORE THE LOAN IS MADE ...				
JOHN DOE			**BANK X**	
Assets	**Liabilities**	**Assets**		**Liabilities**
Deposit account $0	$0	Loans	$0	$0
	Net worth $0			**Net worth** $0

AFTER THE LOAN IS MADE ...				
JOHN DOE			**BANK X**	
Assets	**Liabilities**	**Assets**		**Liabilities**
Deposit account $100,000	Loan $100,000	Loan to John Doe $100,000		John Doe deposit account $100,000
	Net Worth $0			**Net Worth** $0

Of course, loans usually must be repaid. If bank debt is repaid in aggregate, then the money supply decreases – the exact reverse of what we see in Figure 1.2, when a loan is made. In the example of Bank X and John Doe, if John paid off his loan in full, his assets and liabilities would both immediately go down by $100,000, as would the bank's assets and liabilities, and the money supply would decline by that same $100,000. This is what occurred, in a monumental, collective, and destructive fashion, from 1930 to 1933, when depositors withdrew their funds from banks and banks forced borrowers to repay their loans early. The sudden decline in money supply and borrowing were among the main causes of the wrenching contraction in GDP during the Great Depression.[5]

As noted earlier in our example of LoanLand, not all borrowing adds to GDP. If a company uses its loan to buy an already existing asset, for example, a fleet of used cars, then the spending enabled by Bank X's loan will create new money but it will not directly increase GDP.

To examine this more closely, we need to ensure that we divide all borrowing into two main categories – the borrowing for both spending and the purchase of newly created assets that contribute to GDP versus the borrowing for the purchase of existing assets. Borrowing for such things as food, a vacation, or a newly built house falls into the former category – we'll call this *Type 1 debt* – and borrowing to purchase an existing house, shares in a company, or a business falls into the latter category – we'll call this *Type 2 debt*.

This is an imprecise exercise with assumptions regarding, for example, the amount of mortgage debt associated with new versus existing homes, the amount of automobile debt associated with new versus existing cars, and what portion of unsecured household debt such as credit card debt might have been used to purchase assets. This is further compounded by the imprecision inherent in the available macroeconomic data, and any timing lag between the moment of borrowing and the moment of spending. It's even more difficult to divide Type 1 and Type 2 debt when analyzing the economy of countries with less accessible data than the US. Unfortunately, we have to tolerate the timing issues and make do with estimates.

Even within those limitations, and even though the formula has more dimensions than expressed here, we can get reasonably close. We would expect that growth in Type 1 debt, while not the only factor, would be a primary driver of GDP growth, and therefore that increases in GDP would largely reflect increases in Type 1 debt in both direction and amount. For the US, this correlation can be seen in Figure 1.3, which shows the increase in Type 1 debt compared to the increase in GDP. Figure 1.4 shows the ratio of total Type 1 and Type 2 debt to GDP, illustrating that total Type 1 debt adheres more closely to total GDP through time than total Type 2 debt. More detail and explanation on Figures 1.3 and 1.4 is in Appendix D, and note Type 2 debt can add to GDP indirectly.[6]

FIGURE 1.3. GDP and Type 1 debt growth, US, 1984–2021

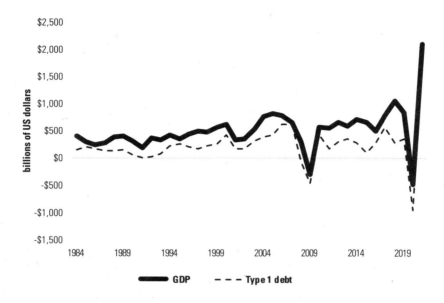

FIGURE 1.4. Type 1 and Type 2 outstanding debt, US, 2000–2021

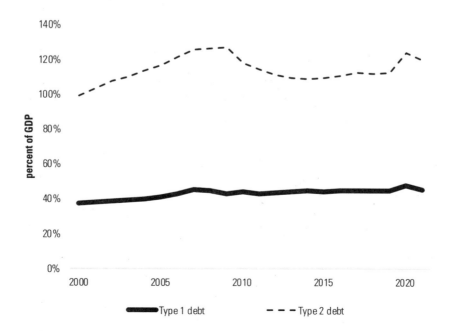

As a practical example, consider a series of linkages between Type 1 debt and GDP. Debt would typically be required to finance the construction of a new mill to produce steel for framing new buildings, and then more debt for a widget manufacturing company to buy the steel framing from the mill in order to build a new factory to make widgets, and then more debt for the widget company to buy the raw material for making the widgets themselves, and then even more debt for a purchaser to buy the finished widgets to use in some process in their business. Increasing debt is fundamental to economic growth. In all of these cases, there will of course be timing differences between when funds are borrowed and when they are spent, but all of the borrowing is *for spending*.

Further, even in an imaginary static economy aspiring to zero growth, debt would remain pervasive because there is almost always a gap between when a product is made and when it is paid for; debt forges a bridge over that gap. Debt is what allows grocers to keep their shelves stocked and manufacturers, like the widget company, to stay supplied with raw materials.

INSIGHTS ABOUT QUANTITATIVE EASING

In addition to bank lending, there is one other major way that money is created: when, in the US example, the Federal Reserve engages in what is called an *open market operation* (OMO). In these operations the Fed buys debt, primarily in the form of US Treasury securities or mortgage securities, from the private sector. When it buys debt from a non-bank seller, whether an institution or a person, the funds the Fed uses to buy that debt become new deposits in the seller's current checking account.[7] Those new deposits are new money, and thus these open market operations increase the money supply.

OMOs are often done to support the policy goal of lowering interest rates. The term *quantitative easing* (QE) describes a type of

OMO first used on a large scale when interest rates were already approaching zero.

The practice is often pejoratively characterized as 'printing money'. The phrase, although popular, is a great misnomer, as the US government last engaged in the actual printing of money of any consequence during the Civil War. It is more accurate to say that the current practice of OMOs is instead an exchange of like for like value in an operation where the Treasury security that the Fed purchases is expected to be sold again – which is in effect a loan.

We've seen that increases in the money supply are often associated with increased economic growth. But is that the case for money created by an OMO? Many economists and political commentators say it is, especially given that lower interest rates are often thought to engender increased borrowing. But there is no compelling evidence for this hypothesis, and therefore OMOs have a limited role in the Type 1 debt growth and GDP growth which concerns us here.

Some of the evidence for a limited role comes from the US and Japan, where money supply increased dramatically in the years following the Global Financial Crisis of 2008. From 2008 until 2018, both Federal Reserve and Bank of Japan assets grew fivefold, but these increases brought little or no boost to spending or lending in the economy. Certainly, lower interest rates can encourage additional borrowing, and if OMOs are part of an overall strategy to do that, then it might have a positive effect. In these two cases, however, interest rates reached zero, and we did not see that result.

In light of this history, it is understandable that some have concluded that OMOs do not incentivize much if any spending. It also fits with an incremental model analysis. Say, for example, John Doe owned a $100,000 US Treasury bill and the Fed bought it from him in an OMO by depositing $100,000 in his bank account. John would be unlikely to spend more, because he has essentially the same net income and net worth – and budget – as before the transaction. He is most likely to simply invest it in some other financial asset, so the $100,000 would not be added to GDP.

There is an argument that OMOs increase spending, because they result in more deposits in banks (John Doe's account at Bank X now has $100,000 more in it), and this incentivizes the banks to lend more, which creates more spending. As a career banker, my observation is that banks are always trying to grow loans and can typically raise funding to do so. More deposits or reserves do not generally create that incentive.

Then why bother with OMOs at all? In fact, OMOs have a crucially important purpose: when debt markets freeze up because of potential catastrophe, threatening to further damage commerce, the Fed can step in with OMOs to prop up the markets, serving as the buyer or lender of last resort, for example, when the Fed bought mortgage securities that no one else wanted in the 2008 financial crisis. That move helped to prevent the failure of an enormous number of institutions. Indeed, this role of buyer or lender of last resort was a key impetus for the creation of the Fed in 1913. OMOs also can help in the management of interest rates.

Whatever the case, over time, the vast majority of new money has been created through bank lending. Over a span of thirty-five years – from 1972, the earliest year for which we have adequate records, to 2007 – more than 90 percent of all money in the US was created by bank loans. It has only been over the last two decades, as the Fed and the US government carried out huge, multitrillion-dollar interventions in response to two extraordinary crises – first the 2008 financial crisis and then the pandemic – that the fraction of money created by bank lending fell, with loans accounting for 35 percent and OMOs for most of the rest. It is possible that, as things return to a semblance of normality post-pandemic, banks may once again create most new money. However, given the high levels of private sector debt in the US today, this may prove elusive.

We can see this same story even more dramatically in the experience of Japan. In the decades leading up to and including the 1980s, most money created in Japan was created through bank lending. Then the 'Lost Decade' arrived in 1991, ushering in a period of economic slowdown and stagnation. From 1997 to 2021, almost all new deposits in Japan have been created by OMOs implemented by the country's central bank. Immediately post-pandemic, as economies around the world began to heat up, bank lending has only created about 30 percent of new deposits in the US. As an economy's private sector gets more heavily laden with debt, it becomes more reliant on central bank activity to create new money.

Incidentally, growth in government debt generally does increase some spending, which in turn increases GDP, but when that debt is sold to households or non-bank entities, it does not increase the money supply. That's because when people or non-bank entities buy these bonds, they use deposits to pay for them, thus shrinking the amount of deposits in circulation.[8] The government then spends the money it has borrowed – usually very quickly – and that money is deposited into bank accounts, which adds deposits back to M2. Thus, the effect of government borrowing on money supply is effectively zero. This is why it's such a great misnomer to refer to the government taking on more debt as 'printing money': government spending creates no net new money.[9] It only increases the money supply when the government debt is bought by a bank, or the Fed.

Figure 1.5 shows how money creation worked during three years of the 1980s. I chose this decade because it is representative of periods pre-dating the Fed's colossal interventions, a time when almost all money was being created by bank loans.[10] At the end of 1983, there were $2.5 trillion in deposits. Banks made $500 billion in loans over the next two years, and there was minimal money creation or other activity by the Fed. Sure enough, deposits totaled $3.0 trillion at the end of 1985. Simple arithmetic.

FIGURE 1.5. Deposit growth, US, 1983–1985

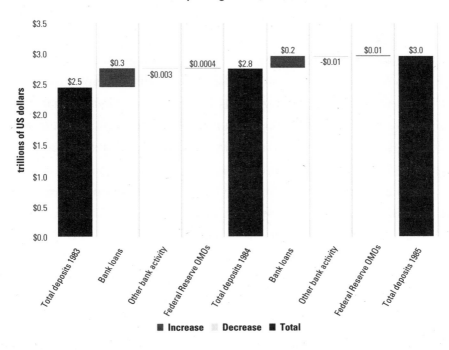

This is the process by which money is created and grows whether inflation is high, low, or somewhere in between. It comes down to the accounting entries for debt and their corresponding deposits, and the other components of M2. *Increased bank loans equals new money supply.*

The pivotal role played by bank debt in money creation accounts for much of the government attention paid to banks in the past decades. No private sector lender other than a depository institution has this capacity to create money. It is an extraordinary power and privilege, and one that (rightly) invites significant regulation.

MORE DEBT THAN GDP

Debt growth in line with or greater than GDP growth is not a coincidence. Because Type 1 debt is interlocked with GDP growth, and

Type 2 debt, which is a large component of total lending, is added on top of Type 1 debt, it follows that, over time, in dollars, total debt will typically grow faster than GDP. This is not the result of specific policies or political ideologies. Nor is it something that might be avoided in an economy where participants aspire to grow their business or their wealth. Instead, debt growing faster than GDP is a feature of our economic system. In the absence of a drastic reconfiguration of economic life, debt growth is essentially perpetual. But why has debt grown so large over the past few decades?

When you differentiate between Type 1 and Type 2 debt in the US national accounts, you can see that Type 2 debt has significantly and consistently outgrown Type 1 debt. In fact, since 1983, Type 2 debt has grown at 1.5 times the rate of GDP, so that Type 2 debt now contributes over 70 percent of total private sector debt. In contrast, Type 1 debt has grown only slightly faster than overall economic growth. In other words, individuals and businesses are leveraged to the hilt. And as we've seen, since the Second World War, total debt has well more than doubled in ratio to GDP, not only for the US but also for the other Big 7 countries. (In Chapter 7, we'll consider some brief but important exceptions to the rule that total debt always outgrows GDP, but these mainly serve to reinforce the general rule.)

People incur Type 2 debt for two primary reasons. One is simply to have more stuff – a larger house, or maybe a vacation home. A second reason is to purchase an income-producing asset such as a business, rental home, or large block of stocks, to increase their wealth or their personal empire. Businesses incur Type 2 debt largely for the same reasons. The general tendency among asset purchasers is to try to increase the amount of leverage in their assets and thus aim to increase the return on their investments, because the more debt they employ, the less capital has to be used. Thus, by definition, their return on the capital is enhanced. This leveraging fuels the overall upwards trendline of total debt.

Another way to think about the growing ratio of Type 2 debt to GDP is that more assets are being purchased and carried by the same relative level of private sector income. This is generally referred to as higher leverage. Just as it would for an individual or business, for a country as a whole, being more highly leveraged has a paradoxical effect: it increases the potential upside from asset appreciation while creating greater risk and economic vulnerability – lower resiliency – because the same income is obligated to service more debt. And, as businesses and individuals get more leveraged, more income is diverted from spending and investing to the payment of interest and principal on debt. This is why greater leverage can ultimately lead to slower growth.

On the household side, at least, this would all be well and good if it were simply a matter of converting apartment renters into home-owners. But in 1980, the homeownership rate was 66 percent and the household mortgage debt to GDP ratio was 32 percent; in 2021, the homeownership rate was 66 percent while household mortgage debt stood at 51 percent of GDP. That's a lot of extra debt for no relative increase in homeownership, which means that households are simply much more leveraged today.

HOW WE CREATE WEALTH

Let's now return to LoanLand, where we can pull these ideas together in a hypothetical economy and see how household wealth is created.

The ten citizens of LoanLand have ten companies. To recall, no one starts with any savings and each person – via their company – makes $50,000 per year, that is, the owner of each company pays themselves a salary equal to the full earnings of their company, or $50,000 annually. Each of the ten people also spends all of the $50,000 they make, so the economy's GDP is $500,000.

To keep the model even simpler, we'll stipulate that the government is run by volunteer citizens, so it has no expenses or need for taxes. Other than real estate and stocks, all the items purchased by citizens of LoanLand are services or perishable items. The government alone owns land. The only cost in each of these companies is the owner's labor. No interest is charged on loans and no interest is paid on deposits. As was the case with our earlier LoanLand scenario, precisely because this model begins with all citizens at a net worth of zero, it will provide us with a clear view of economic activity – here, the creation of wealth.

After LoanLander Ruth borrows $5,000 from the local bank to purchase more food, she spends the extra $5,000 at Mary's Food Company. As Ruth spends her $55,000 over the course of the year, LoanLand's GDP rises to $505,000. With an extra $5,000 of money supply in the economy, it is likely that GDP would remain at least $505,000 in subsequent years as well. The economy would continue to have both more money and more production.

Ruth's loan has other effects. After she receives the loan, she has $5,000 in her bank account, an asset, but she also now owes $5,000 to the bank, a liability. This means her net worth is still zero. After Ruth spends the $5,000 at Mary's Food Company, however, she no longer has $5,000 in her bank account. Now she has a liability to the bank but no corresponding asset, and her net worth is now *negative* $5,000. On the other hand, Mary now has $5,000 in her bank account but no corresponding liability. Her net worth has grown to $5,000. The loan has effectively transferred $5,000 from Ruth's net worth to Mary's net worth, making one negative and the other positive, with the net increase *still* zero, because they offset each other. GDP grows to $505,000 while the net worth of the households as well as the entire economy of LoanLand continue to be zero.

Suppose that the government pays Ruth $5,000 for consulting services on a project. Because no one pays taxes in LoanLand, the

government has to raise the funds to pay Ruth. It does this by selling bonds to an individual or business in the private sector, who will
need to take out a loan from a bank to buy the bonds. As usual, Ruth
spends the money on food at Mary's Food Company, and this again
serves to increase GDP to $505,000, but now both the government
and the private sector investor have $5,000 in debt. When a govern-
ment borrows for debt, twice as much new debt must be created to
attain the same growth in GDP, and, in this particular example, part
of that is Type 2 debt.

The complexion of the nation's wealth also changes. In the case of
LoanLand, after the government sells its bonds and pays Ruth, and
Ruth spends her money at Mary's company, Mary's net worth rises
to $5,000, Ruth's net worth is zero, and the government has debt of
$5,000. The net worth of the entire economy is still zero, but the net
worth of households is not zero – it is positive $5,000; Mary is richer
and no other resident is poorer. The economy as a whole has not
gained wealth, but Mary sure has. Thus, a government taking a loss
most often goes hand in hand with an increase in net income and net
worth for the country's household macrosector.

Suppose Ruth receives the $5,000 as a bonus from a non-financial
business and that business funds the bonus by going into debt. Ruth
again spends the money on food at Mary's Food Company, and this
again serves to increase GDP to $505,000. The end result will be
similar, but now it will be the non-financial businesses rather than the
government which will be in debt and thus have a negative net worth.
Under this scenario, household net worth will again rise by $5,000,
corresponding this time to a reduction in net worth in the country's
non-financial business sector.[11]

So, when we consider households, businesses, and the government
together, the debts incurred and the financial assets created – often
measured by the money in the recipient's accounts – generally cancel
each other out, with no aggregate increase in national wealth.

We can add some twists and variations on these basic scenarios. Suppose Ruth gets her additional loan of $5,000 and spends it, increasing GDP, but then the next year pays back the loan in full. When she pays back her debt, she extinguishes her liability to the bank. As a by-product of this laudable decision, she spends $5,000 less than she would have and GDP contracts by $5,000, about 1 percent, that year. As noted earlier, this is what happened at a grand scale at the onset of the Great Depression, when US banks called in loans en masse, and thus spending was curbed en masse, resulting in US GDP contracting by a crushing 45 percent. It illustrates that although a rise in an economy's debt level can increase spending and therefore GDP, there is always the threat that GDP will revert to its prior level if the debt is repaid.

Another variation on the economics plot might be that Ruth prefers not to go through the hassle of getting a loan and paying it back. Instead, she decides to get the money necessary to buy food at Mary's in the most obvious, responsible way: by saving it over the course of one year before spending it in the next, so Ruth spends $5,000 less this year. The result is unfortunately that $5,000 less is spent in the economy, leading to a minor recession, as LoanLand GDP shrinks to $495,000. With everyone's income declining, Ruth's fellow citizens have less to spend at Ruth's own business. If we assume that GDP continues to be distributed equally as income, then Ruth's income will shrink from $50,000 to $49,500. Ruth thought she was saving $5,000 to spend on extra food, but due to the repercussions of her own saving, she ends up saving only $4,500 – $5,000 minus $500.

To be clear, it's good when individuals save, and in a country like the US, with a population of 330 million people, the effect of one person saving is minimal. The important thing is that saving on a mass scale can have unpleasant consequences: if, for example, 100 million people started to save more, then the economy would certainly contract. As a result, in modern economies the ability to save without causing collateral damage to the economy *depends* on an increase in debt-based spending by others elsewhere.

We now look at another set of scenarios. Suppose that rather than buying extra food, Ruth buys a 25 percent stake in Mary's Food Company with her $5,000 loan from the bank.[12] Ruth is down $5,000 in deposits but, in exchange, she owns $5,000 worth of stock. Mary, conversely, gains $5,000 in deposits but has given up $5,000 in stock. Ruth and Mary therefore have the same net worth they began with, namely, zero. The total valuation of Mary's Food Company is currently $20,000.

The prospects for Mary's Food Company appear to brighten and so another LoanLand citizen, Ed, gets interested in buying some shares in the company. Ruth won't sell her shares to Ed for less than $10,000. Ed borrows $10,000 from the bank and buys the stock. Ed's net worth is still zero. He has $10,000 worth of stock but also $10,000 in debt.

Debt created money – two times – to buy stock in Mary's company.

The series of transactions has also created *wealth*. Once she has sold her stock in Mary's company to Ed, Ruth has the stock sale proceeds of $10,000 in her bank account but only $5,000 in debt. Her net worth is now $5,000. Furthermore, Mary still owns 75 per-cent of her company. Originally, when Ruth bought 25 percent of the company for $5,000, Mary's own shares were worth $15,000 (75 percent of $20,000), but Mary's shares are now valued at $30,000. She has therefore gained $15,000 in additional net worth. LoanLand's household net worth has gone up by $20,000: Ruth's net worth is up $5,000, and Mary's is up $15,000, and no household's net worth is down.[13] (If Ruth now spends this $5,000 at Mary's Food Company, as in the earlier scenarios, then GDP increases by that amount as well.)

This example is crucial to understanding economies. It illustrates how gains in asset valuations can increase household net worth. The phenomenon is important, because, as we'll see, much of the increase in household wealth in a number of countries has come from increases in the valuation of stocks and real estate. It also hints at a deeper issue – the debt-supported ease with which LoanLand citizens can buy stock may actually *facilitate* rises in stock prices. That is, debt for asset purchases might be able to nudge the prices of assets upwards, a point we'll revisit in Chapter 3.

Appreciation in real estate prices operates in a way similar to appreciation in stock prices. If Ruth buys land (from the government, in our model) for $5,000 and her land appreciates in value to $10,000, then through a similar flow of transactions and logic, household net worth in LoanLand would rise by $5,000 as a result.[14] Again, if Ruth now sells her land and spends this $5,000 at Laura's Supermarket, then GDP increases by that amount.

In these examples, I have kept to an incremental model for the sake of clarity, but we could readily add complexity by including interest costs, taxes, other costs of goods sold, different configurations of asset ownership, and many other things. And yet our accounting methodology would still be able to handle the resulting scenarios, and the basic lessons we've learned from LoanLand would all remain the same.

THE SPEED OF SPENDING

I have argued that GDP growth almost always requires the creation of money and thus debt growth. However, there is a scenario in which GDP can grow without debt growth – an economy where spending is increasing in velocity, that is, a given deposit is spent more than once in the same year. For example, I can buy something for $10,000 from Joe. He can then take that same $10,000 and buy something from Sue. In this way, the same $10,000 can be involved in $20,000 worth of spending in the economy in a given year, and so some of the growth in GDP occurs without an increase in the actual amount of money.

Historically, however, spending velocity has stayed within a reasonably narrow range – such that dollars typically do not get spent more than between 1.4 and 2.2 times annually. To support the growth of GDP in the US over the past twenty years, dollars would have had to have been spent more than *twenty* times annually. Velocity has not increased at even a small fraction of the amount necessary to explain the extraordinary growth in US GDP; rather, new money had to be created. In part this is true because velocity itself is dependent on debt: if my income is $100,000, then I can't choose to spend $150,000 or $200,000, much less $1 million, unless I borrow to do so.

So, beyond a limited contribution from spending velocity, the observation holds: we need to increase the supply of money to increase GDP.

THE LIMITS OF PRODUCTIVITY AND INNOVATION

Like velocity, *increased productivity* is often cited as a means of economic growth. Productivity is a great thing, but it cannot create growth without debt, because debt is required to capture or monetize the benefit of any increased productivity.

Let's assume that Jack, a farmer and citizen of LoanLand, finds a way to produce twice as much food from the same farm in the same number of hours through a smarter organization of his work processes. He becomes twice as productive.

He goes to sell his surplus food, but now he has a problem. Because there is still only $500,000 to spend in all of LoanLand, there are only two possibilities: The first is that maybe more people will buy Jack's crops, but do so by spending less on other things, in which case the other citizens will make less income, spend less, and total GDP will remain the same – and some other LoanLand companies, products, or services will languish, unsold. The second possibility is that the other citizens will continue to buy the exact same amounts of products and services from their neighbors and not be willing to spend more on food, and so Jack, despite all of his hard work, will still only get paid $50,000 for his crops. If he does not lower his prices, his extra food will go unsold. In each of these two scenarios, total spending for consumption has not increased apace with 'increased productivity', and so changes in LoanLand's economy – if there any – will not register financially as GDP growth.

In despair, or perhaps seized by a charitable impulse, Jack ends up distributing all of his unsold crops to his LoanLand neighbors for free. In this scenario, all of Jack's neighbors are better off, and Jack himself is not worse off. Jack's generosity has made a big difference to the happiness of LoanLand but not a single dollar more was spent. GDP remains the same.

Jack's farming adventure exemplifies a number of counterintuitive points. A major increase in productivity did not lead to any change in *financial* GDP, the amount recorded in a country's currency. In the first scenario, the consequence of Jack's innovation was his enrichment at the expense of his neighbors but no net increase in GDP. In the second scenario, the primary consequence was a lot of rotting food. In the third scenario, Jack benefited his neighbors, but he did so by acting outside of the usual incentives of the market, and his kindness was not recognized in LoanLand income statistics as a contribution to GDP. The surest way for financial GDP to grow as a result of Jack's increased productivity would have been for someone to go into debt to pay for more of the crops he had grown.[15]

As for innovation, it too can catalyze GDP growth – but only with the help of debt. To pay for research and development (R&D) and other expenses to develop and introduce new products, innovators need to gain access to new money or use savings, and, as we saw earlier, if they use savings, they do so by decreasing spending on other things. Then, when new products or services enter the market, customers must either use debt to acquire them or reduce spending on other things. Much of Apple's success came as people borrowed billions of dollars to buy its iPhones, iPads, and MacBooks. For innovation to grow GDP, debt is necessary.

In a sense, enhanced productivity and innovation are simply ways by which private sector entities compete for a bigger share of the GDP growth that is provided through debt growth.

It's worth noting that some measures of productivity can get entangled with debt in a misleading fashion. For example, from 2001 to 2005, 'total factor productivity', as reported by the Federal Reserve, leapt forward, but much of it came from debt-fueled home-building that would result in millions of empty homes and the recession that came as a result of the Global Financial Crisis of 2008. The economy was in a mirage of productivity, on a road to nowhere.

THE ECONOMY AS A WHOLE

We've seen how households get new money for spending. The other domestic macrosectors in an economy use the same tools – borrowing and getting paid for products and services – but they can do a few things that households cannot. Most notably, a business can raise prices to make a profit – as LoanLand farmer Jack might have done with his crops. If a given business in LoanLand raised its prices, its customers would either have to spend less on something else in order to continue to buy those products and services, or pay the higher price through borrowing. In this way, business profits are largely reliant on net new borrowing.

Or, as we saw in the case of Mary's Food Company, a business might get money by issuing stock. However, if consumers are to buy stock without spending less on something else, new money – debt – is once again required.

A government might tax to get new money to spend. But unless the taxpayers spend less on something else to afford these taxes, debt will have to be incurred.

In short, in all of these very different economic contexts, debt plays a fundamental, all but inherent, and inescapable role.

Debt – especially *certain types of debt* – is a precondition for economic growth and for the creation of wealth for households overall. It takes money to grow GDP, and money is created by debt, so syllogistically, it takes debt to grow an economy. At a more conceptual level, however, debt brings income from the future into the present, in essence by providing the borrower with their future projected income or revenue today, in exchange for a time-based contractual obligation to pay for the associated time value and risk. Debt is the monetization of future income, the largest component of which is labor, whether via the debt incurred to pay an individual's current salary, or their earnings – that is, the income the lender counts on to repay a loan extended to an individual.

With these concepts in mind, we can now turn to the income statement and balance sheet of the US economy.

2

OPENING THE BOOKS ON DEBT

The US has a lot of debt. In 2021, the most recent year for which data was available at the time of writing, the country had $70.8 trillion in total debt, adding together private sector debt and government debt. US debt by sector is depicted in Figure 2.1.[16]

FIGURE 2.1. US private and public debt by sector, 2021

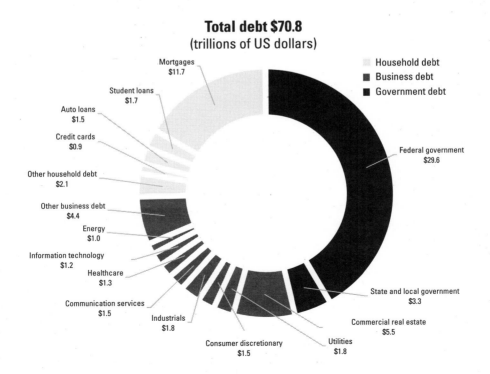

Total debt $70.8
(trillions of US dollars)

Household debt
Business debt
Government debt

Mortgages
$11.7

Student loans
$1.7

Auto loans
$1.5

Credit cards
$0.9

Other household debt
$2.1

Other business debt
$4.4

Energy
$1.0

Information technology
$1.2

Healthcare
$1.3

Communication services
$1.5

Industrials
$1.8

Consumer discretionary
$1.5

Utilities
$1.8

Commercial real estate
$5.5

State and local government
$3.3

Federal government
$29.6

Thousands of books and articles have been written about the causes and consequences of government debt, many brimming with concerns about how such debt will burden future generations. As an example, in its review of fiscal challenges to the US in 2022, the prestigious Peter G. Peterson Foundation argued:

> Federal borrowing competes for funds in the nation's capital markets, thereby raising interest rates and crowding out new investment in business equipment and structures … stifling innovation and slowing the advancement of new breakthroughs that could improve our lives. At some point … [this will] crowd out private investments in capital goods …which would translate to lower productivity and, therefore, lower wages.

Yet, despite abundant attention in the economics literature as well as political discourse, the supposed woes of government deficits are not supported by the data. We have fundamentally misunderstood the role of government debt, and consequentially so. Meanwhile, private sector debt – the more important macroeconomic factor – has largely been ignored.

Both government debt and private debt need to be studied in the context of a country's *balance sheet* and *income statement*. That's a basic principle of this book. By way of analogy, suppose you were to learn that a friend had contracted debts totaling $1 million. You might be mildly worried about her carrying such a large debt – unless, that is, you also knew that she nets $1 million in income each year and had $10 million in deposits and stocks.

In many cases, we can explain the basic principles of a country's macroeconomic statistics, or macrostatistics, by looking at simpler examples that feature just a few individuals, and so it is here. Figure 2.2, for example, shows a personal balance sheet for a proverbial Jane Doe. The first column shows that Jane has a house valued at \$300,000, \$25,000 in stocks, and \$10,000 in her current bank account. However, Jane's total wealth is not \$335,000 because, in addition to these assets, Jane also has liabilities (that is, debts): a mortgage of \$200,000 and credit card debt of \$5,000. If we subtract Jane's total debt of \$205,000 from her assets, we obtain Jane's net worth of \$130,000.

FIGURE 2.2. Jane Doe's balance sheet

	Starting point, year 1	Change in value during year 1	Starting point, year 2
ASSETS			
Home value	\$300,000	\$20,000	\$320,000
Stock value	\$25,000	\$10,000	\$35,000
Current bank account	\$10,000	\$5,000	\$15,000
Total assets	**\$335,000**	**\$35,000**	**\$370,000**
LIABILITIES			
Mortgage	\$200,000	\$0	\$200,000
Credit card debt	\$5,000	\$0	\$5,000
Total liabilities	**\$205,000**	**\$0**	**\$205,000**
FINANCIAL NET WORTH	**-\$170,000**	**\$15,000**	**-\$155,000**
TOTAL NET WORTH	**\$130,000**	**\$35,000**	**\$165,000**

Because net worth is, by definition, assets minus liabilities, it is also true that total assets equal liabilities plus net worth. These direct relationships hold true for all individuals who comprise an economy, or a macrosector of an economy, and they must therefore always be true in the aggregate as well, because a country's macrostatistics are essentially the sum of its businesses, individual households, and other entities.

Let's look at how Jane Doe's wealth might change over time. A year has passed and Jane has received income from a salary and additional sources. She has also spent some, as set out in her household income statement in Figure 2.3.[17]

FIGURE 2.3. Jane Doe's household income statement

HOUSEHOLD INCOME STATEMENT, YEAR 1

INCOME	
Wages or salary	$80,000
Investment income	$5,000
Total income	**$85,000**
EXPENSES	
Housing	$15,000
Utilities	$5,000
Food	$20,000
Transportation	$10,000
Taxes	$20,000
Miscellaneous	$10,000
Total expenses	**$80,000**
NET INCOME	**$5,000**

As we can see, Jane has a salary of $80,000 and investment income from dividends of $5,000. After deducting her expenses of $15,000 for her mortgage payments, $5,000 for utilities bills, $20,000 for food, $10,000 for transportation, $10,000 for miscellaneous things, and $20,000 for taxes, her net income is $5,000. Jane deposits her incoming money into her bank account, which increases her net worth by $5,000. However, she also owns other assets, besides the funds in her account, and it turns out that these have also changed in value. As shown in Figure 2.2, the appraised value of her house increased by $20,000, and the value of her stocks has increased by $10,000, over the course of the year. By adding these to her $5,000 in net income, we can see that her net worth increased by $35,000.

The same logic applies to a country as to an individual. The frightening specter of government debt looks different when you come to understand that an increase in government debt is accompanied, almost in lockstep, by an increase in household net worth.

THE GOVERNMENT'S NUMBERS

The US federal government is different from a household, of course, not least in the scale of its operations and its access to credit, and not all component parts of a country's economy behave in the same ways or are subject to the same constraints. It's therefore reasonable to disaggregate the US economy into a number of macrosectors to gain a deeper understanding of the phenomena of debt. To this end, we have divided the US economy into five macrosectors: households; non-financial businesses; financial institutions; the government, including state and local governments; and the rest of the world (ROW), which is defined as the net of all transactions – especially trade transactions – with foreign households and other foreign entities. These macrosectors allow us to distinguish the contribution to the economy of financial institutions and non-financial businesses. This is important because financial institutions are primarily *lenders* to non-financial businesses and households – that is, because they are the mechanism for creating most private debt, they need to be separately accounted for.

Figure 2.4 shows US income statements broken down by these macrosectors for the years 2019 and 2020, which record the economic transitions which came as a result of the pandemic and the battle to contain the spread of the novel coronavirus. The 'revenue' entry in the income statements corresponds to the 'total income' line in Jane Doe's sample household income statement. The 'expenditure and investment' figures correspond to 'total expenses' in the household statement. Revenue minus expenditure and investment yields 'net income', just as net income in the household income statement is the difference between total income and total expenses. The 'disposable income' entry corresponds to 'total income' less taxes and depreciation. The memo entry 'gross value added' is each sector's contribution to GDP using the output approach.

FIGURE 2.4. US income statement, 2019 and 2020

2019 income by macrosector (trillions of US dollars)	House-hold	Non-financial businesses	Financial institutions	General government	Domestic total	Rest of world	TOTAL
Revenue	$22.38	$10.60	$1.73	$5.91	$40.62	$4.32	$44.95
Expenditure and investment*	$21.51	$10.65	$1.60	$7.28	$41.11	$3.84	$44.95
Memo: Gross value added (GDP)	$6.46	$10.60	$1.73	$2.65	$21.38	$0.00	$21.38
Net disposable income	$15.67	$0.49	$0.19	$1.78	$18.12	$4.32	$22.45
Less: Consumption expenditures*	$14.80	$0.53	$0.06	$3.15	$18.61	$3.84	$22.45
NET INCOME	$0.87	-$0.05	$0.13	-$1.37	-$0.49	$0.49	$0.00
	A		B		C	D	

2020 income by macrosector (trillions of US dollars)	House-hold	Non-financial businesses	Financial institutions	General government	Domestic total	Rest of world	TOTAL
Revenue	$23.38	$10.17	$1.87	$5.98	$41.40	$3.87	$45.28
Expenditure and investment*	$17.11	$9.97	$1.80	$10.10	$42.00	$3.28	$45.28
Memo: Gross value added (GDP)	$6.31	$10.17	$1.87	$2.72	$21.06	$0.00	$21.06
Net disposable income	$16.94	$0.46	$0.12	$0.04	$17.55	$3.87	$21.43
Less: Consumption expenditures*	$14.42	$0.27	$0.03	$3.26	$18.15	$3.28	$21.43
NET INCOME	$2.52	$0.19	$0.09	-$3.21	-$0.59	$0.59	$0.00
	A		B		C	D	

* Includes net capital transfers paid, net fixed capital formation, change in inventory, acquisition of non-produced non-financial assets. Domestic totals include the statistical discrepancy.

Now let's take a wider view. Our hypothetical Jane Doe spent $20,000 on food. If we widen our perspective and contextualize this activity, we realize that each time Jane spent money on food, someone or something else – a supermarket or a restaurant – received the corresponding amount as income. Considering Jane's income statement alone, this $20,000 is an expense, but if we were to combine Jane's income statement with those of all the individuals involved in selling her food, then every expense she incurred would be balanced by an equal and opposite income gained by somebody else. As a result, the effect of Jane's food purchases on the resulting national *net* income statement would be zero.

This illustrates a basic feature of *dual-entry accounting*. As its name implies, dual-entry accounting quite simply involves making two entries. In the world of accounting, when you record income, say the bonus check you received from your company, you also record that money as an expense to your company. You can never make an entry for a liability – your mortgage, for example – without simultaneously making an entry for the corresponding asset – the house you purchased. Everything balances. The invention of dual-entry accounting is widely credited as fundamental to the rise of modern business and the creation of modern economies. Today, dual-entry accounting governs how records are kept for businesses, individuals, and payment systems worldwide.

When studying an entire economy, a key point is that expenses in an income statement are canceled out by corresponding income and thus net to zero only when we include transactions with the ROW. If the net income of the ROW is positive in a country's income statement, that means the ROW is making money at the country's expense. It also suggests that the country has a *current account deficit*, the biggest part of which is normally a trade deficit. If the net income of the ROW is negative in a country's income statement, the country is making money at the expense of other nations. By the rules of dual-entry accounting, the total net income of any given country, when *including* the net income of the ROW, always totals zero.

With these fundamental ideas in place, let's now examine US income statements and balance sheets for 2019 and 2020. This will involve several charts and a few paragraphs of highly detailed description but drilling down in this way will help to convey central concepts for understanding the state of the modern global economy.

In 2019, the total US domestic economy lost $490 billion, or $0.49 trillion (letter C in Figure 2.4). The ROW gained a corresponding $490 billion. In other words, the collective macrosectors of the US economy spent $490 billion more than they earned, which correspondingly implies that the ROW netted $490 billion income in their trade and financing transactions with us. A trade deficit primarily caused this: we imported more German-made BMWs and Chinese-made electronic components, appliances, phones, and other foreign goods than those foreign countries bought in goods and services from the US. The private sector of the US economy had to incur an additional $490 billion in debt largely to fund the purchase of these goods and services. The net income of the entire economy including the ROW equaled zero (letter D in Figure 2.4).

In most countries, the household macrosector has the largest net income. For US households in 2019 that amount was $870 billion (letter A in Figure 2.4). The second largest net income was the $490 billion made by the ROW, which is to the detriment of the domestic macrosectors, because it means less net income for them.

The key year of 2020 brought the largest increase in government spending in US history, and therefore the largest-ever government deficit, also shown in the bottom part of Figure 2.4. The government deficit shows up as a negative value for the government's net income (both letters B in Figure 2.4). A major surge in government spending – primarily spending on pandemic relief programs – increased the government deficit from $1.37 trillion in 2019 to $3.21 trillion in 2020.

As a result, following the principle that income must equal expense, the government's larger net loss, from an accounting perspective, must have been balanced by one or more other macrosectors that saw a corresponding income *gain*. One entity's expense is another entity's income. And in fact, household net income (both letters A) went from $870 billion in 2019 to a whopping $2.52 trillion in 2020.

The unprecedented increase in government spending came hand in hand with an immense raise in income for households.

Indeed, payments to the US private sector, including direct payments to households such as the $1,200 and $1,400 pandemic relief checks that were sent to US citizens and taxpayers, comprised most of the government's expenditures. But even in cases where the government paid a vendor from the US non-financial business sector, a portion of that government spending ended up as that vendor's employee salaries, and thus eventually made its way to the household sector. Government spending results in higher household net income.

Some mainstream economists push back here. Whereas I call the amount of household income in excess of expenses 'net income', they call it 'net saving'. They say that increased government debt is *financed* by the household sector – that is, household 'savings' can be what has caused new government deficit spending and debt. However, government spending during the pandemic was so abrupt and so large it provides us with an ideal context to assess the true causality, which I argue flows in the opposite direction. In the US in 2020, it was not a sudden burst of saving behavior by households that enabled the federal government to spend an additional $4 trillion in two years; instead, it was budgets and other policies enacted by the government that created a flurry of activity – and spending – that landed in household bank accounts.[18]

Naturally, not all of the resulting increase in net income from government spending went to households. Both non-financial businesses and state and local governments improved their overall net income position from 2019 to 2020, albeit by (relatively) small amounts, as seen in Figure 2.4.

I want to be clear as to what I mean by household net income in this context. It certainly means that the household total income exceeds household total expenses by the amount of that net income. It also means that total household revenue has been augmented – in many cases, by payments directly from the government, but also from other macrosectors. So household revenue is higher than it otherwise would have been. Net income shows the increase. Importantly, a positive household net income indicates that households are getting a transfer of wealth from somewhere – in this case (as in many cases), from the government in the amount of the government's spending and deficits.

The US government largely achieved the goals of its pandemic relief programs, not only by helping families in need but also by restoring overall economic growth. It took some time, however: GDP decreased from $21.38 trillion in 2019 to $21.06 trillion in 2020, as Americans sequestered at home for much of 2020 and spending plunged. With the boost from the government's spending, GDP rose to $23.32 trillion in 2021 – essentially where it would have been had the pandemic never happened.

At this writing, in early 2023, the government's special pandemic relief programs have ended, and the net loss on the US income statement has returned to a lower level, with financial institutions and the ROW seeing increases in net income to balance this. We'll return to the aftermath of the government's pandemic spending in Chapter 6. Suffice it to say for now that, during 2022, household net income fell to a level below the historical trend.

THE GOVERNMENT DEBT AND SPENDING MODEL

Let's turn now to the same critical metric – net income – for the five macrosectors in the US, but look at a much longer time frame, from 1946 to 2021. Figure 2.5 shows net income (or loss) by macrosector as a percentage of GDP each year so that we can see the relative change through time. These income statements use the *cash accounting method*, whereby all expenses, including the purchase of a home, are recorded as expenses to the buyer and income to the seller *at the time they are purchased*.

In Figure 2.5, a pattern becomes clear: the two largest macrosectors are typically households and the government, and in most years, households post the highest net income of the five sectors and the government posts the largest loss. The positive net income of households roughly mirrors the negative net income of the federal government.

This is not surprising from an accounting perspective. Because all sectors' income nets to zero, you would expect that the two most significant macrosectors would be strongly negatively correlated.

FIGURE 2.5. US net income by macrosector, 1946–2021

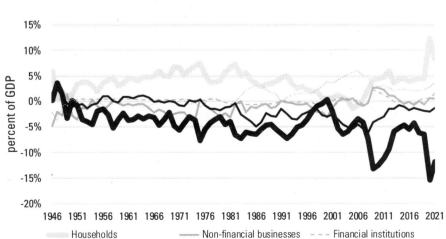

However, during this extended period, there were two periods of time in which this pattern was partly broken, where the household macrosector did not make far more (positive) net income than any other sector. These exceptions occurred during the frenzy immediately preceding the two US banking crises of the post-war period: the savings and loan (S&L) and commercial real estate crisis of the late 1980s and the Global Financial Crisis of 2008. In the years immediately before those two financial crises, rampant growth in lending – including, at times, the irresponsible lending that directly provoked each crisis – fueled a household spending spree. Household net income declined sharply as households spent more on expensive imports and home purchases. A good portion of the benefit of that spending went to the ROW, which posted record high net income.[19] The net income of the other two macrosectors – non-financial businesses and financial institutions – is smaller in comparison.

When we turn to the other Big 7 countries in Chapter 4, we'll see similar patterns, with one of the net income numbers in the graph consistently being the most negative in an economy. In most of the countries the dominant loss is incurred by the government, as it is in the US. In others, a different macrosector consistently has the most negative net income. In those economies, the sector with the most negative net income funds the positive net income of other sectors.

Knowing which macrosector plays this 'funder' role provides you with critical information about the structure of that economy. The US, in which the federal government posts the largest loss, has what we call a *government debt and spending model*. In other countries, other models are in operation, with distinct benefits and drawbacks.

Figure 2.6 shows the 2019 and 2020 balance sheets for the US, broken down by macrosectors. These balance sheets confirm that households are receiving wealth transfers as a result of government spending.

FIGURE 2.6. US balance sheet by macrosector, 2019 and 2020

2019 balance sheet by macrosector (trillions of US dollars)	House-holds	Non-financial businesses	Financial institutions	General government	Domestic total	Rest of world	TOTAL
Total assets	$133.3	$61.8	$110.5	$21.9	$327.5	$34.9	$362.4 H
Real estate	$33.5 A	$27.2	$1.2	$13.3	$75.2	$0.0	$75.2
Other non-financial assets	$6.4	$12.1	$0.9	$2.3	$21.7	$0.0	$21.7
Financial assets	$93.4	$22.5	$108.4	$6.3	$230.6	$34.9	$265.5
Equity assets	$45.2 B	$9.7	$34.8	$0.4	$90.1	$18.0	$108.1
Other assets	$48.1 C	$12.8	$73.6	$5.9	$140.5	$16.9	$157.4
Financial liabilities	$16.5	$84.9	$112.4	$29.9 E	$243.7	$24.2	$267.0 H
Equity liabilities	$0.0	$53.1	$38.0	$0.0	$91.1	$17.0	$108.1
Financial net worth	$76.9	-$62.4	-$4.0	-$23.6	-$13.1	$10.7	-$2.4
TOTAL NET WORTH	$116.8 D	-$23.1	-$1.9	-$8.0 F	$83.8 G	$10.7	$94.5 H

2020 balance sheet by macrosector (trillions of US dollars)	House-holds	Non-financial businesses	Financial institutions	General government	Domestic total	Rest of world	TOTAL
Total assets	$148.5	$72.5	$125.1	$24.7	$370.8	$39.8	$410.6 H
Real estate	$36.8 A	$28.9	$1.2	$13.7	$80.6	$0.0	$80.6
Other non-financial assets	$6.7	$12.6	$1.0	$2.4	$22.7	$0.0	$22.7
Financial assets	$104.9	$31.0	$122.9	$8.6	$267.4	$39.8	$307.2
Equity assets	$52.8 B	$10.7	$39.0	$0.6	$103.0	$21.9	$124.9
Other assets	$52.2 C	$20.3	$83.9	$8.0	$164.4	$17.9	$182.4
Financial liabilities	$17.1	$97.8	$126.2	$34.9 E	$276.0	$26.4	$302.4 H
Equity liabilities	$0.0	$64.1	$42.0	$0.0	$106.1	$18.8	$124.9
Financial net worth	$87.8	-$66.8	-$3.3	-$26.3	-$8.6	$13.4	$4.8
TOTAL NET WORTH	$131.3 D	-$25.3	-$1.1	-$10.2 F	$94.7 G	$13.4	$108.1 H

The 2020 US income statement (Figure 2.4 above) noted that the government had a net loss (deficit) of $3.2 trillion while households had a net income of $2.5 trillion. The dramatic rise in the government deficit is reflected in its balance sheets, with the government's net worth declining from 2019 to 2020. With its loss in that year, the government's net worth declined by $2.2 trillion (both letters F in Figure 2.6), though the government also had an increase in its own assets, which partially offset its significant spending on pandemic relief programs (both letters E in Figure 2.6).

Losing $2.2 trillion in a single year sounds pretty terrible, right? Yet, this government spending did not cause widespread suffering among households. Quite the contrary. Household net worth *increased* from 2019 to 2020 by $14.5 trillion, in large part because government spending added trillions to household bank accounts (both letters C in Figure 2.6).[20]

When we considered the changes in Jane Doe's balance sheet from year 1 to year 2, we saw that, although her net income was only $5,000, her net worth over the period actually increased by $35,000. The additional windfall of $30,000 came from substantial increases in the value of her home and her investment portfolio. A similar explanation for growth in wealth holds for the gains recorded by households in 2020. The value of household-owned stocks[21] and ownership of non-corporate businesses increased by $7.6 trillion (both letters B in Figure 2.6), while the value of household-owned real estate increased by $3.3 trillion (both letters A). Together, these two categories of assets account for $10.9 trillion out of the $14.5 trillion increase from 2019 to 2020 which was posted by the household macrosector (both letters D).

Why did stocks and real estate go up during this period, at a time when government debt was rising? While real estate and stock values change dynamically (and can sometimes be volatile, especially in the case of equities), over the long term *an increase in debt tends to lift the value of both of these asset types.*[22] The flood of US government and Federal Reserve support during the pandemic primed the pump for a surge in stock and real estate prices. (We'll return to this phenomenon in Chapter 4.)

Despite all of the churn and change on the US balance sheet from 2019 to 2020, the accounting axiom that assets equal total liabilities plus net worth still held true (see both letters G and H in Figure 2.6). The ostensibly frightening increase in government debt was accompanied by an even larger increase in household net worth. So, even though total federal government debt reached the record level of $27.7 trillion, there would simply have been that much less in private sector wealth, primarily household wealth, if the government debt had not existed. This is a critical concept: when a government spends, the money does not disappear; instead, most of it ends up in the coffers of households.

We see similar mirroring of household net worth and government debt when we look at the balance sheets of the five US macrosectors through time. Figure 2.7 demonstrates that household net worth trends higher when government net worth trends lower. Contrary to net income, net worth is not zero-sum; it can increase in the economy as a whole.

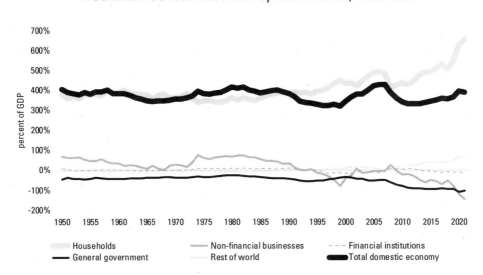

FIGURE 2.7. US total net worth by macrosector, 1950–2021

This trend was particularly pronounced after something I call the Great Debt Explosion, a pronounced rise in total debt to GDP that started in the 1980s. From 1950 to 2021, US household total net worth grew from 376 percent of GDP to 654 percent of GDP, while government total net worth declined from negative 47 percent to negative 104 percent, briefly rising to negative 24 percent along the way.[23] Most of the change in total debt and total net worth occurred from 1980 onwards.

Notice the decline in the net worth of non-financial businesses to a negative value. To some extent this is an artifact of accounting conventions. The equity value of companies shows up in our consolidated balance sheets in the value of stocks owned by households and other parties. To offset this, the equity value is subtracted *as a liability* from the net worth of non-financial businesses.[24]

Another notable trend in the data is the recent rise in the net worth of the ROW. This net worth consists of the amount of foreign ownership of US stocks, Treasury securities, and other financial assets exceeding the amount of US ownership of foreign financial assets. As can be seen in Figure 2.7, the ROW is becoming a much larger slice of the US ownership pie. This began in the early to mid-1980s, when the US current account deficit, and the trade deficit that was the largest part of it, started to rise rapidly – in other words, this is the point at which the ROW began receiving significantly greater net income in its dealings with the US.[25]

Looking at assets and liabilities together, as we've done up to this point, gives a well-rounded picture of total wealth. Next, we'll examine the liabilities, or debt, side more intensively.

THE US DEBT PROFILE

To fully understand the role of debt in an economy, we need to put it in context. The first step is to create a *debt profile* like the one in

Figure 2.8, which shows the key categories of US debt, in ratio to GDP, over time.

As we can see from this debt profile, since 1950 *total debt to GDP* in the US has increased by over 150 percentage points, from 142 percent to 294 percent of GDP. That is an extraordinary, mind-boggling increase. The debt profile also includes a line showing the current account balance in ratio to GDP, which has bearing on debt trends in any economy. If the current account is in deficit, the higher that deficit, the more borrowing the private sector has to do to finance (what is usually) a trade deficit. If the current account is in surplus, there is less need for private debt. For the US, this current account balance went from roughly zero in the 1950s to negative 2 percent to negative 4 percent in recent years.

Looking at the US debt profile over time we can see that total debt has always grown as fast or faster than GDP, *except in periods of*

FIGURE 2.8. US debt profile, 1950–2021

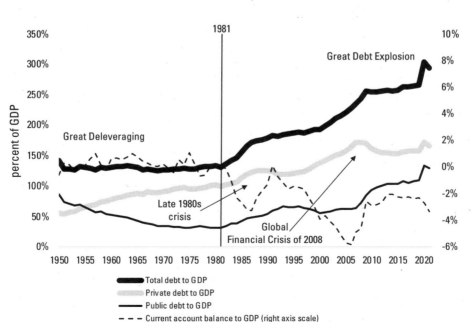

calamity. Debt outgrows income, and this growth is not a cycle, but instead a jagged yet nevertheless *unending upwards march*. The same relationship between debt growth and GDP holds for the other Big 7 economies. This uniformity suggests that debt outgrowing income is not an accident but an inherent feature of the modern economic system.

In Figure 2.8 I have noted a line of demarcation or, better yet, a point of inflection, between the period from 1950 to 1981 – a period referred to as the Great Deleveraging – and the period from 1981 to the present – the Great Debt Explosion. Clear differences can be seen between these two periods.

At the end of the Second World War, the US experienced Depression-era deleveraging and enforced wartime frugality. Furthermore, during the war, the US government had taken over much of the financing of manufacturing from the private sector. As a result, in 1945 private sector debt – the sum of household and non-financial business debt – fell all the way down to a low of 37 percent of GDP while federal government debt hit a peak of 118 percent of GDP, reflecting the enormous expenses of the war.

After the war, the private sector resumed its ordinary role as financier of manufacturing, and households rushed to buy new homes, cars, and other goods. As a result, by 1980 private sector debt had nearly tripled, from 37 percent to 101 percent of GDP. Over the same period, supported by this skyrocketing private debt, American business boomed and US GDP grew by $2.6 trillion.

The government's debt rarely declined in total amount during this period. However, the large rise in GDP, and the 'denominator growth' it afforded, reduced the ratio of government debt to GDP from 117 percent to 40 percent. If there had been no private sector debt growth, US GDP growth would have been largely nonexistent. The term 'Great Deleveraging' therefore refers to the decline in the government debt *ratio*, specifically, the decline from its high as a result of the Second World War. But there was no overall, or *total debt*, deleveraging, because private sector debt grew rapidly and offset government deleveraging. In fact, total debt grew and was more or less stable as a percentage of GDP from 1950 until 1981.

Then, beginning in the 1980s, a markedly different pattern emerged. Under President Ronald Reagan, government debt re-accelerated, and it has continued to grow under presidents of both parties, from 40 percent of GDP in 1980 to 128 percent in 2020. Private debt has not stopped growing either, rising from 101 percent of GDP in 1980 to 171 percent in 2020. In fact, private debt levels far exceeded government debt levels from the 1970s until the Global Financial Crisis of 2008. The government spending enacted to support the economy in the wake of the 2008 financial crisis and during the pandemic allowed the government debt ratio to catch up.

In the early 1980s, many economists made dire predictions about the likely consequences of high levels of government debt. They warned that it would constrain spending, crowd out lending and investment, lead to higher interest rates and inflation, and seriously encumber the country. At the time, inflation had reached 14 percent and interest rates were close to 20 percent.

Since then, government debt has exploded and so we have had ample opportunity to put these predictions to the test. As it turns out, over this time span interest rates have generally plummeted, not risen; investment has remained high, not been constrained; and household net worth has risen, not sunk.

Recently, inflation in the US and the other Big 7 economies has been at levels not seen in a generation, rising to 9.1 percent in the US in June 2022. However, as we shall see in Chapter 6, this was largely due to supply chain issues created by lockdowns in China and other countries to prevent the spread of the novel coronavirus and by supply disruptions in such commodities as oil, natural gas, and wheat caused by the war in Ukraine. If inflation were due to high levels of government debt, then the US would have had frequent bouts of inflation over the last forty years. Instead, inflation has been consistently very low. Similar patterns hold in other major economies. And if history is any guide, inflation will decline once these special circumstances abate.

If it is true that government spending boosts net worth in the household macrosector, then maybe, instead of lamenting debt, we should be applauding it. However, there are several concerns and constraints related to growth in government debt.

Firstly, most economists believe that the level of government debt is limited by real resource constraints. These may be encountered if an economy is at full production, when, for example, every computer or manufacturing plant is running at maximum capacity. At this point, any additional spending will bring inflation. While I can certainly imagine spending scenarios that are so extreme that inflation would inevitably result, current spending levels are far from extreme; in addition, we are not broadly at maximum productive capacity. The pandemic impaired production, and the main focus in the near and mid-term is to return to full production.

Further, the ability – politically and otherwise – of a government to borrow and spend is a precious resource for combating adversities, and high levels of government debt can limit the capacity for additional borrowing and leave a country in a vulnerable position if and when adversity strikes (again). Consider the collapse in the British pound in autumn 2022. The trigger was not as much the UK government's levels of debt but more its adverse current account and trade deficit, which had been in the troubling range of 3 percent to 5 percent for a decade, well before the 2020 pandemic and the 2022 energy crisis.

The collapse in the pound started in September 2020, when new Prime Minister Liz Truss announced steep tax cuts as part of her doomed 'mini budget'. She did this in a context where the UK's trade deficit was already a very high negative 3 percent to negative 4 percent of GDP. The high energy costs which came with the Ukraine war were already exacerbating that trade deficit and putting considerable downwards pressure on the pound. Add to this the already high British government debt, which was over 100 percent of GDP, and the environment was ripe for investor fear. In contrast, when Truss's idol Margaret Thatcher began introducing tax cuts in the early 1980s, the UK had a trade surplus and government debt was less than 45 percent of GDP. The problem for Truss also included the trade deficit, but clearly the UK's high government deficit left the perception that the government had less 'dry powder' to utilize.

Finally, and perhaps most importantly, rising levels of government debt lead to rising inequality, an issue so pivotal – and troubling – that I devote a good portion of Chapter 3 to analyzing it.

OUR FINANCIALIZATION

Now back to the subject of private sector debt – the sum of household and non-financial business debt – which is all too often absent from economic discussions, because government debt tends to be the focus. Yet, I argue, it is private debt which is more vital to understand if you want to understand economies today.

Figure 2.9 shows the composition of US household debt. Since 1980, mortgage debt has towered – you might also say 'loomed' – over other forms of household debt as a percentage of GDP. In 2021, household mortgages totaled nearly two thirds of total household debt – $11.7 out of $18 trillion. All other categories of debt are far smaller: student loans were $1.7 trillion, car loans were $1.5 trillion, and credit card loans were $856 billion. Healthcare debt is interspersed through several categories, so it is difficult to get a separate total, but my colleagues and I estimate it to be approximately $400 billion. (Macrosector debt data, other than commercial real estate debt and household mortgages, is not available for years prior to 1995.)

FIGURE 2.9. US household debt by type, 1981–2021

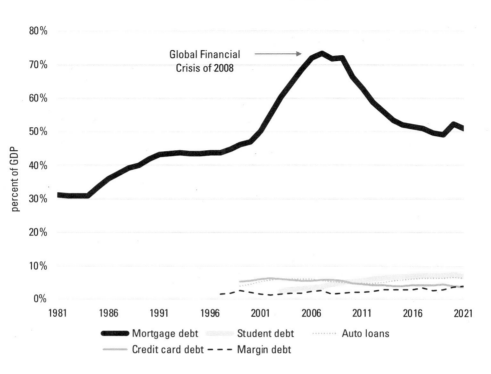

In the lead-up to the Global Financial Crisis of 2008, the US accumulated a gargantuan mountain of new mortgage debt, totaling $5 trillion. This debt was so large it was practically impossible to miss – except that most economists did miss it entirely, and therefore failed to predict the financial crisis.

The household macrosector has not been alone in taking on excessive levels of debt in recent years. Over time, commercial real estate debt has vastly exceeded other forms of non-financial business debt, as shown in Figure 2.10. In 2021, total non-financial business debt was $18.5 trillion, with loans for commercial real estate totaling $5.5 trillion. In contrast, non-financial businesses borrowed $2 trillion in the industrial subsector, $1.9 trillion in utilities, $1.7 trillion in communications, and $1.2 trillion in energy.

FIGURE 2.10. US non-financial business debt by sector, 1980–2021

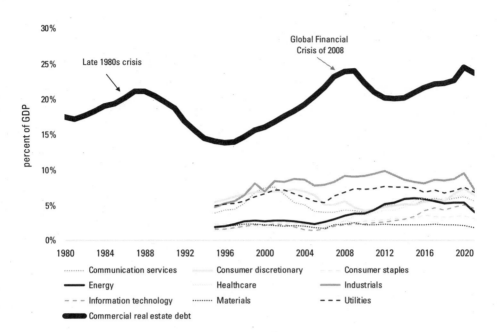

In 2021, household mortgage and commercial real estate mortgage debt, combined, totaled $18 trillion while all private sector debt, which again is the total of household and non-financial business debt, totaled $36 trillion. This means that real estate-related lending was by far the largest component of private sector debt, comprising half of all private debt. With lending of that volume, an adverse trend in the credit quality of real estate loans can disrupt the entire US economy. It's no coincidence that unrestrained, ill-advised real estate lending preceded the banking crises of 1929, the late 1980s, and 2008. By comparison, a major energy lending crisis in 2016 was barely noticed across the broader economy, because energy lending made up only a $1.3 trillion slice of the debt pie – less than 5 percent.

In the overall US debt profile in Figure 2.8, you can see two pronounced 'bumps' in the private debt line, one in the late 1980s and the second around 2007. Both mark the culmination of a short, highly escalated period of private debt growth: the savings and loan and commercial real estate crisis of the late 1980s and the Global Financial Crisis of 2008, respectively. In any debt profile, an acceleration like this in private debt levels typically portends economic adversity, while a decline in private debt levels typically signifies an economic contraction – unless, that is, government spending and debt surge, so as to offset the effect.

I would not go so far as to dismiss the potential long-term dynamics of the government debt ratio, but my concerns about it are subtler than my high level of concern caused by the rapidly accelerating levels of private sector debt. A fast rise in the private debt ratio is a much more immediate, urgent cause for alarm. That is because the government sector can readily refinance its debt – or 'print money', in the misleading parlance of the day – but the private sector is much less able to do so. Torrid growth in private debt was a red flag that predicted – or should have predicted – Japan's Lost Decade, the 2008 financial crisis, and most other major banking crises.

The rise in private sector debt levels is part of what is referred to as *financialization*. In its early stages it can be a sign of the maturation of an economy. But as those levels continue to rise, it can also be a harbinger of potential financial difficulty in the future, including weaker economic growth and financial crisis, as we'll discuss more fully in Chapter 7.

High private debt alone does not bring economic calamity. Instead, it is the rapid acceleration of debt growth to high levels that is the culprit. As shown in these figures, in the period from 2012 onwards, the private sector debt to GDP ratio remained at a comparatively high plateau. That debt was largely the residue of the Global Financial Crisis of 2008. Because that high level did not come on the heels of a rapid run-up in private debt, it did not portend a crisis; however, it did mean that too many businesses and households were so burdened with high debt that their spending and investing were constrained.

The result was that economic growth was also constrained, which helps explain the tepid recovery from the 2008 crisis. Some economists dismiss concerns about this adverse consequence of high private debt, but the reality is that the debt service ratio, which is a household's monthly debt payments in ratio to their income, is today 30 percent higher than it was in the 1950s and 1960s, the two decades with highest growth in the post-war period. The trend in the debt service ratio is worse for households in the lowest income segment, as we'll see. The trend is similar for businesses.

By reorienting our discussion of debt around the basic rules of dual-entry accounting we can better understand the dynamics governing the economy as it operates every day. This approach also provides a well-rounded and balanced perspective on debt, one that is much needed. And it confirms the axiom that one entity's liability is another's asset.

The fact that debt almost always grows as fast or faster than GDP, except in periods of economic calamity, is not an aberrant state or the simple result of poor policy decisions but built into the economy itself. Government deficits, despite having certain potential negative effects, have historically confounded the conventional predictions that they would lead to a catastrophe. The debt growth that we should be worried about is in private sector debt.

Private debt is a major mechanism by which wealth is created. Yet, while it brings increased household wealth, it can also simultaneously lead to increased household wealth inequality. How can both of these things be true? In the next two chapters we turn to this particular paradox of debt.

3

COMPANY SHARES, REAL ESTATE, AND INEQUALITY

Debt brings greater wealth, but it is also the fuel of greater inequality. To understand how this happens, we need to look more closely at how debt creates wealth. We also need to consider why it is that debt – *more* than wealth – which has trickled down to the middle- and lower-income groups, and thus contributed to growing inequality.

WHERE LIES THE WEALTH OF THE NATION

As we saw in Chapter 2, the largest and most important macrosector in the US economy is the household sector. The country's wealth resides there. Figure 3.1 shows the 2020 balance sheet of all US households, with a breakdown of the equity holdings on that balance sheet.

FIGURE 3.1. US households balance sheet, 2020

ASSETS

Total assets	**$148,467**
Non-financial assets	$43,508
Real estate	$36,756
Financial assets	$104,938
Equities	$52,752
Directly Held	$38,998
Corporate	$26,107
Non-corporate	$12,891
Indirectly held	$13,754
Money market fund shares	$2,676
Mutual fund shares	$11,078
Deposits	$13,194
Liabilities	
Total liabilities	**$17,124**
Mortgages	$10,915
Student loans	$1,694
Auto loans	$1,374
Credit card debt	$819
Financial net worth	**$87,814**
TOTAL NET WORTH	**$131,343**

At $52.8 trillion in 2020, the largest household asset is equities, that is, shares of stock or company shares, held directly and indirectly by households, plus equity ownership in non-corporate businesses,[26] such as a family-owned restaurant or retail store. After deducting the $778 billion of margin debt used to purchase equities, the net equity value is $52 trillion. The next largest asset is real estate, primarily houses and land, with a value of $36.8 trillion. Subtracting from this the mortgage debt liability of $10.9 trillion nets a real estate value of $25.9 trillion. Deposits in banks contribute less, at $13.2 trillion.

FIGURE 3.2. US households balance sheet, 1950–2021

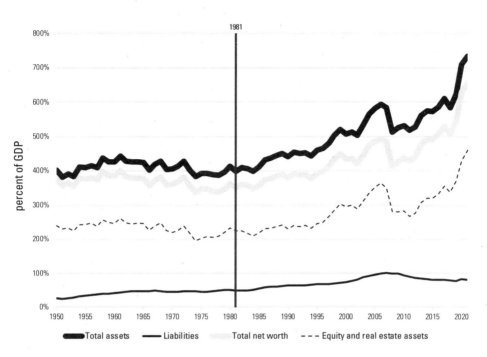

Total net worth of households grew from 376 percent of GDP in 1950 to 654 percent in 2021 (Figure 3.2). That's a dazzling increase. The net worth of households is now 6.5 times GDP.

The two largest contributors to this increase were stocks and real estate, which together constituted 70 percent of US household net worth in 2021. The pronounced rise in the value of these assets began with the start of the Great Debt Explosion in the 1980s and continued into the 1990s, as shown in Figure 3.3. Wealth growth was flat before 1981 in no small part because total debt growth was flat during the Great Deleveraging, with debt growing as fast as GDP, on a ratio basis, but no faster. With the Great Debt Explosion came increased debt, to finance land and stock transactions, and so the relative value of these assets began to climb.

FIGURE 3.3. US total domestic debt and household net worth, 1950–2021

Total debt includes central government, household, and non-financial business sectors

The value of real estate alone as part of US household net worth more than doubled from around 93 percent of GDP in 1950 to 195 percent on the eve of the Global Financial Crisis of 2008, which in part was caused by unrestrained mortgage lending to unqualified or poorly qualified borrowers, that is, households that were taking on much more debt for a house purchase than they could afford, or could be expected to repay, over the longer term. As a result of the 2008 crisis, household real estate assets plummeted to 127 percent of GDP. They have since regained ground to reach 182 percent of GDP as of 2021.

Yet the biggest story of the Great Debt Explosion is stocks. As reported by the OECD, including privately held stocks, US household equity holdings grew from 145 percent of GDP in 1950 to 275 percent in 2021. That is a near doubling in value and the major driver of household net worth in the US. However, it is important to note that the growth in stock values has been anything but smooth. Stocks reached 157 percent of GDP in the so-called go-go years of the 1960s, then fell to a lackluster 96 percent of GDP in the inflationary 1970s, when high interest rates led to discounted valuations. Then, with the Great Debt Explosion starting in the 1980s, their value nearly doubled, as stocks careened on a rocky upwards ascent through three stock market crashes – the junk bond crash of 1987, the dot-com bust of 1999, and the stock market crash which occurred during the Global Financial Crisis of 2008 – reaching 275 percent of GDP in 2021, a record high. Then, the value of stocks declined 22 percent in just the first six months of 2022. Doubtless, the path of stocks will continue to be bumpy.

Combined, the net value of stocks and real estate assets has nearly doubled, rising from 238 percent to 456 percent of GDP. I believe the growth in debt has significantly contributed to these higher asset values. Put simply, if you have more debt-financed buyers of houses, then house prices will rise. That's the law of supply and demand. And, as a matter of fact, household net worth did not take off until after the Great Debt Explosion began.

As it careens upwards, household net worth can sometimes get ahead of itself. This makes it vulnerable to a *correction* – a painful reversal such as an economic downturn or recession. Just before the 2008 financial crisis, which was fueled by overlending in mortgages, household net worth reached an apex, a then record 495 percent of GDP. This gave false reassurance to many economists, but the rapidity of the gains in real estate and stock values should have been a warning.

Most analysts state that this increase in asset values has come from falling interest rates, and view that link as causal. There clearly is such a relationship. My point is that these three things – rising debt, falling rates, and rising asset values – are all powerfully and causally interlinked, an important phenomenon to note because rising debt levels have been falsely thought by many to drive interest rates higher.

THE DISTRIBUTION OF DEBT

Let's now put this wealth in the context of its accompanying debt. In the period from 1945 to 2020, when household net worth nearly doubled, US household debt grew a monumental sixfold, from 13 percent to 79 percent of GDP. However, in relative terms, this increase has fallen harder on middle- and lower-income Americans, with significant economic and political consequence. Debt builds not only wealth but also wealth inequality.

This can be seen in Figure 3.4, which shows the progression of US household total net worth from 2001 to 2021 through a 'reconciliation' in the Federal Reserve's distributional financial accounts

FIGURE 3.4. US household wealth reconciliation, 2001–2021

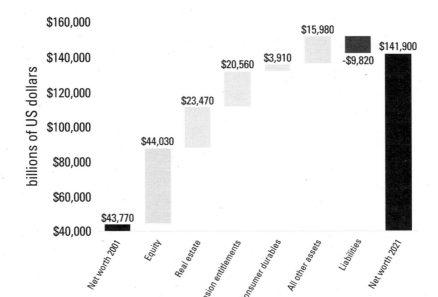

(DFAs). This reconciliation demonstrates how financial net worth grows through disproportionate growth in the value of stocks and real estate in the household macrosector. Real estate and stocks together accounted for 63 percent, or $67.5 trillion, of the $108 trillion in increased household assets in this twenty-year period. Growth in pension fund values constituted 19 percent of this growth, while other assets, including non-equity financial assets such as current checking and savings accounts, comprised just 15 percent. (Some portion of the increase in all other assets – $15.9 trillion from 2001 to 2021 – came as a result of government deficit spending, as discussed in Chapter 2.)

To fully illustrate this downside of debt – debt's disproportionate impact on the less well-off – we must dig down a layer to compare balance sheets and income for different household income segments. I have chosen to look at the top 10 percent of income earners, the next 30 percent, and then the bottom 60 percent in the US population (Figures 3.5, 3.6, and 3.7). This analysis, which utilizes data collected every three years through the Fed's Survey of Consumer Finances, helps to show how debt creates greater inequality even as it creates greater overall household wealth.

Why did my colleagues and I pick the groupings of the top 10 percent of income earners, the next 30 percent, and then the bottom 60 percent, as opposed to, say, the top third, middle third, and bottom third? We tried analyzing different groupings and divisions of wealth holdings and found these groupings to be the most revealing. The unfortunate truth is that the bottom 60 percent own such a relatively small percentage of wealth-building assets – only 14 percent of stocks and real estate in the US – that there is no need, for our purposes here, to subdivide this population. In contrast, the top 10 percent own 61 percent of all stocks and real estate and the next 30 percent own 25 percent. It should not be encouraging or reassuring to anyone that such a broad group of Americans holds so few wealth-building assets, but the distribution is similar in other developed countries, too.

FIGURE 3.5. US net worth to GDP by income percentile, 1989–2019

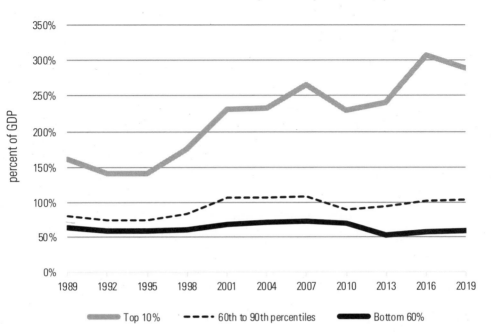

While people can move from one income or wealth band to another, there is relatively little of this type of movement, so looking at these groups over time gives us a reasonable sense of trends. In Figure 3.5, we see that the total net worth of the top 10 percent of US households has increased from 161 percent to 288 percent of GDP, an extraordinary increase of 78 percent. At the same time, the debt to income ratio of the top 10 percent has increased by less than 20 percent, from 52 percent to 61 percent of GDP – a small amount in the context of their overall balance sheets (see Figure 3.6).

In this same period, the total net worth of the bottom 60 percent of households has actually declined, from 63 percent to 59 percent of GDP. However small this decline, it's still stunning when juxtaposed against the 78 percent increase in wealth among the top 10 percent. In fact, many households within this group saw steep declines in their net worth. Further, the debt to income ratio for the bottom 60 percent has nearly doubled, from 38 percent to 72 percent of GDP. Some have argued, with partial merit, that this net worth disparity is less if a present value is ascribed to expected future Social Security benefits in retirement. However, any such analysis should be tempered, given the funding and political challenges faced by Social Security, and the fact that lower-income and lower-wealth individuals typically have a lower life expectancy.

Based on these ratios, debt is a peripheral issue to the top 10 percent of US households but a monumental issue to many in the bottom 60 percent. This bottom 60 percent, by definition, is the majority of Americans, including what could reasonably be considered the 'middle class'. A significant percentage of these households struggle every day to make ends meet. Many experience daily challenges with debt.

This meshes with the often-cited Federal Reserve statistic that 50 percent of all adults in the US would have difficulty paying for a $400 emergency expense, with *one in five* Americans saying they would not be able to pay any expense at all. This dire lack of emergency savings was temporarily alleviated for a large proportion of household through the government's pandemic relief checks.

Figure 3.6 clearly shows that the middle and bottom income groups also bore more of the brunt of the rising mortgage debt that led to the Global Financial Crisis of 2008. Because the Fed survey used to analyze the population by income groups only captures data once every three years, and only started in 1989, this figure does not give us a window onto the effects of the upwards surge in household income during the pandemic. However, although they are less detailed and feature some- what different metrics, the Federal Reserve's distributional financial accounts reveal that from 2019 to 2021, during the years of pandemic largesse, the wealth share of the top 1 percent of income earners alone grew from 25 percent to 27 percent of GDP, the highest value ever recorded by the Fed. As recently as 1989, the wealth share for that small portion of the US population was much lower, at 17 percent.

FIGURE 3.6. US debt to income, by income percentile, 1989–2019

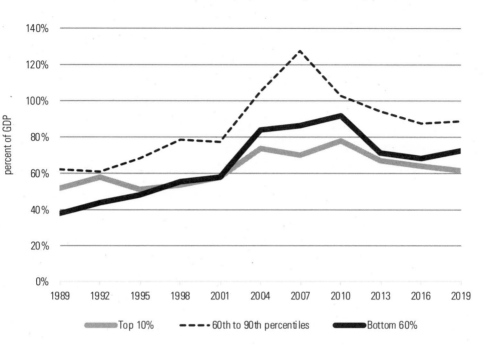

Very quickly as you move down the income distribution, household debt becomes highly burdensome. Tens of millions of both middle- and lower-income households – those in the sixtieth to ninetieth percentiles as well as the bottom 60 percent – have essentially no net worth and high levels of debt. And much of that debt is for purchases of goods and services from companies owned largely by the top 10 percent.

The rising wealth and debt inequality in the US is corroborated by the debt service ratios of the highest and lowest income groups. In the period from 1989 to 2019, that ratio improved for the top 10 percent by 10 percent, while for the bottom 20 percent, it got worse by 15 percent. The very increase in debt that increased household net worth appears to have brought much greater inequality along with it, and thus, the rising net worth in a country brings the likelihood of rising inequality across its population. In other words, those who champion the trickle-down theory of economics are correct – except for one detail: it is debt that has been trickling down, not wealth.

The income trends of these same three groups are shown in Figure 3.7. I have chosen to use average nominal income from 1989 to 2019 here to more accurately glean differences between them.

According to the US Congressional Budget Office (CBO), the income of the top 10 percent rose in this period from $168,000 to $562,000 per household while the income of the bottom 60 percent went from $24,000 to $62,000. Both are remarkable gains, but there's a gap: the top 10 percent's income has gone from being seven times higher than the income of the bottom 60 percent to being nine times higher. This gap will most likely continue to widen.

It is in this rising inequality where the true peril lies for an economy and society. Increasingly stressed lower income–higher debt groups can readily express their discontent by voting for demagogues or even, as in China, rioting against lenders.

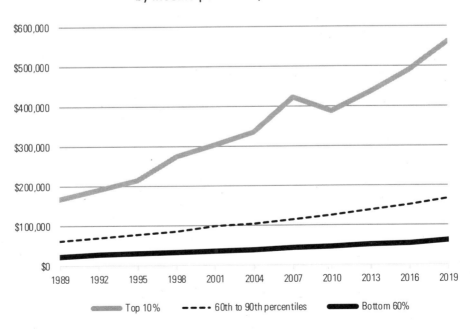

FIGURE 3.7. US average income per household, by income percentile, 1989–2019

DEBT AND ASSET VALUES

With this understanding of US wealth, we can now return to our discussion of the impact of increased debt on asset values. Because growth in the value of stocks and real estate are the prime drivers of growth in household net worth, they both deserve a closer look, focused on how debt affects these valuations.

To an even greater extent than suggested thus far, an increase in debt is a major factor in increasing the value of stocks and real estate over time, even after taking into account the occasional interruption of market corrections and financial crises. Debt is not the only factor, of course; things such as housing inventory, companies' earnings, and population trends also matter greatly. But aggregate debt, and increases in that debt, matter greatly, too, and unfortunately, they are neglected in many analyses.

As we saw in our LoanLand example in Chapter 1, it takes somebody's debt, somewhere, to create the deposits used to purchase stocks or make the down payment on a real estate purchase. But, frequently, a second layer of debt is involved.

Stock is often bought using a *margin loan*, a loan a broker extends to you for purchase of the stock, which is collateralized by the stock itself. The initial margin in the US cannot be more than 50 percent of the value of the stock – that is, you can buy $1,000 worth of stock for only $500 and your broker will lend you the rest. In turn, stockbrokers and investment banks often rely on what is called 'broker loan lending' from a bank to fund margin loans.

For real estate, the use of debt to build wealth usually involves a mortgage loan obtained to buy the house or land. If it's a new home, the developer relied on debt to finance the purchase of materials and other expenses incurred to build it. Indeed, the availability and use of debt is the most important source of high real estate values, and growth in real estate-related debt has the direct effect of elevating prices (with some exceptions, which are discussed in Chapter 7).

The volume of mortgage loans in the economy and the home price index roughly correlate, as shown in Figure 3.8. However, other factors – most recently, for example, housing inventory levels – also affect home prices. If you are selling your house, you will be able to command a higher price if you have more loan-qualified buyers bidding. The number of potential buyers and offers is primarily determined by how many can get a mortgage loan, which is determined by the lending or credit policy of lenders.

There is a direct and causal link between the leniency of lenders' credit policies and higher house prices. For example, if lenders require a 20 percent down payment, then you will have fewer qualified buyers for your home than if lenders reduce the down payment requirement to zero.

Could you imagine trying to sell your house if no one was allowed to take out a mortgage or any other type of debt to fund the purchase? To underscore this point, imagine that no one could buy a

FIGURE 3.8. US mortgage debt outstanding and home price index, 1945–2021

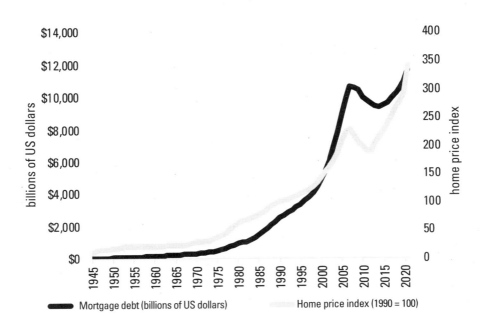

house unless they could pay the entire asking price in cash. How many people could manage that? The number of home buyers would plunge, perhaps by 75 percent or even 90 percent, and home prices would plunge just as precipitously. The change wrought by the complete absence of debt in these transactions would be so fundamental and grim that the real estate market would collapse.

The importance of debt in propping up home values and prices also applies to common stock values and prices. More deposits to fund stock purchases means more potential buyers, which in turn translates into higher stock prices. So the greater the amount of debt, the greater the number of deposits, and the higher the value of stocks.

To be sure, this path towards wealth is punctuated by moments of both irrational enthusiasm and despair. Regardless, debt levels and stock prices are correlated. Figure 3.9 demonstrates the rough correspondence of stock values to three things: company earnings, GDP, and total debt.

FIGURE 3.9. US stock market capitalization, 1945–2021

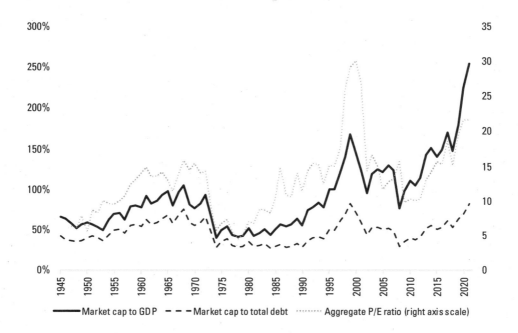

Typically, when trying to decide when to buy and sell stocks, analysts look most closely at company earnings. One widely used barometer here is the ratio of the company's total stock market valuation, also known as *market capitalization* or market cap, to its earnings. This is called the *price to earnings ratio*, or P/E analysis. A second traditional barometer is the ratio of market cap to GDP, the country's total income. Both are plotted in Figure 3.9 alongside the ratio of market capitalization to total debt. The flatter the line in this figure, the better the correlation to stock market valuation. Plainly, debt is far better correlated to stock market valuation than the more conventional metrics of earnings or overall GDP.

Margin loans and stock prices are also closely correlated, as can be seen in Figure 3.10. This is true even though the dollar amount of margin loans is but a small fraction of stock market valuation – 10 percent in 1928 and a mere 2 percent today. Why? On a typical day,

FIGURE 3.10. Dow Jones Industrial Average and margin debt, 1997–2021

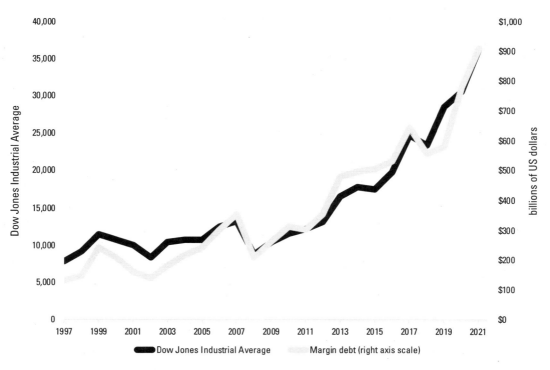

and for a typical stock, only a small percentage of shares are actually traded. The availability of margin debt, though small, therefore has an outsized influence on the volume of the incremental daily transactions which often determine stock prices. So margin debt has a disproportionate influence on overall stock values.

If my theory about the influence of debt levels on wealth levels is correct, then it would follow that most of the increased value of publicly traded stocks over time should come from the rise in prices of existing stocks rather than the addition of new stocks from new companies. And in fact, that has been the case. Initial public offerings (IPOs) have made only a minor contribution to the rise in stock values. Figure 3.11 shows that the increased value of stocks coming from IPOs issued in 2000 or after – not just the value at initial issuance, but the *ongoing* rise in value of those stocks – is a relatively small part of the total. The majority of the increase in the value of publicly

FIGURE 3.11. US stock market valuation for publicly listed stocks, 2000–2021

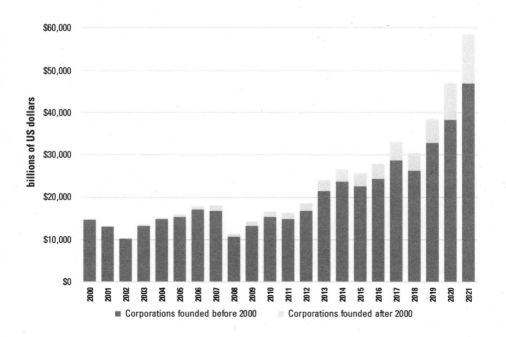

Corporations founded before 2000   Corporations founded after 2000

traded stocks has come from the appreciation in value of existing stocks – stocks that have been in existence and traded for more than twenty years.

Surprisingly, it turns out that over the past two decades, from 2000 to 2021, the value of new stocks at initial issuance was entirely offset – and then some – by the amount of *stock buybacks*, which is when companies purchase their own stock in the open market to reduce the total number of outstanding shares and thus hopefully increase the value of the shares. New stock issued during this period totaled $7.4 trillion while stock buybacks totaled $15 trillion.

At this point you might wonder why companies do not issue significantly more stock if it is such a miraculous wealth creator – indeed, the most significant wealth creator in the US. A powerful constraint is in play. Even though stock creates greater net worth overall, individual companies pay a very real and often very high price when they issue more stock. That price is the ownership they relinquish in their company.

Say you own a restaurant that makes net income of $50,000 per year after paying for your salary. You pay that $50,000 to yourself as a dividend. Suddenly you incur an emergency that requires you to buy new equipment that costs $100,000 but cannot get a loan because of other debt you carry. To get the money, you sell 50 percent of your restaurant for $100,000. That implies a valuation for the whole restaurant of $200,000. You now have the cash you need to buy the equipment but you have also sold half the ownership and you're required to give this new co-owner 50 percent of the restaurant's annual earnings, or $25,000. This is not a great outcome: you sold ownership at a mediocre valuation, perhaps even a poor valuation, only because it was necessary. Alas, such circumstances describe many companies, especially those in need of new capital.

For a happier hypothetical let's say that you start a metaverse company. Your revenues are $1 million but your expenses are $1.5

million, meaning you lose $500,000 per year, but people anticipate that your company is going to be hugely successful, so they are willing to pay a very high price for your stock. You sell $1 million of stock to get operating funds. Because buyers are so enamored, you can set an exorbitant valuation of $50 million for your company (this sort of thing happens sometimes in Silicon Valley, or so I hear), so the buyers altogether get a mere 2 percent ownership of the company. You get to keep 98 percent of the stock and 98 percent of future earnings of the company. Who would say no to that? But this is the happy circumstance for a tiny minority of companies.

Most company owners typically, and obviously, love selling stock at high valuations and hate selling at low valuations. Most transactions are done somewhere in between. The reluctance to cede a percentage of ownership, earnings, and control to others – what stock analysts call 'ownership dilution' – constrains the quantity of new stock that is sold.

BORROWING BY PAUL TO PAY PETER

Borrowing to buy real estate or stocks is the very borrowing to purchase assets, or Type 2 debt, described in Chapter 1. While Type 2 debt is generally applauded when it is used to purchase a residence, there are highly divergent views on its merits when it comes to purchasing other types of assets, including commercial buildings, stocks, commodities, and entire companies. Some view debt spent in these ways as a fundamental, and indispensable, money management strategy; others criticize it as unproductive, or speculative and risky. The critics often argue that borrowing for these purposes *only* serves to inflate values, create bubbles, further enrich the wealthy, and widen wealth inequality.

Note that stocks, like debt – at least from this one perspective – bring money from the future into the present, but in a more speculative way. The current value of a stock is, in essence, the present value of all the future projected earnings of that company – in part, why stocks are so often evaluated on the P/E ratio – even if the estimate of those projected earnings is sometimes optimistic. Unlike debt, stock is future revenue brought into the present without a contractual obligation to pay for the associated time value and risk. Instead, the stockholder simply has a pro rata claim on the ultimate realized value of the company.

Though the price of real estate is a function of how many households can qualify to borrow, and how much they can borrow, all of the parties to a sale – the lender, the borrower/purchaser, and the seller – are guided, directly or indirectly, by the exercise of estimating the present value of potential future income from the real estate. That would include the sale of crops in the case of farmland, the projected lease income in the case of commercial real estate, and the potential sale or lease proceeds in the case of a residential unit. Again, this is true even when those estimates are overly optimistic.

Stocks and real estate are both in large measure dependent upon debt. This reinforces debt's role as the primary mechanism for accessing future income.

Any exercise to estimate future income always involves a projection of interest rates. The lower the interest rate, the higher the present value of future income is. The large-scale debt growth of the past decades has mostly been accompanied by lower interest rates, despite dire warnings to the contrary.[27]

Whether those lower interest rates were introduced by policymakers, or whether instead the rising debt itself brought the change, the direction of rates and the amount of debt appear to be somewhat inversely related, although not in an absolutely linear fashion. In the forty years since the beginning of the Great Debt Explosion, while total debt has been dramatically and inexorably rising, interest rates have gone from between 15 percent and 20 percent down to the mid-2022 level of around 3 percent to 5 percent. While that overall decline was interrupted by brief spikes of several hundred basis points in 1994/95, 2005/06, and again in 2022/23, the first two of those spikes were followed by a renewed downwards drop. Although most economists would not share this view, I believe this helps to demonstrate that more debt pushes down interest rates rather than pushing them up. And if this is in fact true, then the same growth in debt would push up the valuation of stocks and real estate, because lower rates make the discounted value of future earnings higher.

This all adds to our growing inequality dilemma.

WELFARE FOR THE WEALTHY

We've seen that most of the gain in household wealth comes through the increased value of stocks and real estate, which increase in value as debt increases. Because the top 10 percent of US households own most of the stocks and real estate, these rewards fall on them disproportionately while the burdens of increasing debt fall dispro- portionately on the bottom 60 percent. And because growth in debt is essentially perpetual, with only episodic, calamitous reversals, the pressure towards growth in inequality, however fast or slow, is likely also essentially perpetual, absent some major countervailing change, such as a change in tax policy.

A straightforward example from LoanLand illustrates this inequality spiral. In 2020, US households got a multi-trillion-dollar 'raise' through pandemic relief programs. Let's say that as a corollary to these relief programs the LoanLand government borrowed in order to mail a $1,200 check to Sam, an individual who is part of the bottom 60 percent of LoanLand households. Sam lives in an apartment, owns no stock or real estate, and was temporarily laid off from his job because of the pandemic. The pandemic relief check is a lifesaver for Sam.

With his relief money, Sam buys groceries at a supermarket owned by Laura, another LoanLander. Laura is in the wealthiest 10 percent of LoanLanders.[28] Laura's Supermarket records increased profits from Sam's purchases. With this higher revenue, Laura pays herself a higher salary. That is the first benefit to her. And since her supermarket's revenue goes up, its stock price likely gets a boost, too, which increases Laura's net worth. That is the second benefit that accrues to her. Meanwhile, Sam was saved from disaster but spent everything he was given by the LoanLand government. His net worth certainly has not increased and may even have declined.

This illustrates how government welfare and relief programs, including proposals for a universal basic income, can readily end up making the top 10 percent wealthier, though this is certainly not the intended consequence of such policies. I do not mean to suggest that these programs do not also benefit the disadvantaged, providing a critical lifeline during adversity and calamity. It is simply that the proceeds of these programs are largely spent at establishments of which the top 10 percent are either major owners or executives, and occasionally both. Advocates for welfare and universal basic income can argue that a better policy design would prevent the unintended consequence of making the wealthy wealthier, and while this might be somewhat true, because of the *current* levels of wealth inequality, it would be difficult to make it *true enough* to avoid increasing wealth inequality still further.

Note that relief checks such as those sent out during the pandemic are the exception. What happens much more regularly in the economy is that, instead of receiving a check, Sam and others who are similarly situated *borrow* the $1,200 to cover their income shortfall for necessary spending. If we take this same scenario but have Sam getting the funds he needs by borrowing, it is obvious that the debt of lower-income households can, and regularly does, add to the wealth of the top income group. With the money from his loan, Sam buys groceries from Laura's Supermarket, and once again Laura benefits though both higher income and a higher stock price. Meanwhile, Sam spent what he borrowed, so his net worth has likely declined.

In practice, as far back as we can see, the wages of the bottom 60 percent are simply not high enough for that large swath of the population to accumulate a significant stake of real estate or stock, because households in this group largely spend what they make. Even if they receive regular salary increases that exceed inflation, and enjoy improved purchasing power and circumstances as a result, inequality will continue to increase, because of the basic lesson threaded through these chapters: debt always grows faster than GDP, which increases the value of stock and real estate, and the stock and real estate holdings of the top 10 percent are large relative to the holdings of the bottom 60 percent.

Of course, not all inequality is a function of debt trends. Life circumstances, education, family resources, tax and compensation practices, and a number of other factors matter, too, but debt trends are a major – and critically overlooked – part of the equation.

Thomas Piketty, in his highly influential book *Capital in the Twenty-First Century*, similarly observed that inequality will continue to increase because the wealthy hold the largest percentage of wealth-building assets. If the wealthy hold most of the assets, and assets grow faster than income, then inequality will inevitably increase, he argues, so long as the rate of return on investments remains greater than economic growth. In the post-war period in the US, this has definitely been the case. I go one step further by saying that it is the inherent, *perpetual* rise in debt that drives the rate of return on assets to be higher, because it is the debt itself which pushes the value of stocks and real estate to be higher.

THE SUM OF ALL DEBTS

Thus far we have considered three key elements of household net worth value creation:

- the act of bank lending, which creates new money 'out of thin air';
- the issuance of stock, which, through appreciation, can rise in value beyond the total amount of debt and deposits used to pay for it; and
- the appreciation of land values, which is in large part a function of debt, but can also create net worth 'out of thin air'.

Although they may look and sound like financial miracles, they emerge from the exacting and punctilious world of debits, credits, and debt.

We have seen that, in some important respects, debt, equity, and real estate are merely an exercise in bringing income from the future into the present. A person's or entity's net worth is, on the bottom line, a current expression of the future income of the assets owned by them, after deducting for debt. And based on everything discussed in the preceding pages, it seems reasonable to assert that much, perhaps even most, financial value in the economy is predicated, directly or indirectly, on the existence and escalation of debt.

We can now augment the general observations of macroeconomics that I set out in the Introduction (additions are in italics):

- The ratio of debt to income in economies almost always rises, with profound consequences, both good and bad.
- Money is itself created by debt.
- New money, and therefore new debt, is required for economic growth.

- *As a result, debt almost always grows as fast or faster than GDP. This means that all economic systems get increasingly leveraged through time.*
- *Debt always grows faster than GDP because debt for spending – Type 1 debt – corresponds to GDP growth, and debt for asset purchases – Type 2 debt – is added on top of that.*
- *The more the government spends, the more household net income rises.*
- Rising total debt brings an increase in household and national wealth or capital. Most wealth is only possible if other people or entities have debt. As wealth grows, so too must debt. *As part of this, the more government debt increases, the more household net worth rises. This wealth growth comes primarily from increases in the value of real estate and stocks, so it can fluctuate significantly over the short term.*
- *Much, or even most, financial value is predicated on debt. Stated differently, almost all financial value, whether that value is proximately ascribed to income, land, or something else, is realized and monetized through debt.*
- *There is a direct and causal link between the leniency of lenders' credit policies, the rate of debt growth, and the growth in asset values, whether those assets are common stocks, real estate, or entire companies.*
- At the same time, debt growth brings greater inequality, in part because middle- to lower-income households carry a disproportionate share of household debt burden. In fact, in economic systems based on debt – which is the world as it operates now – rising inequality is inevitable, absent some significant countervailing change such as a major change in a nation's tax policy.
- A current account and trade deficit contributes to private sector debt burdens.

- The overall increase in debt, especially private sector debt, eventually slows economic growth and can bring economic calamity.

With this set of economic observations in hand, we'll now turn to the rest of the Big 7 to test how they apply to economies, some of which differ from the US in key ways.

4

GROWTH STRATEGIES

Having explored the key elements driving growth and wealth creation in the US, we now explore the paradox of debt in the other countries of the Big 7. These economies vary in fundamental ways, with the most to learn about how debt functions from the remarkable differences seen between China and Germany, and the other five.

MODEL ECONOMIES

Let's begin by taking a look at the size of these economies and the macrosectors which dominate them. Figure 4.1 shows the relative size of GDP for the Big 7 countries in 2021, on a currency exchange basis, alongside the next three largest economies and the rest of the world (ROW). The economies of the US ($23.0 trillion) and China ($17.7 trillion) tower over all others, but it's worth noting that India[29] is now on par with the 'mature' economies of the UK and France. The next largest economy in size after the Big 7 is Italy, which at $2.1 trillion is well below France, the smallest of the Big 7 at $2.9 trillion. Together, the Big 7 constitute 62 percent of global GDP.

FIGURE 4.1. World GDP, 2021

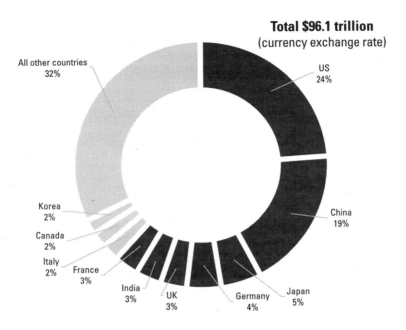

Total $96.1 trillion
(currency exchange rate)

All other countries 32%

US 24%

China 19%

Korea 2%

Canada 2%

Italy 2%

France 3%

India 3%

UK 3%

Germany 4%

Japan 5%

As we define the model for each of the Big 7 economies, it is useful to identify which macrosector most often posts the largest loss, since, as we've discussed, that sector in effect drives the net income of the economy's other macrosectors. Five of the Big 7 follow the US paradigm, whereby government spending and deficits boost private sector net income – primarily household net income – such that the two roughly offset each other. In turn, the government deficit leads to a decline in government net worth that helps to bring about a gain in household and other private sector net worth. This is the classic *government debt and spending model*. In this model, the benefit of government spending can flow to non-financial businesses as well as to households, although to varying degrees. In some countries, such as the US, most government spending goes to the benefit of households, while in others, such as Japan, relatively more goes to non-financial businesses. In addition to the US, the UK, France, India, and Japan operate by the government debt and spending model.

The term 'model' refers to this being a defining, even if unintentional, characteristic of the economy. It is not meant to suggest that the approach is superior or results in better outcomes for the economy, even when it does so, which will become clear as we look at the alternative models.

So far, I've referred to a country having a government debt and spending *strategy*. By this I mean that the economy in fact operates primarily following that particular model, not that the country's politicians and policymakers have intentionally pursued, or even been aware of, that model. Indeed, it's reasonable to say that some governments do not fully comprehend that they have adopted a government debt and spending strategy and may have arrived at it inadvertently. It is equally reasonable to say that some governments may have no deliberate economic strategy at all; their approach is simply the by-product of wider economic and social circumstances, as well as political compromise and negotiation.

I hasten to add that the government debt and spending model works most readily in large, developed economies, which have deep and established markets for government debt. Smaller, less developed countries, particularly those that borrow in a foreign currency and are net importers, are much less well suited for the government debt and spending model. A small country government that borrows in a foreign currency and runs a trade deficit is pursuing a high-risk strategy that can easily lead to a devaluation and a borrowing crisis. But the dynamics of smaller economies are a story for another book.

For Germany, in stark contrast to the US, the macrosector with the largest loss has been the ROW, given that Germany's partners in trade collectively post a large net loss in their net trade with Germany. In other words, Germany sells more to other countries than other countries sell to Germany. This is the *net export model*. Here, I'm using the terms 'net income' and 'net loss' (instead of 'net surplus' and 'net deficit') to underscore that Germany's private sector makes more than it spends in trade, to the German economy's immense benefit, and Germany's trading partners spend more than they make, and generally must borrow to cover the shortfall, to their general detriment. Using a term like 'net deficit' makes the process seem benign, when in reality the deficit is to the disadvantage of the net importer.

China departs from both the government debt and spending model and the net export model because China's non-financial business sector posts the largest net loss of its macrosectors, as we'll see in the income statements later in this chapter. China uses the very high net losses of this sector to boost household net income. China's non-financial businesses post a large loss because the income statements for the country have been largely prepared on a cash basis; however, most non-financial businesses report their results using *accrual accounting*, which means they defer or avoid the recognition of certain expenses, and thus they show a profit. We'll discuss this crucial distinction later in this chapter. For now, it is useful to know that China's non-financial business losses are entirely funded by borrowing from banks and other lenders, so that the cash needs of this macrosector are fully met.

The loans made by China's banks and other lenders to China's non-financial businesses often fall far outside the parameters of sound credit used by lenders in other Big 7 economies. Loans to the developer Evergrande (officially, the China Evergrande Group), which defaulted in 2021 and 2022, are symptomatic of the widespread over-lending in China; the loans were so far out of the bounds of prudent credit that Evergrande became the world's most indebted company. By 2021, Evergrande had amassed the equivalent of more than $300 billion in debt and other liabilities, which was likely greater than the realistic value of its assets. This debt was all to build residences, many of which went unsold, and some of which were pre-sold but still unbuilt – part of a nationwide accumulation of somewhere between 50 million and 100 million housing units which stand empty in

China. Meanwhile, as Evergrande piled up debt, it paid out billions in dividends to wealthy stockholders. The company obtained loans even though it dangerously exceeded China's own recently articulated 'three red lines' policy for property developers, which mandates a liability to asset ratio of less than 70 percent, a net debt to equity ratio of less than 100 percent, and a cash to short-term debt ratio of more than 100 percent.

In short, China's non-financial business sector, in lieu of the central government, is used by the Chinese government to pump income into the household sector (though that may or may not have been the government's original intention). This is the *business debt and spending model*, and it is unique to China among the Big 7. In fact, it would be hard for any country to use this approach without China's extraordinary government control over both its non-financial businesses and its banks and other lenders. And given the degree of government control over non-financial businesses in China, some might argue this is simply a variation on the government debt and spending theme.

China has followed this economic strategy ever since the government adopted elements of a capitalist economy in the 1980s. It's easy to imagine that the leaders of the Communist government at that time were eager to catch up to the developed world, and one way to do this was to prod an emerging sector of non-financial businesses to build a lot of houses, buildings, and infrastructure, all of which were funded by bank lending. Along the way they made the happy discovery that China's households as a whole were getting a bump in income from this in the form of salaries, and GDP was growing briskly. So the government simply doubled down on the practice.

All three of these models require significant growth in debt to boost household net income and net worth: government debt in the case of the US and other government debt and spending economies; private sector debt across the ROW in the case of Germany; and non-financial business debt in the case of China. The limits on growth for each of these types of debt represent the limits of each economic model.

As we take a closer look at each of the debt approaches taken across the Big 7 economies, we'll consider each country's debt profile to understand its debt in the context of income and assets, as we did for the US in Figure 2.8.[30]

I would like to make one last note before we turn to examining each of these countries. It is easiest for a country to grow GDP when population growth is high and – as many before me have said – typically, fast economic growth solves problems and slow growth causes them. But for most of these countries, most notably China, Germany, and Japan, population growth is decelerating or actually in decline, portending slower GDP growth. Decelerating population growth will increasingly present challenges to GDP growth in these countries and, as such, deserves its own study, complementary to the ideas presented in this book. Among major, developed countries, the US has the most favorable population growth trends in the context of GDP growth.[31] India, a developing country, has a comparatively young demographic profile with comparatively high population growth.

FRANCE – A CASE OF DÉJÀ VU

We start with the economy of France because, like the US, it is representative of the government debt and spending model. Thus many of the insights about debt in the US economy gleaned from the analysis in Chapter 2 can be seen in play here, too.

Over the past half century, France's total debt has grown rapidly, as shown in Figure 4.2. Total debt rocketed from 115 percent to 346 percent of GDP between 1970 and 2021. Very high private debt growth from 1986 until 1993 and from 2003 until 2009 brought overcapacity, retrenchment, and recession to France in the early 1990s and then

FIGURE 4.2. France debt profile, 1970–2021

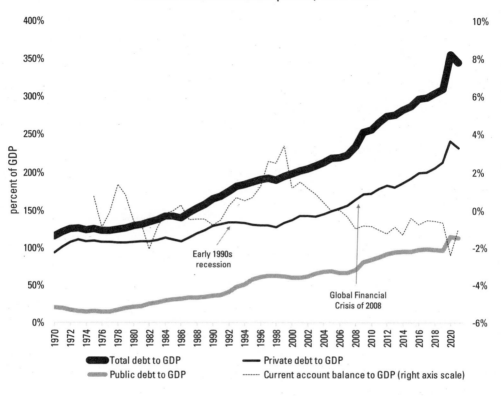

again after the Global Financial Crisis of 2008. Immediately after both of these difficult periods, government debt growth increased, as the government incurred higher deficits to help support economic recovery. From 2013 onwards, private debt in France has continued to be high, potentially resulting in harmful overcapacity. The spike in debt seen in 2020 reflects a combination of pandemic relief spending, including higher payments from France's unemployment schemes, and a drop in GDP. So while the causes, timing, and scale are different, France has had an overall experience of debt similar to the US over the past few decades.

This is also the case when we drill down to the data for France's macrosectors over time. France's net income trends clearly show the same paradigm as in the US: increased government spending has boosted the net income of the household sector, as can be seen by how the household and government income lines in Figure 4.3 are near reflections of each other.

Total domestic net income in France is slightly negative because of the country's small but persistent trade deficit with the ROW. As in the US, total domestic net income and the net income in the ROW are inversions of each other.

Just as in the US, the dramatic increase in government pandemic spending translated into an equally dramatic increase in household net income and net worth. We can also see that a notable and perhaps uncomfortable – for France – amount of this relief ended up in the hands of the ROW, largely because France's exports declined more than its imports during the pandemic.

FIGURE 4.3. France net income by macrosector, 1995–2021

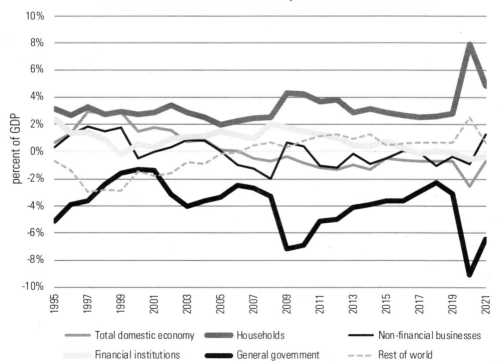

The data available at this writing is not sufficiently current to know with certainty whether the government boost in spending increased inequality in France – or, for that matter, in any of the other Big 7 economies. This must wait until inequality metrics, such as asset concentration amounts in the top percentiles, and tax databases are updated. For now, it's reasonable to hypothesize that inequality did increase, perhaps significantly. Recall that in the US, the top 10 percent holds more than 60 percent of the total stock and real estate and stock owned by households and the bottom 60 percent holds less than 15 percent.

Further, as we saw from the Federal Reserve's distributional financial accounts data, from 2019 to 2021 the wealth share of the top 1 percent in the US hit the highest value ever posted to date. Thomas Piketty, utilizing tax records, concludes that other major countries, not just the US, have had similarly unequal distribution of assets across their citizenry. Figure 4.4 is drawn from the World Inequality Database that stems from his research. It shows the ownership of wealth by the wealthiest 10 percent in the Big 7 economies increasing

FIGURE 4.4. Wealth share of the Big 7's top 10 percentile of wealth, 1980–2019

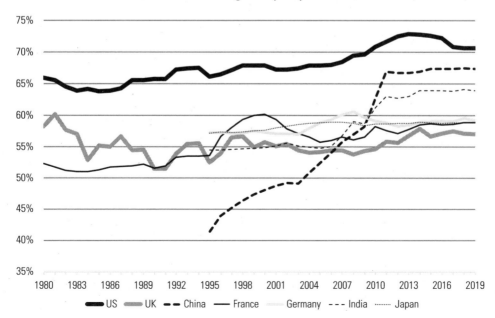

from the 1980s, marking the start of the Great Debt Explosion, after having largely decreased for years prior. The proportion of wealth owned by the top 10 percent is very high across all of the Big 7, ranging from 57 percent in the UK to 71 percent in the US. As data becomes available for years beyond the ones included here, I anticipate that we'll see continued high or increasing wealth concentrations for the reasons outlined previously. The highest levels of wealth inequality are seen in the US and China, which are the very countries in which we have seen the largest increase in asset valuations.

Because the top 10 percent in all Big 7 economies hold such a large share of the key wealth-building assets, and the value of these assets went up during the pandemic as a result of government and central bank support, it is reasonable to conclude that the top 10 percent of households in the Big 7 countries received most of the benefit of government pandemic relief spending. It's also reasonable to conclude that, as in the example of LoanLander Sam discussed in Chapter 3, a disproportionate amount of the spending of pandemic relief occurred at establishments largely owned, directly or indirectly, and managed by the top 10 percent. If the data show that these things held true, then the pandemic will have delivered increased wealth inequality not only to the US but also to France and the other Big 7 economies.

Deficit spending in France caused a slight decline in the net worth of the government, as more government debt was issued. However, this decline was more than offset by strong gains in the net worth of the household and non-financial business macrosectors. As shown in Figure 4.5, from 2000 to 2020, the net worth of households in France increased from 339 percent to 584 percent of GDP, while the net worth of the government declined from 29 percent to 10 percent of GDP.

This net worth gain in the household and non-financial business sectors was tied to increased government debt in two ways. First, much of the government's spending ended up in the bank accounts of households.

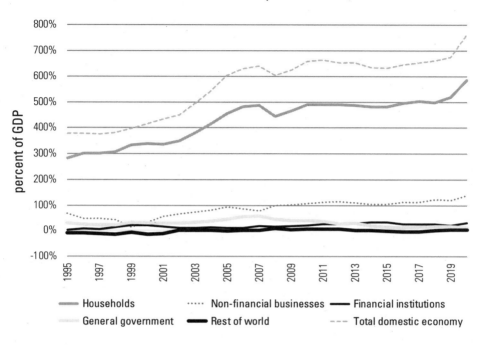

FIGURE 4.5. France net worth by macrosector, 1995–2020

Second, the flood of relief cash had the effect of boosting the value of stocks and real estate. Again we see a key principle of dual-entry accounting at work at the level of a national economy: a decline in government net worth is part of what brings an increase in household net worth.

One notable difference between France and the US is that the French government macrosector has a positive net worth, albeit one that is rapidly declining as government indebtedness increases. In contrast, the US government has significant negative net worth. Much of this can be traced to the fact that the French government, including local government entities, owns substantial quantities of stock and other financial assets while the US government holds almost none. In fact, the US government holds far fewer assets relative to GDP than all of the other Big 7 governments, although that contrast may be somewhat misleading given the difficulty of valuing real estate in each country.

In addition to France, three other Big 7 governments have a positive net worth, despite their debt. The government's net worth in China and Germany is solidly positive. Japan also has a positive government net worth but, as for France, it has been shrinking due to the addition of debt, and indeed may flip to being negative in the near future. Like the US, the governments of the UK and India have negative net worth. It's not clear whether this difference is of great consequence, however, given that economic trends more so than asset holdings determine the creditworthiness of nations. At the very least, these asset holdings represent additional capacity for spending, and are evidence of the level of government support for financial markets.

Through this analysis of debt position, we can see that France is a solid example of how most large, developed countries operate: it has both very high total debt growth and high reliance on government debt growth to increase household net income, the definition of the government debt and spending model. The most concerning factor for France as of this writing is the high growth trend in its private sector debt, which portends potential overcapacity in select areas of the economy, with the possibility of a financial reversal of some sort within the next few years.

THE UK – NO ECONOMY IS AN ISLAND

The UK is yet another Big 7 economy that follows the government debt and spending model. And like France, the debt profile of the UK is reasonably similar to that of the US: greater government losses have meant more household net income and greater household net worth.

The UK's total debt has also grown dramatically over the past fifty years. Total debt doubled from 133 percent to 261 percent of GDP between 1970 and 2021. And like in France, explosive private sector debt growth from 1979 to 1991, and again from 1997 to 2008,

FIGURE 4.6. UK debt profile, 1970–2021

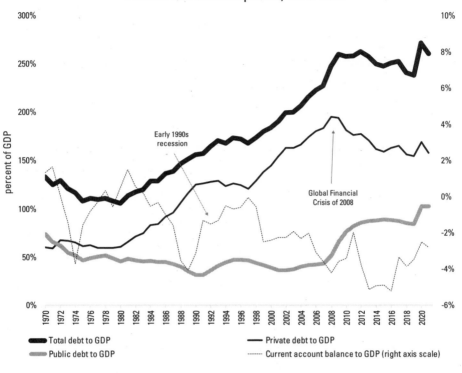

brought overcapacity, retrenchment, and recession in the early 1990s and in the wake of the Global Financial Crisis of 2008, respectively. As we saw with the US and France, government debt grew in the aftermath of both periods, as tax receipts fell and the UK government spent to bolster the economy.

Looking at the UK's macrosector net income over time (Figure 4.7), we can see that the household and government net income lines roughly mirror each other, with increases in government losses causing an increase in household net income, as in the US and France. But look more closely and note that households in the UK *lost* money from 2017 to 2019. This odd phenomenon was also evident in the US in the years immediately preceding the crashes of 1987 and 2008. In those cases, very high household spending, including a significant increase in the purchase of houses and luxury imports, was registered in the nation's cash-based net income statements as a large increase in household expenses, and thus manifested as a net loss over the period. In the UK, these pre-pandemic household losses appear to have been due to a large, perhaps even excessive, increase in household spending, primarily in the form of real estate purchases.

More important, however, is the high level of net income for the ROW in the UK, a disadvantageous trend that is captured in the large, persistent trade and current account deficit in the UK's debt profile (Figure 4.6). This deficit has had the effect of depressing the UK's household and non-financial business net income. It also helps to explain the discontent and concern over an unfair trade disadvantage that may have tipped the scales in the 2016 referendum vote over whether to remain in or leave the EU. Unfortunately for the UK, a debt profile analysis does not necessarily support Brexit as the best strategy to redress this disadvantage.

FIGURE 4.7. UK net income by macrosector, 1995–2021

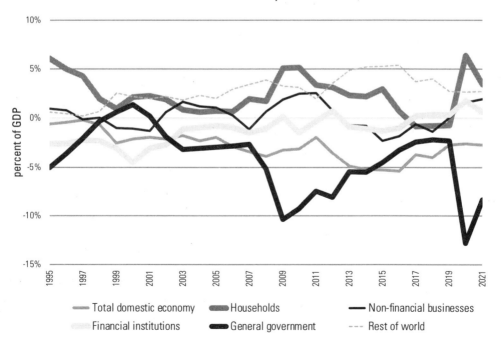

As noted earlier, because of the UK's dependence on natural gas imports, its trade deficit worsened as a result of the war in Ukraine and subsequent economic sanctions against Russia, which led to a dramatic increase in natural gas prices in 2022. Persistent trade deficits create vulnerability to this very sort of adversity. When the exchange rate of the pound versus the dollar collapsed in late 2022, imports became even more expensive for the UK, at a time when higher, Covid-linked inflation was already decimating many household budgets. This is a cautionary tale for economic planners everywhere: trade deficits warrant the full attention of a government because they constrain the tools available for boosting an economy.

The UK government, like the US and French governments, spent significant amounts on pandemic relief in 2020, with the government deficit rising to 13 percent of GDP. This increase in government debt caused the net income of households and non-financial businesses combined to rise to 8.5 percent of GDP. The relative amount of pandemic relief resembled that in the US; however, because the UK government chose to focus on supports such as income replacement for workers furloughed from their jobs during lockdowns rather than on sending checks directly to households, the benefits of this spending included more benefit to non-financial businesses by comparison. In a change of approach, in autumn 2022 the government offered subsidies for rising household energy expenses. This spending was at a level similar to the country's pandemic relief.

All of this has had, and will have, implications for the UK's net worth by macrosector over time. As shown in Figure 4.8, government net worth in the UK has been declining, for the same reason as in the US and France: because government debt is increasing. And as in the US and France, the decline in government net worth is more than offset by an increase in household net worth. From 2000 to 2020, the net worth of Britain's households increased from 404 percent to 535 percent of GDP, while the net worth of the government decreased from negative 4 percent to negative 69 percent of GDP. This has happened directly, in the form of increased non-equity-related financial assets such as deposit accounts and bonds, but also indirectly, in the form of land and pension assets, as increased cash and purchases from pandemic relief spending lifted the value of those assets. However, we can see an even larger increase in the net worth of the ROW macrosector – a function of the UK's trade disadvantage. This reflects increased holdings by the ROW of UK non-equity financial assets, including deposits.

The UK exemplifies a country with both very high total debt growth and high reliance on the government debt and spending model. Compared to France, however, its total debt growth has moderated over the last decade, reflecting different recent practices in its lending sector.

FIGURE 4.8. UK net worth by macrosector, 1995–2020

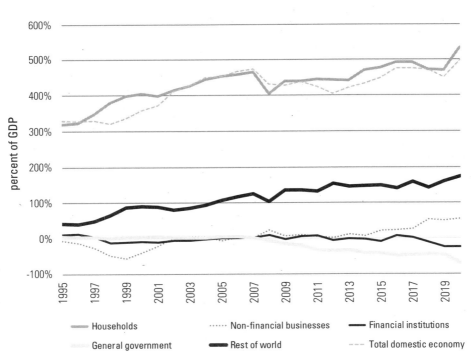

INDIA – LESS DEBT, LESS DATA

India's total debt is considerably lower than the other Big 7 economies, a marker of the economy's less developed status. This lower total
debt is a prime illustration of one of the principles of debt economics
that I outlined in the Introduction: that GDP growth results from
debt growth.

Let's consider the evidence of this through a comparison of
India with the other developing economy in the Big 7, China.
The GDPs of India and China were at rough parity in 1987, at
which point China's debt growth began to take off, facilitating the
record-breaking GDP growth that has led to China's economy
being five times the size of India's today. Even after adjusting the
figures for relative currency valuations (that is, on a purchasing
power parity, or PPP, basis), China's economy is three times the
size of India's. China's much larger debt growth in comparison to
India powered China's much greater GDP growth, too. The rub is
that China's level of non-government debt is now so high it stands
as a potential impediment to the economy's future growth. India,
by contrast, has the capacity to grow GDP significantly over the
next decades.

Although India's debt is starting from a lower base, its growth in
debt has still been high. Its total debt has gone from below 50 percent
of GDP in 1970 – a best estimate, given the data available – to 176
percent of GDP in 2021.

Net income information for India is only available for 2004 to
2021 (Figure 4.10). Despite the narrow timespan, the figure shows
the same mirroring of government and household net income seen
elsewhere. Surprisingly, India has a trade and current account deficit,
as it has not translated its low wage profile into a net trade advantage.
This can be seen in the positive net income of the ROW over this
period.

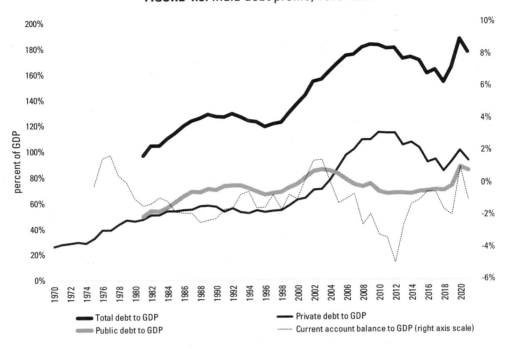

FIGURE 4.9. India debt profile, 1970–2021

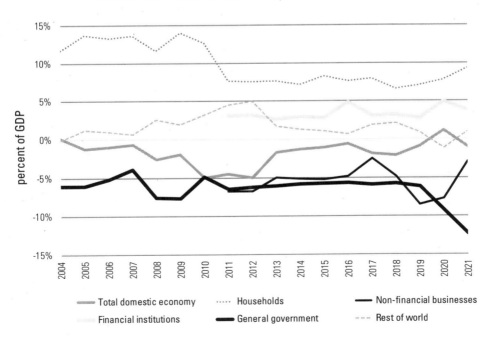

FIGURE 4.10. India net income by macrosector, 2004–2021

FIGURE 4.11. India net worth by macrosector, 2011–2018

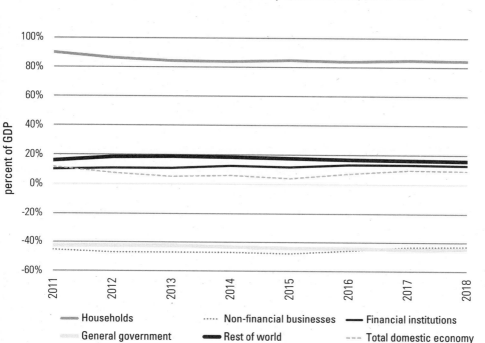

The balance sheets for India also cover a short window of economic history, from 2011 to 2018 (Figure 4.11). With this end date, it is not yet possible to know how the pandemic affected macrosectors of the economy. In addition, the data available does not include any non-financial assets, such as real estate. Net worth trends show a slight decline from 2008, but the picture is far from complete.

India is the singular example of a less developed country among the Big 7 today. Less developed countries have less debt, and as such, much of India's debt accumulation will happen in the future as it increases spending on development. India could benefit greatly from studying the experience of other Big 7 countries and strategically considering the paths that could be taken to guide its economy going forward.

JAPAN – THE COST OF HIGH-FLYING DEBT

Japan is the most vivid illustration among the Big 7 of the debt economics principle that the ratio of debt to income almost always rises. What makes it different, however, is the unprecedented substitution of public debt in place of private debt as the larger constituent in the debt ratio.

This is particularly striking because Japan's total debt is the highest among the Big 7. As shown in Figure 4.12, from 1970 to 2021 the economy's debt grew from 130 percent to 430 percent of GDP. Roughly 90 percentage points of that debt increase has been used not to fund deficits but instead to fund the Japanese Treasury's purchase of financial assets, which it has done to support financial markets, including stocks. This makes the net lower.

From 1981 to 1991, private sector debt in Japan rose at an extraordinary pace, with real estate and stock market valuations reaching meteoric heights before they collapsed in the early 1990s. By 1997, private debt had peaked. It has declined steadily as a percentage of

FIGURE 4.12. Japan debt profile, 1970–2021

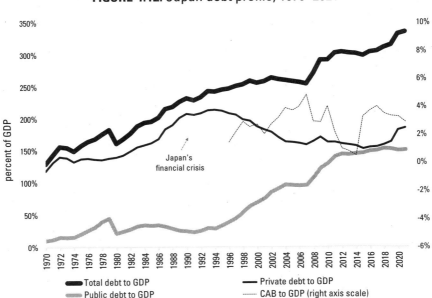

GDP since then, exerting a grim downwards pressure on the country's GDP growth. The excesses were so pronounced that in the aftermath of peak private debt, Japan's nominal GDP was essentially flat all the way until 2017. This extended period of little or no GDP growth is variously referred to as the Lost Decade, the Lost Decades, or the Lost Generation. Since the 1990s, the government's policy has been to offset the losses in private debt creation through radical increases in government debt and spending.

Net income in Japan tells the same story as in the US, the UK, and France, illustrating that a government deficit can be a key source for increased household income. However, non-financial businesses in Japan get as much of the benefit of government deficit spending as do households. So instead of charting separate lines for the income of households and non-financial businesses, Figure 4.13 shows income for these two macrosectors combined. This combined line roughly mirrors the general government line.

FIGURE 4.13. Japan net income by macrosector, 1994–2020

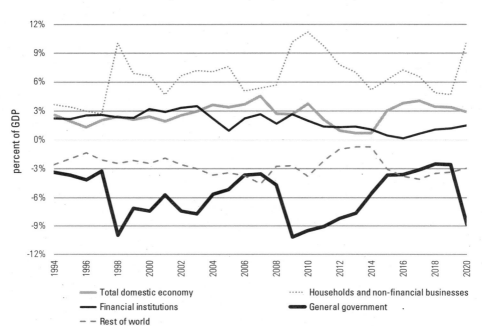

Total domestic economy .... Households and non-financial businesses
—— Financial institutions ●●● General government
– – Rest of world

To help combat the economic impact of the pandemic, in 2020 the Japanese government increased spending, with government debt growth rising to more than ¥50 trillion – twice the level of growth over the previous five years. This increased net loss in government income translated into significantly increased net income for households and non-financial businesses that year.

The trend in the net worth of Japan's macrosectors over the past three decades is much flatter than in most of the other countries examined here, as shown in Figure 4.14. This is the case despite Japan's high total debt growth, largely because the country's private sector has spent most of the past twenty-five years deleveraging from the 1990s peak in private debt levels.

Note, too, that much of Japan's debt growth came in the form of government purchase of debt, which does not typically boost the value of real estate or stocks. So while the Nikkei Stock Average has

FIGURE 4.14. Japan net worth by macrosector, 1994–2020

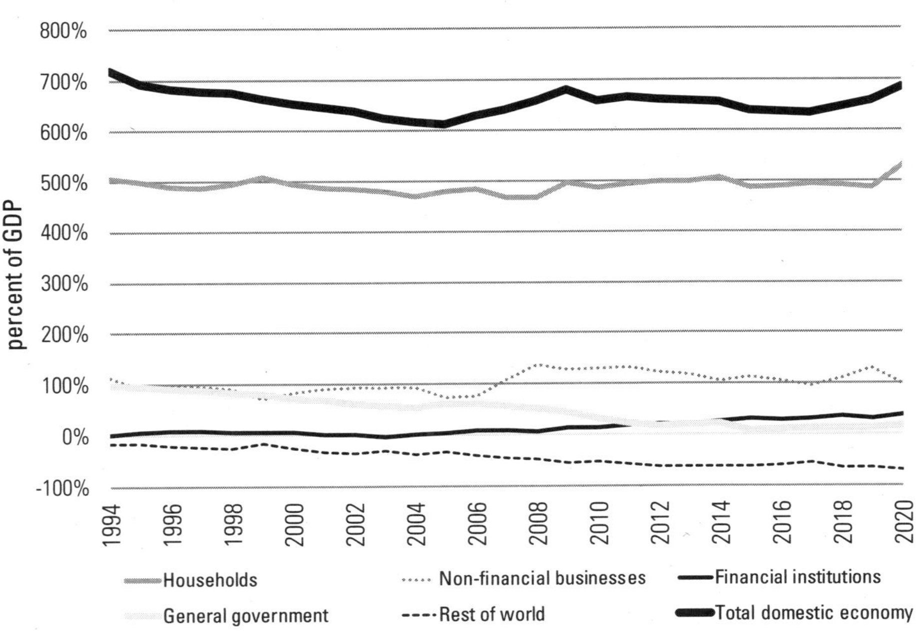

been rallying upwards (with some ups and downs) since the Global Financial Crisis of 2008, it has been well shy of its asset price bubble high of 38,957 posted in December 1989. The closest it has come to those heights was in February 2021, when the Bank of Japan infused the asset markets with cash in response to the pandemic and the Nikkei topped 30,000.

There is another interesting anomaly in Japan's experience of debt and wealth. Although the government's net worth has declined over time due to ongoing deficits, it actually went up in 2020 – and this despite increasing borrowing. This was possible because the Japanese government holds a significant quantity of financial assets and the value of these assets went up during the pandemic. Yet, notwithstanding its idiosyncrasies, the paradigm we see elsewhere holds here, too, for 2020: decreasing government net worth brings increasing private sector net worth.

In many respects, Japan may be a harbinger of the future for Big 7 economies. It had its cataclysmic debt crisis in the 1990s, well over a decade before the Global Financial Crisis of 2008, which disproportionately affected the US and Western Europe, and a generation before any financial crisis that China might experience in the 'Evergrande era'. Instead, Japan was forced to enter a period of deleveraging from its too-lofty heights of 1990s private debt while the rest of the Big 7 went along for a longer ride on the Great Debt Explosion.

Without the GDP growth boost that would normally have come from private debt growth but was absent because of private debt deleveraging, Japan became reliant on government debt growth, and thus has the dubious distinction of leading the Big 7 in this regard. It relies on government debt growth not just to prop up household income but also to prop up the country's financial markets, doing so through extraordinarily large government purchases of stocks and other financial assets.

Japan is a sobering example of the diminishing impact of rising debt on asset values once they reach extraordinarily high levels – a topic we'll return to in Chapter 8, when we consider the limits of debt in an economy.

GERMANY – IN TRADE, ÜBER ALLES

Germany's total debt is the lowest among the developed countries of the Big 7, as shown in Figure 4.15. An exceptionally favorable trade balance from 1981 to 1990, and even more so in the period from 2003 through 2021, allowed Germany to have favorable economic growth without relying too much, in relative terms, on total debt growth. Still, its total debt growth has been high as well, rising from 102 percent to 199 percent of GDP from 1970 to 2001.

FIGURE 4.15. Germany debt profile, 1970–2021

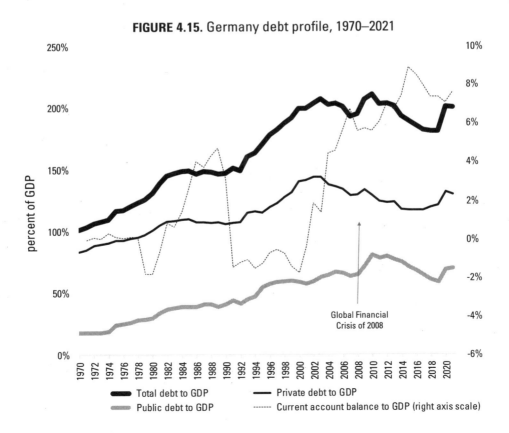

To understand Germany (and also, as we'll see later, China), we need to take a brief detour and discuss how households achieve positive net income. Across the five countries that adhere to the government debt and spending model, increased government debt has provided much of the positive net income to households. While, in total, it is true that most of the increased spending of households comes from increased household debt and not from increased government debt, household debt and spending alone do not and cannot bring increased household net income because the spending from one household to another is offsetting and thus nets to zero. We saw this in LoanLand in Chapter 1, where Ruth's spending with Mary was an expense for Ruth and income for Mary but neutral for all LoanLand households when considered in aggregate. To post positive net income in the household macrosector, some payments to households must come from outside the household sector. The candidates for supplying these payments are government debt and spending, business debt and spending, or net exports. Most typically, among these three options, government debt and spending has had the greatest positive impact on household net income and net worth in most of the countries we're examining.

And so we see that in five of the Big 7 economies, government spending is the strategy that has increased net income. But it is not the only way. An economy can also grow through business spending and debt, household spending and debt, or a net trade surplus. This clarification is vital to understanding why generally – but not always – it takes government spending for household income to exceed household expenses.

Now, let's return to one of the two exceptions, Germany, which has grown its economy through a net trade surplus. Figure 4.16 shows Germany's macrosector net income through time. Here we can clearly see that the macrosector with by far the largest net loss is the ROW. So, the rough inversion in this figure is between the ROW's losses and the gains of German households and non-financial businesses combined. The relationship is not quite as perfectly mirrored as for the Big 7 economies we have studied so far, but it is still reasonably evident.

The ROW loss in net income has been very good news for Germany, because the additional net income for Germany's private sector translates into a trade surplus which results in GDP growth not dependent on domestic private debt growth – and more taxes for Germany's government. Exports provide an economy with income that is not reliant on domestic debt growth. Instead, this growth comes from private debt growth in importing countries. Simultaneously, Germany is able to post slightly positive government net income. That is the considerable prize of the net export model.

I said near the top of this chapter that the term 'model' was not meant to suggest that one of these approaches to debt and growth was better than any others, and, despite its obvious economic benefits,

FIGURE 4.16. Germany net income by macrosector, 1995–2021

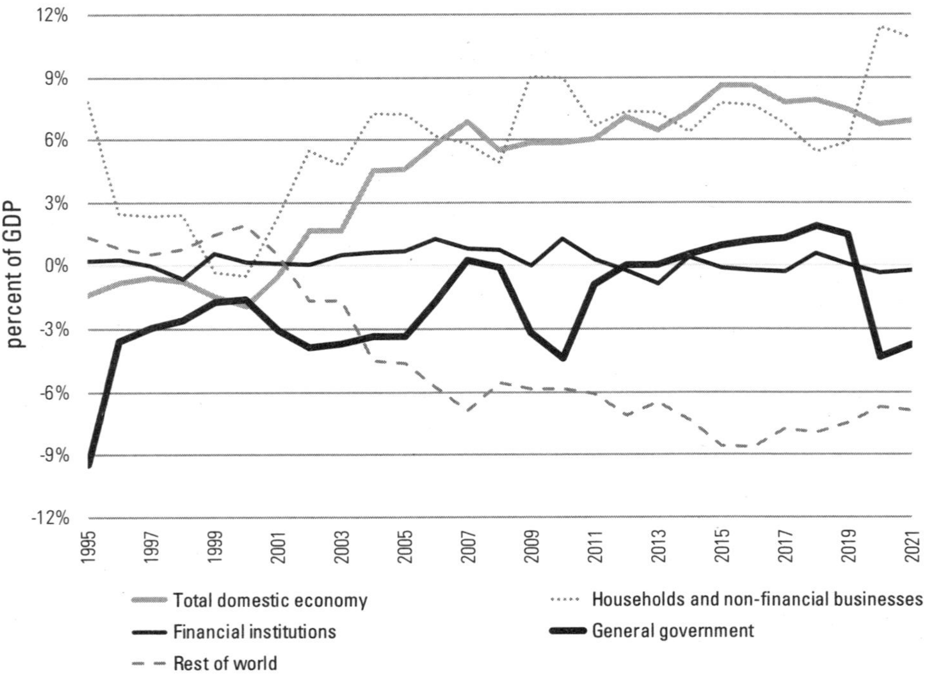

Legend:
— Total domestic economy
····· Households and non-financial businesses
— Financial institutions
— General government
– – Rest of world

I do not advocate for the adoption of the net export strategy by government planners. It's hard to achieve, just as difficult to sustain, and can make for tumultuous foreign relations. Still, it is a helpful thing, when you have it.

It is also constrained by the economic fortunes of a country's trading partners. Even with all of the benefits of accruing a ROW net income loss, the German economy needed to be propped up with pandemic relief in 2020. Although the rise in German government spending was at a lower level than in the US, it had much the same effect as in the other Big 7 economies: it boosted Germany's household net income and reduced the government's net worth.

Germany's net worth, shown in Figure 4.17, has looked different as well. Every macrosector's net worth has gone up in the twelve years since the Global Financial Crisis of 2008, including the government's – every macrosector's net worth has gone up, that is, except

FIGURE 4.17. Germany net worth by macrosector, 1995–2020

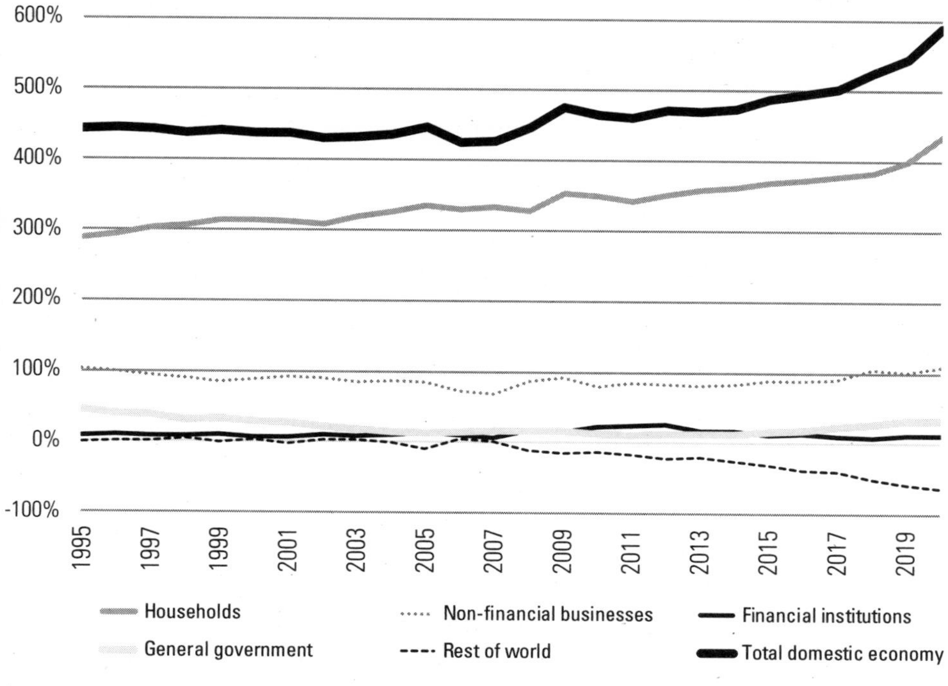

the ROW's. The ROW's slight decline, a consequence of Germany's trade surplus, added to the rising tide that lifted all other macrosectors in the economy.

Germany's trade advantage began as a windfall with its entry into the European currency union in the early 2000s. Because of the strictures of the currency union, the trade advantage was partially protected in ways that would not be available to a country operating outside a currency union. Greece, for example, could not devalue its currency to mitigate its trade disadvantage with Germany. To its credit, Germany sustained its trade advantage within the currency union and then expanded it, to reap rewards from its vast net trading surplus with many trading partners around the globe. In recent years, Germany's net exports have been buttressed significantly by China's turbocharged debt growth. Now that China's debt growth is decelerating, Germany may start to feel some tightening in its net income.

Indeed, Germany's reign as a giant net exporter is finally being challenged. In 2022, imports to Germany have exploded as an expense, largely due to rising energy costs, and as a result, the country's trade surplus declined markedly. What if that change persists and Germany's trade advantage starts to unravel? What if Germany were to begin to face not only higher import prices but also tariffs, quotas, devaluations, and other barriers to exports in key export markets across the globe – not just China, but also the US and other European countries? What if Germany's overreliance on Russian energy exports takes years to rectify? And what if one or some or all of these things happen just as Germany's overreliance on China starts to be felt, given China's decelerated growth? Any among these turns of events would likely force Germany to make some stark economic choices. Surely it would – and, given the outlook for China's GDP growth, I'm tempted to say it will – suffer a contraction, unless the government quickly encourages large increases in private sector spending, funded by increased business and household debt, or, alternatively, enacts large increases in government spending. These would be a significant departure from Germany's past practices, and potentially remake the German economy.

Germany's asset values, especially for stocks, its total net worth, and its household net worth, are somewhat low in comparison to the other developed countries of the Big 7. Germany's public stocks have tended to trade at lower valuations than US stocks, and some economists contend that Germany's privately held stocks are carried at too low a valuation. This might help to explain why Germany's household net worth is only 436 percent of GDP as compared to 584 percent of GDP for France and 654 percent for the US. But there's also another way to look at this: because less debt contributes to lower asset values, Germany's lower debt levels might be holding down the value of its stocks.

Germany has been the prime example of the net export model among the Big 7. During the 2000s, China briefly operated on the net export model, but its trade surplus came from the West's epochal debt binge and evaporated with the Global Financial Crisis of 2008. Perhaps a good portion of Germany's current trade benefit has come from China's extraordinary debt growth. Over the longer term, it remains to be seen how potentially lower debt growth in China, sanctions against Russia, and other changes in Russia's export practices will impact the German net export model.

The prognosis is not favorable.

CHINA – FEEDING THE CAPITAL DRAGON

China follows a radically different strategy for boosting household net income growth, one that is unlike any other major country, and consequently, I spend more time examining this country's financial statements. Though it seems strange in contrast to other countries, the big picture is that China relies to an extraordinary degree on business sector losses and debt. The country's government, at all levels, has an almost absolute authority over both non-financial businesses and lenders – not just over state-owned enterprises, but all businesses, banks, and other lenders. Its economic strategy would be next to impossible otherwise.

Figure 4.18 shows China's macrosector net income. Of particular note is the enormous, sustained cash-flow net loss for non-financial businesses, which exceeded 12 percent of GDP in 2019.[32] In the other Big 7 economies, this number is closer to zero or somewhat positive, so the difference here is highly significant.

China's non-financial business loss is offset by a proportionate increase in household net income, which was also roughly 12 percent of GDP in 2019. From 1992 to 2019, the two mirrored each other – that is, in China the inverse relationship applies more to non-financial

FIGURE 4.18. China net income by macrosector, 1992–2019

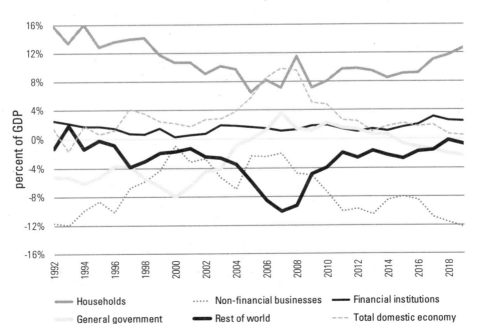

business net losses and household net income rather than to government net losses and household net income. As non-financial business sector net losses grow, household net income increases. This increase in non-financial business losses has in turn delivered an increase in household net income through payment of salaries and other disbursements.

To be sure, government spending is present, too, and includes spending and debt of local governments. These lower-level authorities get a lot of attention from economists who specialize in studying China. While local government spending in the other Big 7 economies is dwarfed by central government spending, things are more complicated in China, because of the heavy borrowing and spending that goes through local government financing vehicles (LGFVs). These entities fund the construction of roads, railways, airports, power plants, and other infrastructure, and in late 2022 were being leaned on heavily to help China's economy to recover from the impact of the pandemic and other, more self-inflicted, financial challenges. Regardless, this infrastructure spending has in recent years been exceeded by non-financial business debt and spending, for an important reason: local governments in China have grown dependent on the debt-financed purchase of local government land by non-financial businesses, with real estate developers providing roughly 40 percent of local government annual revenue. These land sales are necessary for servicing LGFV debt, which in 2021 was estimated to total ¥54 trillion, or $8 trillion, compared with non-financial business debt of ¥174 trillion, or $26 trillion. This means that the finances of local governments and China's commercial real estate development sector are now inextricably intertwined, and are the biggest contributor to non-financial business losses in China.

These losses are shown on a cash basis in Figure 4.18. China's banks and other lenders accommodate this loss by lending whatever is needed to fully cover it and keep its non-financial businesses operating. Of course, this is why business loans have grown so rapidly for so many years in China, and now stand at 158 percent of GDP, twice the relative level of business loans to GDP in the US, and a truly problematic level.

As with all the net income figures presented in this book, my colleagues and I have shown these net income losses on a cash basis rather than on the accrual basis that Chinese businesses use to handle certain expenses. As noted earlier, accrual accounting means that companies defer or accelerate certain expenses to match them to the period in which that expense provides benefit or has its intended impact rather than accounting for them when they are actually paid. With accrual accounting, a company that built a $10 million building or factory would post the $10 million to its balance sheet as an asset instead of subtracting it as an expense, and then perhaps recognize some small portion of the $10 million as an expense in following years, such that the expense is either incurred gradually over future years, or not at all. Those expenses are considered investment expenses, and posting them as an asset instead of an expense is referred to as *capitalizing the expense*. The cash-based income statements used in this book are much less complicated. Funds that are spent, whether for a house, some software, a dividend to investors, or some other purpose, are recorded as an expense at the moment they are spent.

The data for China used to generate the net income by macrosector presented in Figure 14.18 was gathered by the OECD and shows, for example, that China's non-financial businesses had a cash loss of ¥9 trillion, or about $1.3 trillion, in 2017. However, that figure was after deducting all the investment expenses that are usually capitalized in companies' public earnings reports, which according to the OECD would have totaled around ¥24 trillion, or $3.7 trillion, that year. The OECD calls this cash loss the 'net borrowing total', but I've opted to use the business nomenclature over the OECD terminology.

The publicly reported aggregate net income for China's non-financial businesses, most if not all of which use accrual accounting, was ¥7.9 trillion, or $1.2 trillion. If you add non-reporting companies, the total would likely be around ¥12 trillion, or $1.8 trillion. By contrast, US non-financial businesses had a cash loss of $310 billion in 2017, after deducting investment expenses of $2.1 trillion, and publicly reported aggregate net income in the US using accrual accounting was $2.0 trillion.

The cash loss of China's non-financial business sector has been reported as negative 11 percent of GDP in 2017 (negative 12 percent in both 2018 and 2019), which strikes me as being surprisingly high, though it has hugged close to that percentage for a number of years. US non-financial businesses, by comparison, posted a cash loss of only negative 1.6 percent of GDP in 2017, a level that is not dissimilar to other Western economies.

But as we've seen, the OECD also reports that the 11 percent cash loss for China's non-financial businesses was offset by household net income of roughly 11 percent of GDP. So in China, both the business loss and household net income are notably higher than in other major countries, and are inversions.

The bottom line of this unusual accounting and debt profile is that China is building, or investing, far more relative to the size of its economy than any other Big 7 country. Figure 4.19 illustrates this. In accounting, such expenses are known as *capital expenditures* or *fixed investment*, and this type of economic production is referred to as *capital formation*. Spending must meet certain criteria to be counted as a capital expenditure – namely, the spending must create an asset, such as a factory, building, or intellectual property, whose benefit is expected to last for years. The biggest part of this category of investment for China, as for most countries, is usually new real estate construction, funded almost entirely through increased debt.

FIGURE 4.19. Capital expenditures to GDP, by country, 1995–2021

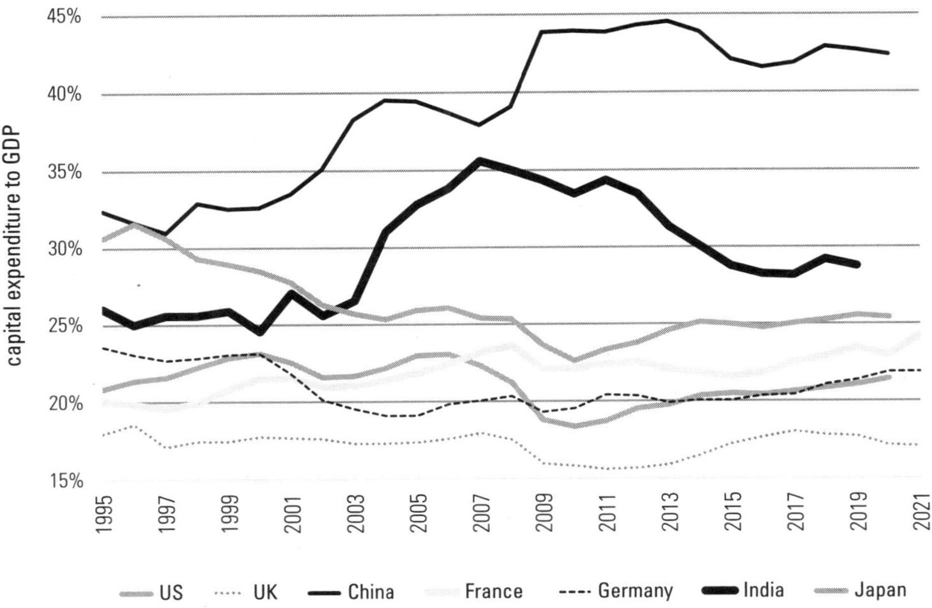

Some analysts have lauded, or at least excused, China for relying so heavily on this approach to capital formation. They argue that the expense of new houses, buildings, and factories will pay off handsomely for the economy in the future by satisfying the need for infrastructure that will improve the standard of living for China's households. For China, pursuing a strategy of high capital formation was certainly valid in the 1980s, when the country did not have anywhere near enough housing, manufacturing, or infrastructure. It was still partly valid through at least the mid-2010s. But in 2022? China already has far more investments in many areas than it needs. Indeed, we know from the Evergrande story that China's capital formation – *which has been financed by debt* – resulted in the construction of tens of millions of dwellings that now stand empty. As noted above, estimates of the exact number of housing units vary widely, but my view is that the actual number is likely to be closer to 100 million than 50 million, and in any case, far more than can be occupied in any reasonable time frame, especially with China's imploding demographics. This is why Evergrande and dozens of other real estate developers in China defaulted on their debt in 2022. It is also the key revelation we can glean from China's debt profile: the negative difference between the cash and accounting earnings of non-financial businesses in China increasingly, and perversely, is a proxy measure of China's stubborn creation of unproductive overcapacity, primarily in real estate.

At stake here is something more than arcane accounting rules about debt. Some economists have viewed capital formation as being purely positive, but much of what gets counted as capital formation is simply the real estate machine churning. This can lead to unproductive excess when it escalates too fast and goes too far. There are at least some instances when a *decline* in capital formation is an appropriate development in an economy, for example, when it signals conservatism in preparation for a perceived slowdown to avoid overcapacity. A decline in capital formation might also be a crisis-averting, protective response to overcapacity.

The value of China's empty dwellings has been propped up by at least two things: first, the government's guidance to lenders to continue to fund builders and home buyers; and second, the widespread belief among Chinese citizens that the value of real estate will always go up. Because house prices have only very recently gone down, China's developers and its households have continued to build and purchase new homes, regardless of the market for them. At some point, however, the fiction of ever-increasing value will unravel – and that point may now be arriving. The Evergrande collapse almost certainly weakened people's confidence in real estate as an asset. Official figures show home sales in China fell nearly 30 percent in the first half of 2022, and as of late 2022, the National Bureau of Statistics of China was reporting that homes had declined in value in seventy cities. On at least one hundred projects, spread across more than fifty cities, homebuyers stopped making mortgage payments. These protesters included a large number of buyers who had paid for homes before they were built and were still waiting for them to be completed – or, in some cases, for building to start. The fall in housing values may have left many mortgages and other real estate loans underwater, meaning that the value of the home was at least 10 percent lower than the amount of the loan on it. It's no wonder that anger around unfinished housing projects was one of the spurs for the mass protests by borrowers against banks that occurred in July 2022 – an almost unprecedented event for China in every respect.

For over forty years, China's non-financial business macrosector has had negative cash earnings. How can the country sustain this practice, which would undoubtedly create more empty, unused structures; more uncompleted building projects; and potentially more unrest?

It's worth noting that, many times over the last decade, China's policymakers have attempted to reassure credit markets worried about the economy having too much private sector lending to state-owned enterprises and other non-financial businesses. They have repeatedly asserted that China is going to slow down and reduce its dependence on non-financial business debt growth. But this would be tantamount to slowing the growth of household income – yuan for yuan.[33]

If the cash loss of China's non-financial businesses were reduced – which could readily be done by throttling back new construction – both household net income and GDP growth would slow or contract. To overcome this, China's central government would then be forced to consider covering a big part of the reduction by increasing its own spending (and loss), which was negative 2 percent of GDP in 2019. If, for example, non-financial business 'investments' were cut in half, the government would need to increase its spending by 6 percent of GDP to offset the resulting economic contraction – an admittedly enormous step. But on what would the government spend this money? Increased direct subsidies to households? Increased military spending? Something else? Whatever its target, increasing government spending is the most likely compensatory strategy to decelerate China's non-financial business debt growth and losses when that day inevitably arrives.

Perhaps China's household macrosector itself could shoulder some of the burden of creating growth by increasing its own borrowing, but the inconvenient fact is that households have already been loading up on debt. Since 2008, China's household macrosector has increased its level of debt from a mere 19 percent of GDP during the Global Financial Crisis of 2008 to 62 percent of GDP in 2020, a level approaching household debt in the US. (In contrast, over the same period, US household debt declined from 99 percent to 80 percent of GDP.) This means that household debt growth already accounts for a large part of China's GDP growth. If China's rapid increase in household debt continues at this pace for five more years, then it will stand at 80 percent to 90 percent of GDP, surpassing the US and reaching the highest level of any major economy. On the other hand, if it does not continue to grow at this pace, then China's GDP growth will decelerate.

It is clear that China has been employing every economic strategy available to it – non-financial business debt growth, household debt growth, and government debt growth – and yet it is still posting smaller and smaller annual growth in GDP, a problem compounded by its heavy-handed approach to managing the pandemic. Some of the reduction in GDP growth is the natural result of decelerating debt growth, but it also suggests that a good portion of China's business debt is going to things that do not increase GDP. One of those things, for example, is the insidious practice of making loans to companies to give them the cash to pay interest and posting the interest due as an asset rather than an expense – a practice known as *capitalizing interest*. In a blatant maneuver to inflate income, some non-financial businesses capitalize their interest expenses when the interest has in fact not been paid and is still owed. Taking this approach, Evergrande's earnings were a positive ¥8 billion in 2020 instead of a negative ¥61 billion. There is no way to rationalize or justify this practice. It is a brazen, highly misleading accounting sleight of hand.

Figure 4.20 depicts China's net worth by macrosector. We can see that the net worth of all 'private sector' macrosegments continued to rise through 2019 while the net worth of the government, which includes LGFVs, appears to have remained stable, though the validity of certain valuations within this is subject to debate. The ROW net worth continues to be negative, as in Germany, but that negative value has become less negative, reflecting a declining benefit to China as its trade surplus has gone down.

FIGURE 4.20. China net worth by macrosector, 2000–2019

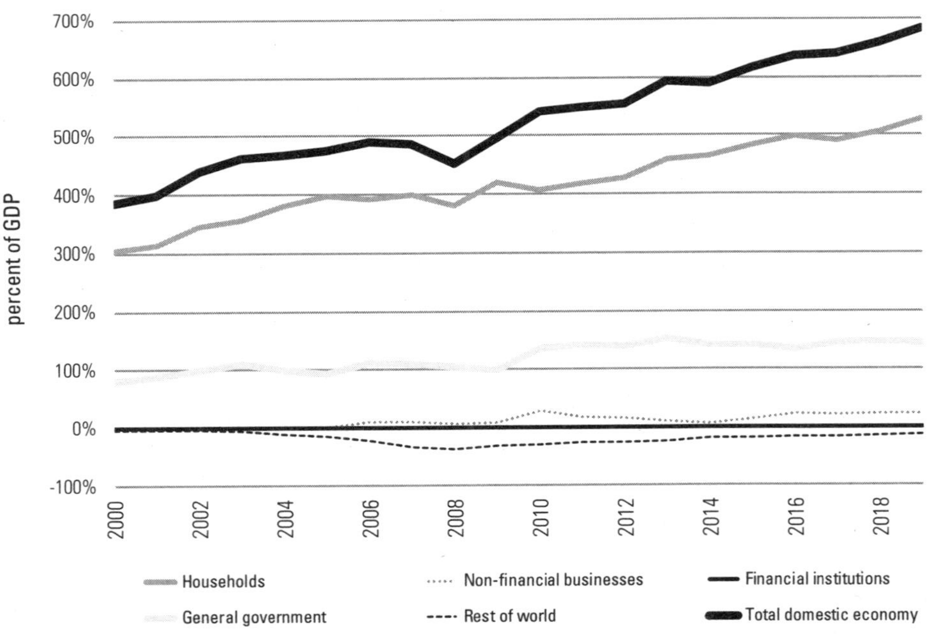

I leave it to more specialized analysts to judge whether the net worth of non-financial businesses and households shown here holds up to scrutiny. A large component of that wealth appears to be those 100 million empty houses, which my colleagues and I have estimated to have been valued – or overvalued – at between ¥25 trillion and ¥40 trillion, or roughly 25 percent to 40 percent of GDP. That is a manageable number in the context of a total household net worth of 527 percent of GDP and a country net worth of 682 percent of GDP, but it is a big caveat to attach to China's macrosector net worth. Are these empty houses actually worth that much? If yes, then the values in Figure 4.20 are valid; if not, then they should be discounted accordingly. Another key question any dedicated analyst must resolve is the feasibility or plausibility that the non-financial business sector could post huge cash income losses of the magnitude seen here while also posting net worth gains.

A closer look at the events leading up to China's economic pivot in 2008 will help us to better understand the country's current economic straits. China's non-financial business losses reduced from 12 percent of GDP in 1992 to 2 percent of GDP in 2007 (Figure 4.18). This was an enormous, positive change that coincided exactly with, and was a direct result of, the voracious debt binge in the West that provoked the Global Financial Crisis of 2008. Flush with cash from its frantic borrowing, the West's private sector bought huge volumes of goods made in China, so that China saw its net exports and current account balance surge from 2 percent to 10 percent of GDP between 2000 and 2007. China's private debt ratio stopped increasing during this period because domestic private debt growth was not needed to kindle GDP growth; increased exports were bringing in more than enough without growth in internal debt and spending. (Some in the US blamed this imbalance on currency manipulation, but the West's debt growth was far more the precipitating factor.) In short, China emerged as the winner from the series of events that brought crisis to the US and other Western economies.

With the 2008 financial crisis, the West's private debt growth came to a screeching halt, and GDP growth collapsed with it. China's exports quickly dried up. China's own GDP would have collapsed, too, if it had not pivoted – and fast. And pivot it did, by quickly ramping up borrowing in its non-financial business sector and also, for the first time, ramping up household borrowing as well. This combined borrowing created an echo of the West's debt binge which saved China's economy from contraction, but it also created that oversupply of somewhere in the neighborhood of 100 million empty dwellings that we see today.

This is captured in the debt profile for China (Figure 4.21). Here we can see that private debt to GDP escalated markedly

FIGURE 4.21. China debt profile, 1985–2021

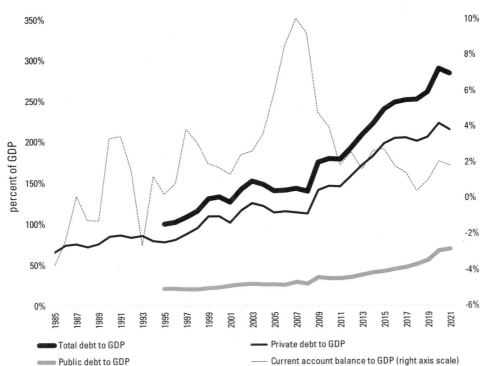

in China between 1994 and 1999, ushering in the country's first major financial crisis. It was rescued from that crisis in part by the West's debt binge. This is indicated in the line for the ratio of the current account balance, which is largely net exports, to GDP. Note that the ratio of private debt to GDP actually declined in these years because of the robust growth supplied by those net exports.

This debt profile also shows that, starting in 2008, China's private debt growth vaulted higher, to compensate for the plunge in net exports. The trend in private debt to GDP continued to rise steeply during the pandemic, powering China's GDP growth but also contributing to the vast excess now evident in the economy. We can also see that total debt almost tripled from 1995 to 2021, rising from 100 percent to 285 percent of GDP. In this way, China also exemplifies one of the principles of debt economics: the continuous upwards march in total debt.

With its business debt and spending model, China is a country of enormous size with a distinct playbook. But the vast overcapacity in its real estate sector may signal that this approach is no longer enough to sustain China's household net income growth – at least, not at anywhere near the levels of the past twenty years. China's leaders may very well need to devise a new plan.

Businesses will be hard pressed to continue to increase borrowing to create even more overcapacity. China's households do not have the same latitude to lose money and not repay loans that the country's non-financial businesses have enjoyed, so household capacity to increase borrowing has a practical ceiling – and the Chinese people are increasingly showing resistance to their lenders and their lenders' policies. China already has a trade surplus and is unlikely to be able to expand it much, especially given the geopolitical headwinds it faces. The only other choices, then, are for China's government to start spending much more or, more creatively, to start forgiving or restructuring a very large amount of private sector debt – an option we'll consider in detail in Chapter 8.

It is mystifying to me that financial analysts have not focused more on the extraordinarily negative cash flow of China's non-financial businesses, or on the equally stunning increase in the country's debt each year relative to its GDP. But as too often seen in other economies, in other contexts, and in other times, investors have a stunning capacity to ignore inconvenient facts as long as money is being made.

BY PLAN, OR BY ACCIDENT OF HISTORY

In this chapter, I've set out the four main approaches an economy can use to grow and increase GDP: debt-led business spending, debt-led household spending, debt-led government spending, or an improved net export position. Economies rarely rely solely on one of these strategies. Instead, they usually combine strategies, albeit weighted more to one (or perhaps two) of the four.

All of these models for growth are plagued by two issues. The first problem is that, once you start using a given model, you must continue to use it, and even increase your use of it, or else suffer an economic reversal. For example, if the US were to have lower deficits, or if China's businesses had lower losses, or if Germany's exports were to decline (as was starting to happen in late 2022), this would result in slower GDP growth and lower household net income, unless these countries assertively boosted the macrosector that was flagging or assertively adopted another model for growth.

The second problem is that, regardless of the model, GDP growth must be fueled by growth in debt. Whichever category of debt drives the model must continue to accumulate. If China continues with its business debt and spending model, it will inevitably create more excess and more Evergrande-type disasters. Debt economics holds that excessive private debt growth eventually slows economic growth and, worse, can bring economic crisis. By the same token, the US can continue with its government debt and spending model but, over the long term, unless crafted in previously unheard-of ways, it will inevitably drive wealth inequality higher.

In theory, the government debt and spending strategy which describes five of the Big 7 economies is not *necessary*. An economy could run just fine with only businesses and individuals buying and selling to each other. Of course, under such circumstances, the net income of the private sector would be zero, because income in that economic ecology would, by definition, exactly equal expense. For the sake of argument, I'll call this the *self-contained private sector model*, or SCPS.

Within an SCPS economy, there would still be winners and losers. They would emerge just as they did in our hypothetical LoanLand – that is to say, the economy could chug along in equilibrium, with all participants spending exactly as much as they made, but just as soon as someone wanted to consume more or produce more, the economy would evolve to have debt. Hence, the economy would start to feature increasing inequality. Those who bought more products and services of others would have borrowed to buy them. Those who could not borrow would have less – both less money and fewer services and products.

However, in my research, supported by my colleagues, I have not been able to identify any countries today that operate using the SCPS model. Some, including the US in the 1800s, relied on the model in the past, but they did so only briefly. Frequent wars led to periods in which the government debt and spending model predominated.

It is my observation that, historically, no countries have started with the stated goal and intention of pursuing a government loss model. In fact, most countries have explicitly pursued the opposite policy, with a goal of having a balanced budget and avoiding government debt, given the popular view that a balanced budget is both a virtue and a necessity. Inevitably, however, either wars or the desire of legislators to spend gradually eroded the aversion to deficits. As this happened across a number of countries, it became clear that lower interest rates, lower inflation, and other acceptable economic trends were associated with higher government debt. As Vice President Dick Cheney said in 2004: 'Reagan proved that deficits don't matter.' US legislators may not like a government deficit, but they believe they are doing the right thing when they recommend spending programs – and in many contexts, they are. In turn, a growing number of economists, including proponents of modern monetary theory, have made the intellectual case for, and even endorsed, some level of deficit spending. Among other things, modern monetary theory carefully describes the process whereby deficit spending is not limited and can usefully boost growth when an economy is operating below capacity.

Keeping in mind the benefits and limitations of these models for wealth and economic growth, in the next chapter we'll further compare the Big 7 economies to see how they perform in relation to each other.

5

THE RELATIVE
WEALTH OF NATIONS

If the net worth of households and countries matters – and I argue that it both matters greatly and is fundamental to understanding macroeconomics – then a key tool for deepening our understanding is how the balance sheets of the Big 7 stack up against one another.[34] So, in this chapter, we turn to comparing the key elements of net worth for the household macrosector in each of these economies.[35]

Some quick caveats before we begin: I undertake these comparisons with some trepidation because they are genuinely, and to some extent inescapably, fraught with difficulty. There are many differences in the underlying markets, and divergent data collection practices and methodologies. There are also a range of proverbial apples-to-oranges issues. For example, is the US capital markets model really applicable to all other countries, and can country-by-country comparisons properly account for the melding of markets in the Eurozone? To make the analysis as robust as possible, my colleagues and I have relied on primary data from the Federal Reserve, the OECD, and other key government authorities, and notwithstanding the pitfalls and perils of cross-country comparison, it would be remiss if we did not use the data as presented by these established authorities. The goal is to deepen our exploration of similarities and differences between economies rather than to critique data sources. The solution to comparison challenges is not to avoid making comparisons altogether but instead to make and use them as a platform for analysis and debate, and, most importantly, as an invitation to deeper study.

Where applicable, the figures in this chapter convert other currencies to dollars on a purchasing power parity basis as opposed to a currency exchange basis. This does two things – it largely eliminates distortions caused by currency exchange fluctuations, and it gives an advantage to less developed nations as compared to the currency exchange approach.[36]

Some of these figures were prepared on a percent of GDP basis or on a per capita basis, which makes the data from country to country more comparable. However, some figures are prepared on a total US dollars basis, and in these cases we can easily see the overwhelming size of the US and China relative to all other countries. We've chosen total amounts deliberately in these cases to highlight the scale of these two economies, which is immense. The US and China do in fact dominate today's global economy.

THE WEALTH OF HOUSEHOLDS

With these caveats in mind, we can turn to what the comparisons yield. The most basic insight is that the net worth for most of the Big 7 economies increased markedly during the Great Debt Explosion, the period beginning roughly in 1981 when debt to GDP ratio increased dramatically in the US. And for all seven countries, the macrosector with by far the largest net worth was households. To a very real and practical extent, governments act, or at least normatively *should* act, as mechanisms to facilitate the accumulation of income and net worth by households and, to a lesser extent, non-financial businesses, and this accumulation has indeed occurred.

Figure 5.1 shows the net worth of households in ratio to GDP for the Big 7. Here, the US leads the pack, but only slightly, with five of the seven countries tightly bunched. Germany lags somewhat behind, largely because of the low relative value of its stocks. However, as noted in Chapter 4, some scholars attribute this to the low valuation afforded to privately held stocks, which constitute a larger proportion of all stocks in Germany (and some other countries) compared to the US. India registers far below the other six, in part because we have no reliable estimate of real estate values for India.

Comparing household net worth across the Big 7 in terms of total US dollars (Figure 5.2), we can see that the US and China stand apart, with the others grouped together well below them. This data, along with the figures on stock ownership and real estate ownership, demonstrates the sheer economic dominance and size of these two countries. They truly soar above the rest of the world.

FIGURE 5.1. Big 7 household net worth by country, 1994–2021

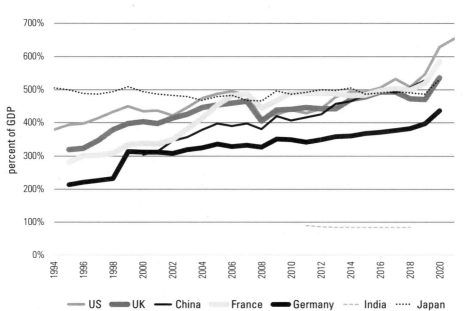

FIGURE 5.2. Big 7 household net worth, 1994–2021

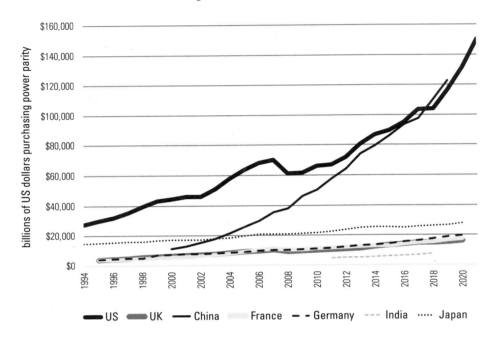

FIGURE 5.3. Big 7 household net worth per capita, 1994–2021

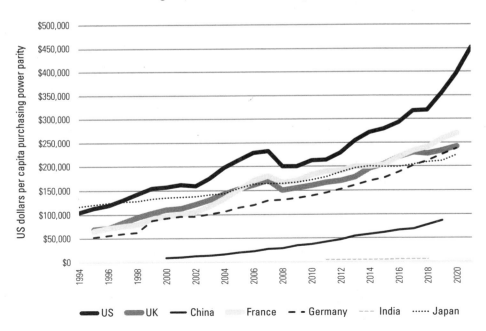

Figure 5.3 gives the comparison of household net worth on a per capita basis, to illustrate the relative economic wellbeing of people across the Big 7. Although China is dominant in aggregate size, its people are far less well off than those in more developed economies, and in fact are not much better off from a wealth standpoint than the people of India, where net worth is a much lower percentage of GDP, even after accounting for the poor real estate data.

To make this clear, Figure 5.4 shows household net worth on a per capita basis excluding real estate. India continues to lie at the bottom of charts. Without real estate, the US clearly pulls away from the other countries and China descends closer to the level of India.

These per capita figures without real estate also contradict the longstanding notion that Americans are poor savers. This misunderstanding reflects a difference in the ordinary, commonsense understanding of the term 'savings', which is the amount individuals have in

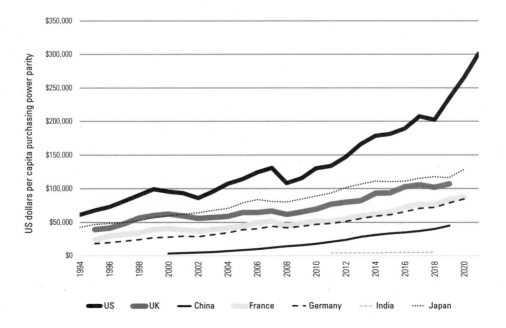

FIGURE 5.4. Big 7 household financial net worth per capita without real estate, 1994–2021

their current checking and savings accounts, plus the money they have invested with brokers and in pension and other retirement accounts (which is a 'stock' in the specialized parlance of economists) – as compared to economists' definition, which is the amount by which household income exceeds expenses (called 'flows' by economists). Using their jargon, some economists have repeatedly bemoaned that Americans are poor savers.

However, by the more ordinary definition, Americans are un-equivocally the best savers in the Big 7, with the next best, Japan, lagging far behind. Net income – or 'net saving', among economists – is a zero-sum game within an economy, which is why I argue that this approach to measuring household saving is, in some respects, a function of measuring the government deficit. We've seen that when households' aggregate income exceeds their expenses, it is due in large part to government deficit spending. So what is lauded as 'improved saving' by the economists' definition is simply the product of more government spending.

TAKING STOCK OF THE BIG 7

Because between 60 percent and 70 percent of the net worth in each of these economies is held in the form of either stocks or land, differ-ences in household net worth are largely explained by differences in the valuations of these two categories of assets. Figure 5.5 shows the difference in the size, over time, of the stock markets – also referred to as equities markets – in each Big 7 economy as a percentage of GDP. (To better account for differences across countries, I've included insurance and pension assets, as well.[37]) The US shows the highest overall level, and the sharpest increases in value, for equities wealth relative to GDP. However, all six of the more developed countries show significant gains during these decades.

FIGURE 5.5. Big 7 household equity and investment assets, including insurance and pensions, 1995–2021

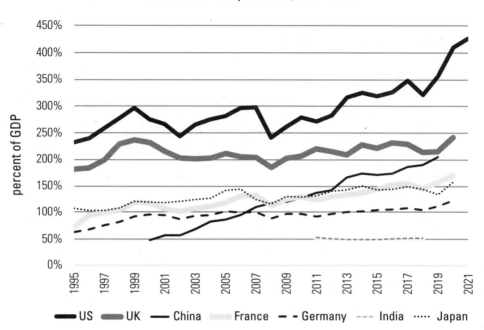

Figure 5.6 also provides information about stocks in each country. This is something of an apples-to-oranges figure. For each country, the lefthand column shows the total market valuation, or market cap, of publicly traded stocks in comparison to GDP. This includes equity owned by households, non-financial businesses, financial institutions, foreign investors, and other entities. Cross-border ownership of stocks among EU countries is easier and more common, and can distort a country-by-country analysis, so the totals for France and Germany should be viewed with this in mind.

The righthand column for each country in the figure shows the household macrosector's total ownership of stocks. This includes both publicly traded and privately held stocks, as well as investment fund shares, pension and other retirement entitlements, and insurance, even though the latter categories are only partially comprised of stocks.

I have taken this approach in an attempt to create a better – though imperfect – proxy for stock ownership across the Big 7 economies, given the broad variety of preferences and structures for equity ownership. For example, countries have different channels for conveyance of equity ownership and for equity accumulation.

FIGURE 5.6. Big 7 stock market cap and household equity ownership as percentage of GDP, 2020

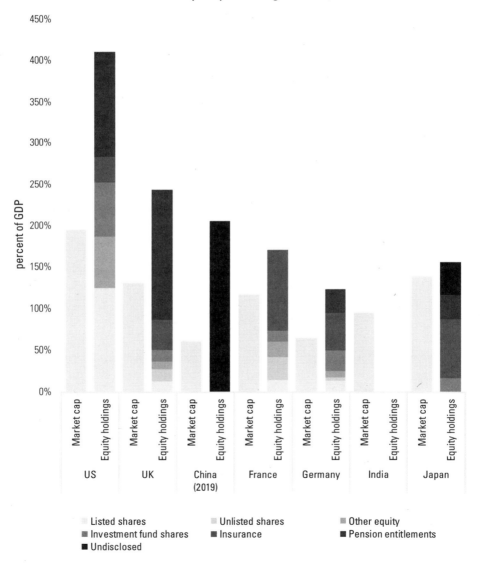

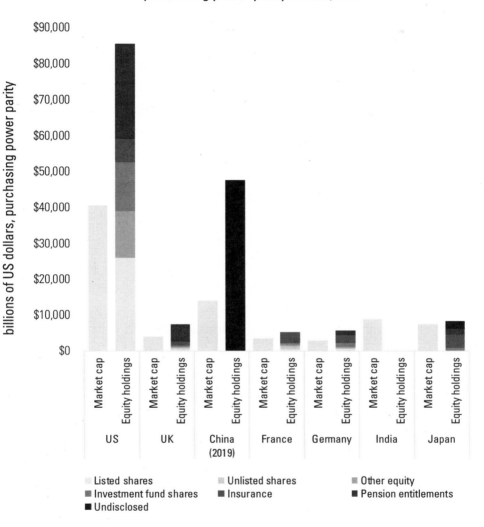

FIGURE 5.7. Big 7 stock market cap and household equity ownership in purchasing power parity dollars, 2020

The US leads the world by a wide margin in the total value of listed, or publicly traded, stocks. The country with the second highest market cap is Japan, with Germany and China lagging behind the other Big 7 economies. The German shortfall may, as noted earlier, in part reflect the low valuation of the country's privately held stocks. The fact that China's households own so much more in stock than the value of its publicly traded stocks means either that its households own an enormous slice of privately held stocks or that the reported number is a misrepresentation of this value. Household equity ownership information is not available for India.

Figure 5.7 presents the same information, except this time in US dollars on a purchasing power parity basis. Here US market cap towers over all other publicly listed stock markets, in part because it is a more established destination for overseas investment. In fact, the value of publicly traded shares in the US is as large or larger than the other six countries combined.

There is also a radical difference in who owns stock in the US as compared to the other six countries. For the US, and only to a slightly lesser extent China, stock ownership is largely the province of households. For the others, large amounts of stock are owned by the government, non-financial businesses, and financial institutions, in some cases related to tax policies.

In fact, government ownership of assets in the US differs markedly from the other countries in the Big 7. In Figure 5.8, we see the ownership of assets by each country's government and central bank, though for France and Germany, the central bank is the European Central Bank, which covers the entire EU.

Of course, due to its very form, the government of China owns a lot of its companies' stock, in particular, shares in the country's state-owned enterprises. But what is striking, and somewhat more surprising, is that both Japan's central government and its central bank also own an immense amount of these domestic financial assets. Equally notable is the relatively large ownership of domestic stocks by the governments of France and Germany.

We might ask if government ownership of stocks creates a conflict of interest in these countries. If a government owns stocks in entities it regulates, is it less likely to intervene against bad business practices? Is it more likely to try to prop up the valuations of non-financial businesses?

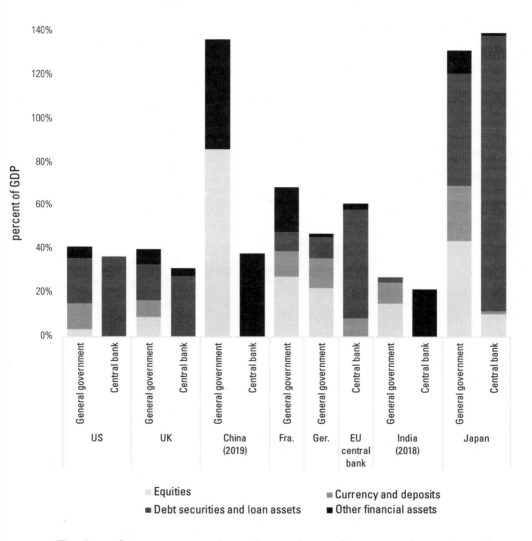

FIGURE 5.8. Big 7 ownership of financial assets by governments and central banks, 2020

Further, if a government has a big stake in the country's stocks and other financial assets, does this artificially inflate those markets and related valuations, and is this a help or a hindrance to the economy? On the surface it would seem a large government stake would boost markets, but the US stock markets, which do not enjoy much government ownership, have had much higher comparative valuations over recent decades. And, in general, the US stock markets tend to command higher valuations for publicly listed companies than do other countries', even when the companies being compared are very similar. This is revealed in the higher price to earnings (P/E) ratios of the comparable stocks.

This may be partly why, as of May 2022, you could find nearly five hundred non-US stocks from forty-five countries listed on the New York Stock Exchange (NYSE). However, a variety of reasons may explain the higher P/E ratios, as well as the decision these non-US companies have made to list their stocks there. It could simply be that, because the NYSE is the world's largest equities market, it attracts the most investment. Investors may have greater confidence in the quality of audits and oversight provided by the Securities and Exchange Commission (SEC) and other US-based regulatory entities. Or conversely, perhaps companies prefer to list shares on the NYSE because they perceive it to have relatively lower levels of regulation compared to domestic markets.

It's also worth lingering for a moment on the valuation of listed and unlisted stocks for China's non-financial business macrosector, which is unlike any other in the world. Given the large cash losses in this sector (laid out in Chapter 4), these stocks appear to be problematically overvalued in aggregate. Figure 5.9 compares non-financial business income in China and the US in 2019, the most recent year for which data for China is available. This comparison, done on both a currency exchange and a purchasing power parity basis, shows that, with similar gross revenues, China's non-financial businesses have almost twice the debt and thirteen times the net loss of US non-financial businesses. That alone should be cause for concern for China and investors in the country's non-financial business sector.

FIGURE 5.9. Key non-financial business macrosector
statistics, US and China, 2019

	US	CHINA	
	billions of US dollars	billions of US dollars (currency exchange)	billions of US dollars (purchasing power parity)
GDP	$21,373	$13,927	$23,083
Gross non-financial business revenue	$14,394	$8,642	$14,324
Household equity holdings	$45,221	$28,778	$47,699
Total market cap listed shares	$38,471	$8,434	$13,979
Total gross value of listed and unlisted shares	$78,455	$43,150	$71,519
Total net value of listed and unlisted shares	$57,094	n/a	n/a
Total business debt	$17,441	$20,867	$34,587
Total non-financial business income	$(215)	$(1,716)	$(2,845)
	percent of GDP	percent of GDP	percent of GDP
Gross non-financial business revenue	67%	62%	62%
Household equity holdings	212%	205%	205%
Total market cap listed shares	180%	61%	61%
Total gross value of listed and unlisted shares	367%	310%	310%
Total net value of listed and unlisted shares	267%	n/a	n/a
Total business debt	82%	150%	150%
Total non-financial business income	-1%	-12%	-12%

Beyond this is the question of the relative valuation of all stocks in China as compared to US stocks. It's highly difficult to compare total value of the stocks in the US to those in China for two major reasons. First, it appears that, according to China's National Institution for Finance and Development, a good deal more of China's stocks are privately held than in the US. This makes China's total equities holdings inherently more difficult to value. Second, with the available data it is not possible to accurately identify any assets held by private financial institutions that are also held by households to properly eliminate double counting. However, with what we can see, I would tentatively suggest that the aggregate value of all such stocks in China is valued at a level reasonably close to US stock values, even with the much higher debt and losses in China, which would suggest they *are* significantly overvalued. If this is so, it can only have happened through a tolerant or complicit central government.

LAND RICH

The other key category of a country's net worth is real estate. Figure 5.10 shows the value of total real estate as a percentage of GDP for each of the Big 7 economies.

Real estate is one of the more problematic categories to assess confidently in the aggregate. It is difficult to assess whether the Federal Reserve, the OECD, and other established sources have included all real estate and used appropriate valuations. But even with these limitations, the data can give us a general sense of the relative holdings of real estate across the seven countries, and seem reasonable and useful.

Total household real estate value as a percentage of GDP is tightly bunched among the countries. France leads the group, and its strong real estate values explain why France's overall household net worth to GDP ratio is high despite its low household ownership of stocks

FIGURE 5.10. Big 7 household real estate assets, 1994–2021

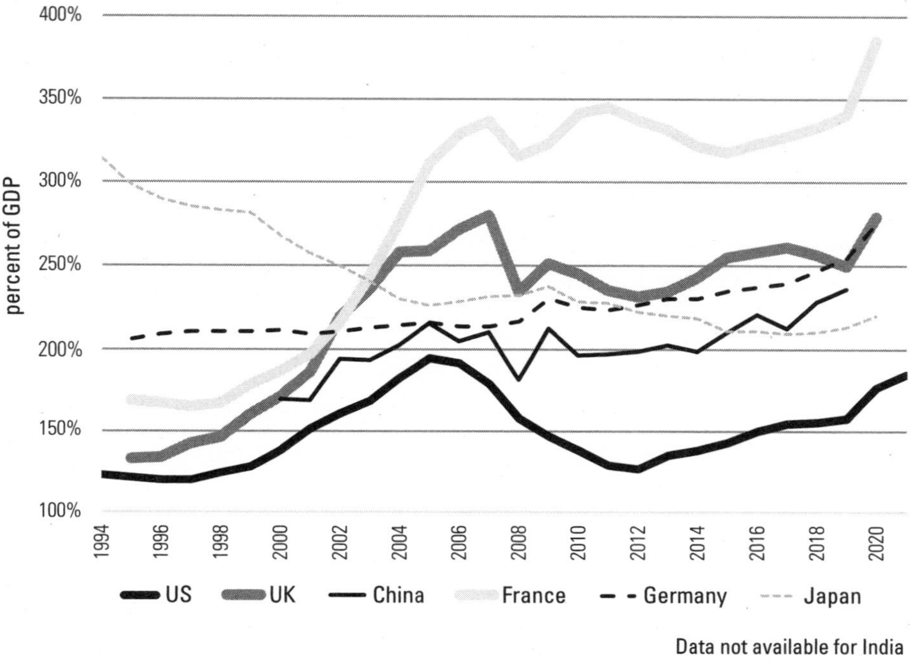

Data not available for India

(see Figure 5.1). We can also see a low value for US real estate. The extraordinary valuation of stocks owned by US households explains why the US leads all other countries in household net worth despite these comparatively weak real estate values.

While real estate values have been increasing in six of the seven countries in recent years, in Japan they have mostly been declining. In the late 1980s, in the midst of Japan's lending euphoria, real estate in Tokyo sold for prices as high as $139,000 per square foot, nearly 350 times as much as in Manhattan. Using that valuation, the land under the Imperial Palace in Tokyo was worth as much as all of California – at least for a short period – and the total Japanese property market was worth four times more than the total US property market. Savvy analysts recognized that this was an egregiously unrealistic level and took it as a warning at the time.

After that notably absurd peak, and the massive banking crisis that followed, Japan's real estate prices collapsed. Since this correction in the early 1990s, prices have stagnated as a percentage of Japan's GDP. Finally, in 2022, Japan's real estate posted the first gains in more than twenty years. Because real estate values reached such preposterous levels and have been on such a prolonged downwards drift, Japan stands as an exception to the general debt economics principle that rising debt levels bring higher asset levels. Japan's experience is compounded by the fact that the debt growth which brings higher asset growth is growth in private sector Type 2 debt, and this type of debt growth has been a declining percentage of Japan's overall growth in debt. Finally, these trends may suggest that there is a law of diminishing returns: when debt levels get extraordinarily high, an economy experiences diminishing asset growth from debt growth.

Notably, Japan's population has been declining, and that is relevant to the equation; indeed, it may be a key part of it. Depopulation could lead to moderating or declining asset values, no matter how much debt increases. Japan has 11 million empty homes, not because of a recent episode of overbuilding but because of declining population.

Figure 5.11 shows the value of real estate assets, excluding land, across the Big 7 economies for which data is available. The US and China again lead the league, with China's valuation accelerating rapidly since 2008 as a function of the increase in lending for real estate development and acquisition. Values in every country save Japan have been rising for many years, albeit not so dramatically. Presumably, however, the recent reversal in some real estate values in China will begin to show up in a flat or downwards trajectory for these assets, in keeping with the correction in real estate values seen in Japan in the early 1990s (prior to the period shown in Figure 5.11).

FIGURE 5.11. Big 7 household real estate assets excluding land, 1994–2021

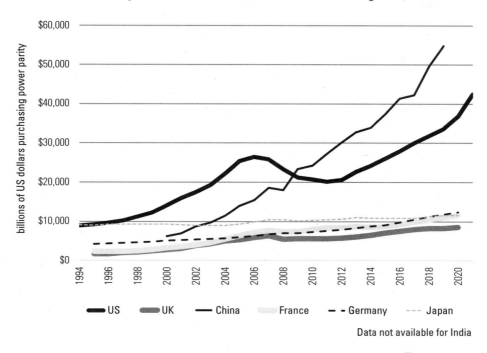

Data not available for India

FIGURE 5.12. Big 7 household real estate assets per capita, 1994–2021

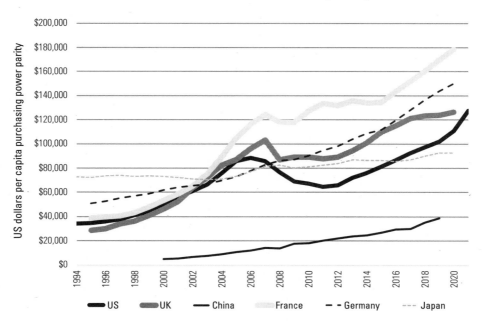

Data not available for India

Figure 5.12 charts the same data but on a per capita basis. This helps to put these household assets in greater context, particularly for China's population of 1.4 billion. Here, all of the Big 7 household macrosectors show a higher, upwards trend in recent years, even Japan's. In China, values are rising but are very low, a function of the population denominator. Note that this figure does not indicate anything about the concentration of these assets within the wealthiest 10 percent of the population.

DATA AND POLICY

These comparisons of the Big 7 economies yield important, and sometimes counterintuitive, insights – including some correctives to common assumptions. As noted above, and contrary to conventional wisdom, Americans are the best savers of the bunch. Likewise, the US emerges as the country with the greatest per capita net worth and as the country where, in contrast to China and Japan, most equities are owned by households rather than governments. Overall, net worth has gone up rapidly during the Great Debt Explosion, and most of that worth is held by households.

For our purposes, these contrasts also help to illuminate the effects – and effectiveness – of economic policies across the Big 7 countries. As one small example, China has had little or no tax on residential real estate, thus lowering the carrying costs of buying a second or third home, which has contributed to the country's real estate boom. That boom is now fraught with risk of reversal and default. A recent pilot program to introduce residential real estate taxes in China, designed in part to curb speculation, if adopted and implemented, could exacerbate the unprecedented declines in real estate prices the country has recently been seeing. Comparing aggregate trends in asset levels helps us to more fully understand the consequences of them.

The data in this chapter also reinforces the observation that the Great Debt Explosion has been accompanied by an increase in household net worth. Because the greatest increases in net worth have arisen in the two countries with the greatest concentration of wealth in the top 10 percent of their population – the US and China – it stands to reason that growth in aggregate wealth is typically correlated with rising inequality.

These macroeconomic relationships shape the financial fortunes of a country's households and businesses, no more so than when adversity arrives. Next, we move to an analysis of the tumultuous year of 2022 – a topic, and year, sufficiently dramatic and eventful that it merits its own chapter.

6

THE COVID BUBBLE, INFLATION, AND REVERSAL

In 2020, for a few months, it seemed like the world as we know it might end, as we watched the first wave of an eventual 6 million global deaths from Covid-19 and the collapse of both spending and stock values. But, in what is surely one of the more unexpected outcomes in recent history, we can now characterize 2020 and 2021 – even with the millions who died and the millions more who were badly hurt financially – as nothing short of boom years, because in the US and elsewhere, legislatures and central banks rose to the economic challenges of the pandemic, instantly and decisively.

In the US, trillions of dollars in support from Congress, coupled with lower interest rates and a flood of quantitative easing from the Federal Reserve, helped propel stock and real estate prices to record highs. Though US GDP was down slightly at the end of 2020 compared to 2019, pandemic relief checks and other support programs meant that GDP rebounded in 2021, landing where it would have been expected to be if we had never had a pandemic. Further, after first collapsing in value by 21 percent in the bleak uncertainty of spring 2020, US equities markets also rebounded, hitting an all-time high valuation of 254 percent of GDP at their peak in 2021. This was all the more remarkable because in 2019 stock markets in the US had hit their previous all-time high of 180 percent of GDP, a level already considered by many to be overvalued.

For those with significant holdings of stocks and real estate, 2020 to 2021 was a dramatic example of how a flood of new debt can lift household net worth. The total US nominal debt growth, which totaled a fairly typical $2.6 trillion in 2019, vaulted upwards by $6.9 trillion in 2020 and by $4 trillion in 2021.

A QUARTET OF ECONOMIC CHALLENGES

Unfortunately, early 2022 brought a collision of bad news. By June, the value of the stock market as reported by the Federal Reserve had tumbled by 22 percent, though in ratio to GDP its valuation was still above the pre-pandemic levels of December 2019.

The first piece of bad news was that the Fed was adopting a policy of *reverse quantitative easing*, also known as *quantitative tightening* (QT). This involved the Fed withdrawing its support for US debt markets by removing deposits from the system. Alongside this change in monetary policy, most of the payment forbearance granted to apartment renters, mortgage holders, student loan borrowers, and others ended, which inaugurated a period of reckoning with payments in arrears. And with the end of the federal government's pandemic relief payments, households were back on their own for the first time since early 2020, making softer growth more likely. The government's fiscal largesse appeared to have evaporated.

Second, price inflation, which had started to emerge in mid-2021, accelerated. The worldwide absence of workers from many manu-facturing and distribution businesses due to pandemic lockdowns depleted the supply chain. The lack of workers rippled out to the economy as product shortages, and these product shortages rippled out to households and businesses as higher prices. For the first time in forty years, the US and other large, developed countries contended with the fearsome specter of sustained, high inflation. Although inflation had begun to register in the Consumer Price Index (CPI) in 2021, it was not so high as to provoke the Fed to respond. The broadly held view was that pandemic-related worker and supply chain problems would be largely resolved within one to two years, and then prices would fall. The Fed held back from raising interest rates, on the reasoning that this could cause unneeded damage to a fragile economy.

But then, in a third piece of bad news, in February Russia invaded Ukraine. Russia is the number one exporter of wheat to the world and the number one exporter of oil and natural gas to Europe, and Ukraine is the number five exporter of wheat to the world, so this war was destined to have global price implications. As early as November 2021 the prospect of such an invasion was rattling markets and elevating the prices of wheat, energy, and other commodities. When the invasion itself actually occurred, Europe and the US responded with a slate of aggressive sanctions against Russia that, together, further blocked supplies and drove up prices.

The global supply chain disruption from the pandemic had only been partially repaired by the time of the Ukraine invasion, and now the war exacerbated it, portending a longer and more difficult process to resolve the problem of high global inflation. An estimated one third of the inflation reported for mid-2022 related to the war, and economists warned that inflation would likely increase further as the war continued. So, just as workers were returning to factories, pandemic-related inflation morphed into war-aggravated inflation, and quickly rose from 5 percent to 8 percent in the US.

Fourth, and finally, the Fed took action on interest rates. A number of economists had been arguing that raising interest rates had become all but mandatory in order to bring down inflation; raising rates would bludgeon any excess consumption demand in the economy and pull down prices. Now, the Fed agreed with them – or acquiesced to growing public pressure – even though it was unclear how higher interest rates could hasten the end of the war or resolve any lingering or new issues in the supply chain. Seven times in 2022, the Fed bumped up interest rates, with rates rising from 0.25 percent in March to 4.5 percent in December – the highest interest rate level in the US since 2007. The first of these interest rate hikes was announced the day after the Fed began quantitative tightening.

Higher interest rates increase the cost of borrowing to buy a home or stocks, and thus exert downwards pressure on home sales and stock prices. Just as adding deposits through quantitative easing boosted asset prices of homes and stocks, removing deposits through quantitative tightening curbed them.

The financial markets tumbled.

THE AFTERMATH

These factors were a gut punch to households, whose wages in the twelve months ending in June 2022 had increased far less than inflation. The US economy now faced a continuing pandemic, higher prices, and higher interest rates – all in the absence of government support. And it was not alone among the Big 7. By September 2022, the impact was clear: net income and household net worth in the US, as shown in the income statements and balance sheets in Figures 6.1 and 6.2, were down.

FIGURE 6.1. US income statement, 2021 and 2022 third quarter year to date

2021 income by macrosector (trillions of US dollars)*	House-hold	Non-financial businesses	Financial institutions	General government	Domestic total	Rest of world	TOTAL
Revenue	$25.18	$11.77	$2.13	$6.73	$45.82	$4.66	$50.49
Expenditure and investment*	$23.42	$11.48	$2.11	$9.55	$46.69	$3.80	$50.49
Memo: Gross value added (GDP)	$6.76	$11.77	$2.13	$2.91	$23.58	$0.00	$23.58
Net disposable income	$18.15	$0.65	$0.08	$0.74	$19.61	$4.66	$24.28
Less: Consumption expenditures*	$16.38	$0.35	$0.06	$3.56	$20.35	$3.80	$24.15
NET INCOME	$1.77	$0.30	$0.02	-$2.82	-$0.86	$0.86	$0.00

2022 3Q income by macrosector (trillions of US dollars)	House-hold	Non-financial businesses	Financial institutions	General government	Domestic total	Rest of world	TOTAL
Revenue	$19.38	$9.74	$2.05	$5.69	$36.86	$4.05	$40.91
Expenditure and investment*	$19.26	$9.79	$2.03	$6.39	$37.63	$3.28	$40.91
Memo: Gross value added (GDP)	$5.52	$9.74	$2.05	$2.66	$19.97	$0.00	$19.97
Net disposable income	$13.39	$0.50	$0.06	$1.95	$15.90	$4.05	$19.95
Less: Consumption expenditures*	$13.27	$0.55	$0.04	$2.65	$16.51	$3.28	$19.78
NET INCOME	$0.12	-$0.04	$0.02	-$0.70	-$0.77	$0.77	$0.00

* Includes net capital transfers paid, net fixed capital formation, change in inventory, acquisition of non-produced non-financial assets. Domestic totals include the statistical discrepancy.

Household net income, consistent with the logic of my argument in this book, was destined to shrink simply as a function of reduced federal government spending. Consequently, household net income was a mere $120 billion for the first nine months of 2022, a steep decline from the $1.77 trillion posted for the full year of 2021. Total federal, state, and local government debt growth still remained high, even with stronger tax receipts, but much of the net benefit in this period went to the ROW and, at least at some level, state-level infrastructure spending, rather than directly to households.

FIGURE 6.2. US balance sheet, 2021 and 2022 third quarter

2021 balance sheet by macrosector (trillions of US dollars)	House-holds	Non-financial businesses	Financial institutions	General government	Domestic total	Rest of world	TOTAL
Total assets	$168.5	$79.6	$137.9	$26.3	$412.2	$47.4	$459.7
Real estate	$42.5	$33.6	$1.5	$15.6	$93.2	$0.0	$93.2
Other non-financial assets	$7.9	$13.8	$1.0	$2.6	$25.3	$0.0	$25.3
Financial assets	$118.1	$32.1	$135.5	$8.0	$293.8	$47.4	$341.2
Equity assets	$63.0	$12.6	$42.2	$0.6	$118.4	$27.9	$146.3
Other assets	$55.1	$19.6	$93.2	$7.4	$175.3	$19.5	$194.9
Financial liabilities	$18.4	$111.7	$141.5	$36.0	$307.5	$30.0	$337.5
Equity liabilities	$0.0	$78.2	$48.6	$0.0	$126.7	$21.8	$148.6
Financial net worth	$99.8	-$79.6	-$6.0	-$28.0	-$13.8	$17.5	$3.7
TOTAL NET WORTH	**$150.1**	**-$32.2**	**-$3.5**	**-$9.7**	**$104.7**	**$17.5**	**$122.2**

2022 Q3 balance sheet by macrosector (trillions of US dollars)	House-holds	Non-financial businesses	Financial institutions	General government	Domestic total	Rest of world	TOTAL
Total assets	$162.5	$82.3	$127.2	$28.3	$400.3	$40.0	$440.3
Real estate	$46.4	$34.9	$1.7	$17.3	$100.2	$0.0	$100.2
Other non-financial assets	$8.4	$15.2	$1.1	$2.8	$27.4	$0.0	$27.4
Financial assets	$107.7	$32.3	$124.5	$8.2	$272.7	$40.0	$312.7
Equity assets	$53.4	$9.4	$36.0	$0.5	$99.3	$21.4	$120.7
Other assets	$54.4	$22.9	$88.4	$7.7	$173.4	$18.6	$192.0
Financial liabilities	$19.2	$98.2	$131.2	$38.2	$286.9	$23.9	$310.8
Equity liabilities	$0.0	$63.2	$40.9	$0.0	$104.1	$16.4	$120.5
Financial net worth	$88.5	-$65.9	-$6.7	-$30.0	-$14.2	$16.0	$1.8
TOTAL NET WORTH	**$143.3**	**-$15.9**	**-$4.0**	**-$10.0**	**$113.4**	**$16.0**	**$129.4**

With inflated prices, nominal GDP grew, but this was because private sector debt increased sharply, from $931 billion to $1.5 trillion, while total government debt, including state-level and local debt, continued to grow higher. GDP adjusted for inflation – *real GDP* – was down in the first two quarters of 2022 as compared to the final quarter of 2021; for the first three quarters of 2022 it was up only a modest 1.9 percent as compared to the first three quarters of 2021. Higher inflation took a large bite out of *real* growth.

On the net worth side, the trends were more unfavorable, as shown in Figure 6.2. By September 2022, the value of household equities had tumbled in value and trends in real estate prices were mixed. The overall effect was that household net worth was down by 4.6 percent for the snapshot taken at the end of the third quarter of 2022, from $150.1 trillion to $143.3 trillion.[38]

Yet, these values were still well above the levels in 2019, just before the pandemic (see Figure 2.6). And those 2019 levels were themselves highs for the period following the Global Financial Crisis of 2008. For these reasons, it was implausible to characterize these assets on the US balance sheet as being undervalued, even after correction. This left many economic observers concerned that household net worth would continue to reverse, at least somewhat, in the near future.

Such a drop in net worth has ample precedent. During the 2008 financial crisis, net worth as a percentage of GDP fell by 16 percent and then took a full eight years to return to its pre-crisis level. The largest drop in household net worth to GDP before then was 12 percent, which occurred from 1972 to 1974, during the worst years of the 1970s oil and inflation crises. Then, net worth also took a number of years to return to its previous peak.

NEXT STEPS

A key difference between 2022 and the aftermath of the Global Financial Crisis of 2008 is that, by 2009, all the damage to the economy had been done. The concerted efforts of the government and the private sector could be focused solely on repairing and recapitalizing the economy. In late 2022, however, the economic damage was still a work in progress. Although President Joe Biden had declared the pandemic to be over, and it was much less disruptive to daily life, it nonetheless had an impact on the economy, as supply chains were not yet fully restored to their pre-pandemic condition. The war in Ukraine continued, and sanctions against Russia remained in force, without an obvious path to resolution.

As a result, at the end of 2022, the US was experiencing modest growth, higher inflation, and low unemployment at the same time, stoking broad-based fears of a potential recession.

Restoring and sustaining growth in the future will also be more challenging due to two secular, long-term trends. The first is slower population growth. It is easier to grow GDP if a country's population growth is accelerating; this is not an endorsement of population growth but an acknowledgment of one of its effects. The second is near-record levels of private debt in relation to US aggregate income. It is harder to grow debt rapidly if an economy is already overleveraged.

In this context, what's the most likely path for boosting GDP growth in the near future? Which sector of the economy appeared best positioned to increase spending fueled by increased debt? As we've seen, there are only four possible options: businesses, households, the rest of the world, or the government.

The first option, a major increase in business debt and spending, could theoretically be viable. Non-financial business debt growth became somewhat more brisk in the first months of 2022 compared to previous years. However, the likelihood that we'll see further acceleration is low because businesses are weighing the odds of recession, continued high inflation, and potentially high interest rates. Collectively, these factors mean that businesses are going to be somewhat more cautious and conservative in managing their own individual income statements and balance sheets. A surge in lending to the non-financial business macrosector seemed unlikely in the immediate future, from the perspective of both lenders and businesses.

The second option, household debt growth, would be plagued by similar hesitation. So although household debt for the first nine months of 2022 showed stronger growth than in previous years, the outlook for growth was muted because the advent of higher mortgage rates had led to a collapse in new mortgage applications, putting this lending volume at multi-decade lows. The appetite for debt among households was clearly dampened, and this appeared likely to be the case over the near term. Add the fact that government pandemic supports had been discontinued, ending an immediate channel for wealth transfer into households, and that a backlog of unpaid rent, mortgages, and other bills had suddenly become due – and we have a recipe for moderation or retrenchment, rather than borrowing.

The third option, a major improvement to the US net trade position, also seemed unlikely. President Donald Trump's tariffs and other trade policies did not put the US in good stead with many of its regular trading partners. A deeper problem was that improving the US trade position would take years of concerted efforts across a broad set of initiatives, including 'reshoring' manufacturing and other jobs, to bring about a change of the magnitude needed to meaningfully impact overall GDP growth. In 2022, the US trade deficit remained high.

And then there was the fourth approach, a major increase in government debt and spending. This seemed to be an unlikely path forward at the start of 2022, after pandemic relief programs were allowed to come to an end and the political will to increase spending appeared quite low. But the Biden administration and Congress rallied energetically, passing into law the CHIPS and Science Act, which provided $280 billion in incentives to businesses making new semiconductors in the US, the Inflation Reduction Act, which includes upwards of $437 billion to fund projects to address climate change and energy issues, and a $1.7 trillion omnibus appropriations bill for the 2022/23 fiscal year.

Another potential wealth transfer would come directly from the Executive Branch in the form of the Biden administration's large student debt forgiveness program, if the Supreme Court allows it to move forward. With the Republican Party taking control of the House of Representatives and a return to divided government in the US, it appeared highly unlikely that major spending bills would make it to the president's desk for signature over the near term, and even where the administration moves to act on its own – doing things like attempting to forgive debt – under the Constitution, Congress controls federal government spending, and it would surely be challenged.

None of the four models for debt growth has an easy road ahead, at least so far as things stood at the time of this writing in early 2023. Growth, therefore, looked likely to remain moderate to tepid, if not recessionary, in the near term.

THE FEAR OF INFLATION

Because inflation became such a prominent issue in 2021 and 2022, I want to spend some time dispelling the pervasive notion that government debt and spending causes inflation. Indeed, this misperception about inflation illustrates nicely the underlying misperceptions about government debt which too often cause poor policy choices and skew our capacity to predict or understand economic crises.

During summer 2022, when inflation reached 9 percent in the US, inflation was the number one concern among US households. It was gnawing away at family budgets, so much so that some said they feared inflation more than any other economic woe, even a stock market crash or deep recession. Fears of inflation arise in part from the fact that its sources seem mysterious and uncontrollable at the same time that it extracts immediate, adverse effects on essentially all people's lives and household budgets.

The impact was felt acutely each time Americans went to check out at the supermarket or fill up the gas tanks of their cars. The sanctions against Russia constrained the availability of oil, natural gas, and wheat worldwide. The price of oil, which had been $60 per barrel before the pandemic, climbed to $70 during the pandemic, and peaked at over $120 after the invasion of Ukraine. By December 2022, it had retreated down to just under $80 – still well above its pre-pandemic price. The price of natural gas, which had been $2 per million British thermal units (BTUs) before the pandemic, climbed to $4 during the pandemic, and peaked at over $9 with the advent of the war. By December 2022, it was just $3.50 per million BTUs, still above the pre-pandemic price. The price of wheat, which was $4 to $5 per bushel before the pandemic, climbed to $8 to $10 during the pandemic, and peaked at $16 with the advent of the war. By November 2022, it was still costing an exorbitant $10 per bushel. The war-related premiums had abated, but prices were still both high, volatile, and susceptible to further developments in the war.

These three commodities play an outsized role in determining inflation levels around the world. Analysts have estimated that about one third of the US inflation rate in summer 2022 was due to the Ukraine war. Yet there was an almost universal conviction that government spending, government debt, and profligate 'printing' of money were the *real* culprits, on the logic that more money chasing the same quantity of goods would translate into that money buying less – the very definition of inflation. This meant that the primary solution being employed was to raise interest rates. Some were even convinced that the Fed had waited too long to raise rates and thus had missed its opportunity to control inflation. Setting aside the inconvenient fact that the first rate increase occurred less than one month after the Russian invasion, these critics argued that if the Fed had only moved more decisively and more aggressively, inflation could have been leashed, but now that it was on the loose, there was no way to contain it except with even higher interest rates.

This theory was widely espoused in the 1970s, and has subsequently taken the form of dogma. But we have had four decades of new experience and data, spread across a wide number of countries, since then, and the data refutes the dogma. Resoundingly.

Consider these four basic points:

1) Inflation has been infrequent in US economic history. It has usually receded quickly once the true underlying cause of the inflation was addressed, without the need for high interest rates.
2) Inflation is not a monetary phenomenon – in other words, it is not a function, or artifact, of the Fed putting copious amounts of new money into the economy.
3) Although raising rates will indeed help to tame inflation, it does so only in the most blunt and painful way, and high inflation in the US has usually been resolved without recourse to crushingly high interest rates.
4) The current wave of inflation is largely the combined product of the pandemic and the war in Ukraine. It will resolve once these are resolved – or, at least, mitigated in some fashion.

Before we look at each of these points in turn, I want to be clear that, although the discussion which follows is focused on the US experience, there is no reason to believe these observations would not apply to most of the other Big 7 countries and other large, developed economies. The context is different for smaller, less developed nations, but again, that is a topic beyond the scope of this book.

Inflation is infrequent

Over the course of the nation's history, from 1800 up until 2021, the US economy has been challenged by a bout of inflation only eight times, and this inflation has usually dissipated within a few short years, without the need for high interest rates. For example, in 1864, during the Civil War, inflation reached 34.4 percent, but by 1865, it was a *negative* 1.6 percent, and short-term interest rates prior to that period of high inflation bounced up and down between 6 percent and 8 percent, never rising above that. In 1947, the inflation that accompanied the Second World War reached 14 percent, but by 1949 inflation was again negative, at negative 1 percent. This happened as interest rates were at 2.4 percent, or steadily on the decline. The exception to this pattern was the inflation of the First World War, which in 1917 reached 19 percent. Inflation was again negative, at negative 11 percent, by 1921, but from 1917 to 1921, interest rates rose painfully, from 4 percent to 8 percent. Money supply does not appear to have been an issue in any of these cases. Instead, each of these involved *supply-depletion inflation*, caused almost entirely by wartime decimation of farms and factories, quite similar to the supply depletion at the root of current inflation.

The US has experienced two more recent bouts of inflation. The mildest of these occurred from 1969 to 1970, when annual inflation peaked at 5.9 percent. Some blamed this inflation on 'guns and butter' spending during the war in Vietnam, but the ratio of federal government debt to GDP was actually *declining*, from 43 percent in 1965 to (a very low) 33 percent in 1972. The war in Vietnam was confined to a small geographic area that was not central to the world's supplies or supply chains. Instead, the most notable macroeconomic factor was the US defense of the gold standard as the dollar had begun to weaken. This allowed foreign governments to redeem their dollars for gold at $35 to $40 an ounce and then sell the gold at a higher price in foreign markets. Despite efforts to intervene, especially by raising interest rates to make holding dollars more attractive, over the decade of the 1960s US gold supplies plunged from 20,000 metric tons to less than 10,000 metric tons. The sale of so many dollars further weakened the currency, making imports more expensive, thus contributing to inflation. Interest rates peaked at 6.7 percent in 1969, and inflation peaked at 5.9 percent in 1970. The interest rate hikes did not staunch the gold outflow, so President Richard Nixon took the US off the gold standard in 1971. Only then, once the actual cause of the inflation was addressed, did inflation fall, in this case to 3 percent in 1972.

The bout of US inflation that bewitched a generation of economists, and which has come to define the conventional view of inflation writ large, lasted from 1973 to 1982. This inflation was largely a function of high oil prices, which came as the Organization of the Petroleum Exporting Countries (OPEC) strangled oil production in retaliation for the US stance in support of Israel in the 1973 Yom Kippur War. The Iranian Revolution in 1979 further disrupted oil production. These events drove the price of oil from $4 to $39 per barrel, a tenfold increase that pushed inflation to a peak of 13.5 percent in 1980.

This inflation was vanquished not by high interest rates, as many believe, but by domestic oil price deregulation, which allowed domestic producers to sell their oil at over $30 per barrel instead of the regulated price of $6 to $15 (depending on the type of oil). With that enhanced profit opportunity, the domestic industry scrambled to discover new oil fields, with the number of oil and gas drilling rigs rising 202 percent, from 1,496 rigs in 1977 to 4,521 rigs in 1982. As a result of all this new drilling, North American oil production jumped from 12.2 million barrels per day in the late 1970s to 15.4 million barrels per day by 1984. Predictably, the surge in production brought down the price of oil, to $12 per barrel by 1986 – and this sent inflation tumbling to 2 percent. (The tumbling price of oil also left a lot of bankrupt drillers in its wake.) Infamously, however, Federal Reserve Chairman Paul Volcker, following in large part the positions espoused by influential economist Milton Friedman, believed the period's inflation had been more a product of the country's money supply than the growth in oil prices, and so in 1979 hiked interest rates to double digits. That act helped to precipitate the severe US recession of the early 1980s.

The Friedman–Volcker view of inflation does not hold up particularly well under scrutiny. Data from the largest countries of the world from over the last seventy years demonstrates that periods of low inflation have sometimes been preceded by high money supply growth, and that episodes of high inflation often occur without high money supply growth. The data also shows a similar lack of correlation between high government debt growth and inflation. In fact, US money supply growth was still high in 1986, and government debt growth was exploding, when inflation dropped to 2 percent, which means that Volcker did not succeed in reducing money supply growth by much and yet inflation still plummeted. As oil prices rose and fell, so did inflation. This proves that it was OPEC's stranglehold on the price of oil that triggered high inflation and US deregulation that broke it.

As this short history underscores, inflation – especially the sort of high double-digit or triple-digit inflation that has plagued many less developed nations – has rarely been a problem in the US. Among economic calamities, including banking crises, stock market crashes, currency collapses, and other disasters, inflation has impacted the world the least on a GDP-weighted basis. However, because its impact on households is so direct and painful, it is politically consequential, which is why it's been viewed as being such a terrible calamity. In the US and other Big 7 economies, we would be well advised by history to approach bouts of inflation with the expectation that they can be brief – if the underlying causes are addressed.

Inflation is not a monetary phenomenon

During the pandemic, the Federal Reserve took monetary action to support the US economy through open market operations (OMOs), purchasing $3.5 trillion in Treasury securities and $1 trillion in mortgage and other securities between the beginning of 2020 and the end of 2021. This quantitative easing was entirely separate from the legislative relief in which the government gave money directly to households. However, because these two separate things – Congressional spending and the Fed's OMO – happened simultaneously, they have been confusingly conflated by almost all commentators since.

The Fed chose to undertake quantitative easing primarily to provide support for the US public and private bond markets, to prevent them from 'freezing up' due to a dearth of private sector buyers. Quantitative easing was also seen as a way to increase access to deposits in the private sector – deposits that were highly liquid and readily available for spending. Further, it was considered to be a mechanism for reducing interest rates. The OMOs were structured to buy securities with a full payment of equal value with the expectation that the securities would eventually be sold back, in effect a loan where one liability is exchanged for another. This is very different from the $1,200 and $1,400 checks that the federal government issued as pandemic relief.

I do not believe that the Fed's massive pandemic OMOs contributed to inflation, although many economists assume they did. Again, our best evidence for this comes from history. As mentioned earlier, Japan's ratio of money supply to GDP increased almost 35 percent in the years after the Global Financial Crisis of 2008 and yet the Japanese economy has seen zero inflation. In the same span of time, US money supply almost doubled and the US economy averaged 2 percent inflation.

Between 1994 and 1999, Japan's equivalent to the Fed, the Bank of Japan, bought a huge quantity of Japanese Treasury bonds with the aim of increasing inflation and ending the country's financial languor. This monetary activity doubled the size of the Bank of Japan's balance sheet by 1999, and tripled it by 2003. Japan's inflation did not budge from zero. Desperate to engender even a tiny amount of inflation, the Bank of Japan doubled the size of its balance sheet yet again between 2011 and 2014, and had almost quintupled it by 2018. Inflation still remained near zero. By 2022, the balance sheet had increased by another third from 2018, and the country was finally showing modestly higher inflation compared to the near-zero inflation of the prior two decades, but inflation was still only a comparatively low 3 percent. This happened at the same time that inflation was rising around the world because of production and supply chain depletions and war, which is why I believe this late-in-the-day, slight increase in inflation was not due to the Bank of Japan's monetary actions.

As further context, Japan's government spending and monetary growth over this period vastly exceeded government spending and monetary growth in the US. At the end of 2020, government debt in Japan was 247 percent of GDP, compared to 133 percent of GDP in the US. Japan's money supply was 211 percent of GDP compared to 91 percent of GDP for the US. Likewise, monetary actions to combat the aftershocks of the Global Financial Crisis of 2008 more than doubled the size of the US balance sheet between 2009 and 2014, and yet inflation remained stubbornly stuck at 2 percent.

While the extraordinary growth in the US money supply during the pandemic is unique, when my colleagues and I scoured a database covering macrostatistics for forty-seven countries we found only thirty instances where money supply doubled in five or less years. Of these, only seven were followed by inflation – meaning that more than three quarters of the time, high money supply growth was not followed by high inflation and high inflation was not preceded by high money supply growth. A similar pattern holds for high government debt growth.

We should take a moment to revisit why the idea of 'printing money' should be retired from the contemporary economics lexicon. In contrast to the greenbacks printed during the Civil War – which truly were money printed *de novo* in order to make payments on government debts – the Fed's OMOs only ever involve the purchase of securities, with a credit to the seller and the expectation that the securities will be resold. As noted earlier, OMOs are an exchange of things of equal value, in essence, the equivalent of a loan.

Money supply does not change in amount when the government issues debt and spends the proceeds. As discussed, if John Doe buys Treasury debt, he pays with a deposit – which actually reduces the money supply. When the Treasury then spends that money by, for example, paying salaries to employees, it comes in the form of deposits to employees' bank accounts, which then increases the money supply. The *net* result of those two events – the issuance of debt and the spending of the proceeds – is that the money supply remains unchanged.

While OMOs do not lead to price inflation, they appear to play a role in asset inflation – increasing the prices of stocks and real estate, or at least arresting any decline in their value, such as seen in Japan in the 2000s, when the private sector was deleveraging. The individuals or investment companies that have sold bonds to the Fed are inclined to reinvest the proceeds in something – and that something is often other assets, such as equities.

Raising interest rates is a blunt and painful tool

Interest rates can help to quell inflation, but only in the clumsiest, most bruising way. Rising interest rates hurt millions across an economy, curbing household and non-financial business spending and throttling demand for goods and services offered both domestically and by the ROW. Less spending can help reduce inflation somewhat, but it cannot repair broken supply chains or replace shortages caused by a pandemic, war, or similar world event. This has become so obvious that even some who advocate for higher interest rates to lower inflation concede that this tool should be used in moderation.

It's important to note that interest rate increases in the early 2020s have had more than twice the economic braking impact than they did in 1979, during Volcker's tenure at the Fed, because total US debt as a percentage of GDP had risen dramatically, standing at 132 percent in 1979 compared to 273 percent as of the third quarter of 2022, the most recent available data as of writing. In this context, the increase in interest rates from near zero at the start of the pandemic to nearly 5 percent at the end of 2022 will likely squelch as much growth as when Volcker's actions pushed short-term Treasury bill rates from 5 percent to 14 percent in 1981. The damage to demand of the Fed's rate hikes since 2020 were, by mid-2020, acutely felt in many households and businesses.

As part of the Fed's overall policy of increasing interest rates, it has indicated plans to shrink the US balance sheet from $9 trillion in 2021 closer to the pre-pandemic 2019 level of $4 trillion. But this action will exert downwards pressure on stock markets and other asset values, and is not strictly necessary. At 37 percent, the ratio of Federal Reserve assets to GDP was actually low in 2020 compared to the holdings of other Big 7 central banks. By contrast, this ratio was 38 percent for the People's Bank of China, 57 percent for the European Central Bank, and 139 percent for the Bank of

Japan (see Figure 5.8). These ratios, especially Japan's, have been higher than the Fed's for years, without any adverse inflationary consequence in the US economy. The Fed does not have to shrink its balance sheet.

To resolve inflation, resolve its underlying causes

This may be one of the more difficult challenges in addressing our current bout of inflation, because, as discussed earlier, the high inflation of 2022 has come in two waves with two different causes. The pandemic drove the first wave of inflation, and the war in Ukraine drove the second. Although by the end of 2022, war-related price increases had abated, a continuing war in Ukraine could trigger more price shocks, with global implications. For example, if a tanker carrying Russian oil to export destinations were to be torpedoed and sunk, the price of oil would likely rise sharply.

And it is not just the price of the key commodities of oil, natural gas, and wheat that remain at high risk. Russia is a major supplier of many of the world's raw manufacturing materials – iron; potash and boron for fertilizers; neon, which is essential for the lasers used to etch semiconductors; vanadium, which is used to produce superconducting magnets; and the list goes on. A higher price for petroleum products also constrains the production of some fertilizers. When fertilizer prices go up, food prices go up, too.

We have seen from history how inflation typically tumbles from high to low levels without high interest rates when the underlying causes of the inflation are addressed. It is reasonable to think that this would have been the case in 2022 had the war in Ukraine not exacerbated pandemic-related production and supply chain issues.

It is also reasonable to believe that high inflation will persist, at least to some extent, as long as the war disrupts the oil, natural gas, and wheat markets. But pandemic-related production and supply chain disruptions will likely take longer to untangle because of the global complications wrought by the war. More war could readily mean upwards pressure on prices and inflation.

ENDING INFLATION

There are many reasons to be concerned about inflation. Inflation rates could very well stick above the Fed's 2 percent target for some time, even if the war in Ukraine comes to an end, or at least a stalemate. The most pronounced issue is the 'decoupling' of the economies of the West from China and Russia as a result of rising political tensions, which will likely continue even if the war ends and sanctions against Russia are lifted.

Outsourcing to China has long been a key strategy used by US non-financial businesses to keep operating expenses, and end-consumer prices, low. Decoupling could spell higher prices for everyone. And as the Ukraine war has made plain, Russia has become an important source for a number of vital commodities, which may remain more expensive and more difficult to obtain with decoupling. The antagonism between China and Russia on the one side and the West on the other is, in many respects, the ultimate supply chain disruption. There's no escaping the short-term impacts here.

But I believe decoupling from China and Russia will lead to new couplings – or enhanced recouplings – with countries such as India and Vietnam. It could even provide the financial and political incentives for reshoring some high-end manufacturing, particularly where automation has largely eliminated wage disadvantages for the US, the UK, and other major, developed economies. If one or both of these possibilities come to fruition, the difficult consequences of decoupling will eventually abate, after some period of transition. Notably, the US has had low inflation in periods of high tariffs, low trade, and high wages – a relatively full gamut of economic circumstances.

As an aside, some economists have argued that slowing US, UK, and EU population growth will add to inflation. The logic is that fewer workers means higher salaries, which means higher costs. But Japan's population growth slowed to a crawl and even declined while the country's inflation hovered near zero for years. This happened because slowing population growth decreases demand as well as the size of the labor force. So slowing population growth could create short-term pressure on inflation that can be resolved once countries learn how to better utilize their workforce, including through the use of automation.

Helpfully, since 1997, the Federal Reserve has published the Global Supply Chain Pressure Index (GSCPI), which integrates transportation cost data and manufacturing indicators to gauge global supply chain conditions. Changes in the GSCPI are associated with goods and producer price inflation. The index calculates standard deviations from average value, with zero meaning the supply chain is operating at a normal level. The index catapulted from zero to 3.15 in spring 2020, and recorded 4.31 standard deviations, its highest value ever, in December 2021. It dropped to 2.4 by February 2022 before rising again to 3.29 in April due to the impact of Russia's invasion of Ukraine. By September 2022, it had fallen back to 0.94, which suggested that supply chains were about two thirds of the way back to normal, before resurgent Covid-19 cases spurred supply chain issues and social unrest in China. In December 2022, the GSCPI was around 1.2, according to the latest Fed estimates available at the time of writing, indicating that we still have some ways to go in repairing the global supply chain.

Today's solution to inflation is the same as it has always been: we need to address the underlying causes. Unfortunately, the Ukraine war may be an intractable problem for years.

The many wild cards here make it difficult to predict the duration and path of inflation in the near term. Nevertheless, as the causes of inflation are resolved, or at least mitigated, inflation will return to lower levels. This is the lesson of debt economics, and of history.

7

THE DARK SIDE OF DEBT

At a number of points in this book we've seen that a very rapid rise in private sector debt over a short number of years is likely to result in overcapacity, bad debt, and economic reversal, sometimes even to the point of a banking crisis. In this chapter, I examine these calamities in greater detail because they are one of the defining attributes of debt growth in an economy, and the culmination of debt's destructive power. Indeed, one of the principles of debt economics is that total debt always grows as fast or faster than GDP – except in periods of great calamity. Some of these banking crises were of such magnitude as to constitute one of these exceptions.

Almost all banking crises follow the same simple if unforgiving logic: widespread overlending leads to widespread overcapacity which leads to widespread bad loans and then bank and other lender failures. These are the dominos that fall one after the other until the moment of crisis.

My colleagues and I have examined all of the major banking crises of the last two hundred years in the six largest economies of the world: the US, the UK, China, France, Germany, and Japan. To do this, we reviewed the work of a number of economic historians, identifying forty-three banking crises – including the 1836 crisis that spanned the US and Britain; the 1866 crisis in the UK; the 1873 crisis in the

US, Germany, and Austria; and the Great Depression – all of which are described and analyzed in my 2019 book, *A Brief History of Doom*. The US alone had lending booms that culminated in banking crises – usually referred to as 'panics' – in 1819, 1837, 1857, 1873, 1893, 1929, 1987, and 2008. Such banking crises deserve heightened scrutiny because, among the major types of economic crisis – including those related to inflation, currency, and stock markets – they have been by far the most severely damaging to major, developed economies.

For example, US total private debt as a percentage of GDP declined from 43 percent to 31 percent after the Panic of 1837, from 65 percent to 56 percent after the Panic of 1873, and from 120 percent in 1930 to 103 percent in 1936, the bookend years of the Great Depression,[39] and as we've seen, a decline in private debt causes a contraction in GDP such that each of these sharp declines brought protracted, painful, era-defining depressions. In contrast, in many of the banking crises which have occurred globally since the Second World War, policymakers and the Federal Reserve have learned to respond quickly and forcefully, using government spending and debt growth to compensate for the decline in private sector debt, such that the overall ratio of total debt to GDP has continued to grow and GDP has contracted comparatively little, even if it has not felt that way at the time.

Of the many banking crises in major, developed countries since the Second World War, the two most severe were the 1990s financial crisis in Japan and the Global Financial Crisis of 2008. For this reason, I dissect these crises in detail in this chapter.

HOW JAPAN LOST ITS DECADE (AND MORE)

The 1990s financial crisis in Japan was primarily the result of an extraordinary burst of private sector lending in the late 1980s. Japan's private debt – comprised of both household and non-financial business loans – increased by ¥343 trillion, or $2.4 trillion, ballooning private debt from 143 percent of GDP in 1985 to a then unprecedented 181 percent of GDP in 1990.

This increased lending came largely in the commercial real estate sector through overconstruction, overdevelopment, and out-of-control acquisition of land, office buildings, hotels, and apartments, in both Japan and select markets overseas, especially the US. From 1985 to 1990, commercial real estate loans grew from ¥75 trillion to ¥187 trillion, creating innumerable new buildings that would not be filled or sold for decades.

The lending frenzy drove real estate prices up by 300 percent over those five years. It brought a short-term surge that, at the time, was applauded as an economic miracle.

The euphoria extended well beyond real estate projects. Real estate was so central to Japan's lending boom that bank loans for things other than real estate, such as small businesses and finance and leasing companies, were often secured by real estate. Japan's economy grew to become the second largest in the world, at 18 percent of global GDP. With this lending boom, five of the world's ten largest commercial banks by total assets were Japanese. People in the US and elsewhere thought that Japan was on a path to become the world's leading economy, and some zealous US parents enrolled their children in Japanese language classes to prepare for this future.

But the miracle proved to be a mirage. Japan's banks, businesses, and households quickly became overleveraged. The country was fully overbuilt no later than 1990, as were other Japanese lending targets, such as California and Hawaii. After its 1980s boom, Japan endured a slow-motion bust in the 1990s, as the economy reckoned with the consequences of its overlending. Today, Japan stands at only 5 percent of global GDP.

FIGURE 7.1. Japan construction value, real estate prices, and private debt, 1980–2020

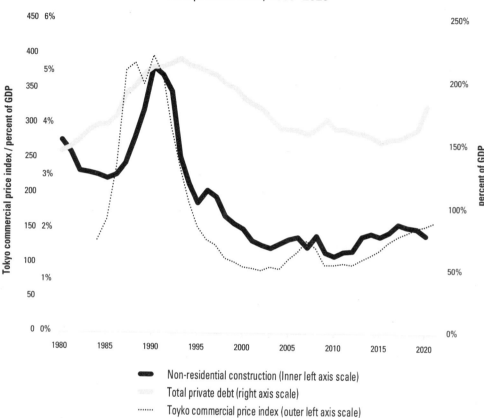

Figure 7.1 shows Japan's boom-and-bust trajectory from 1980 to 2020. As lending began to pick up in pace, both construction activity and prices began to soar. Prices tripled, and from 1986 to 1990, spending on non-residential commercial real estate construction grew from 3 percent to 5 percent of GDP.

When it became clear that ever more of these newly constructed buildings would not be fully leased or sold, and that the loans made to build them would not be fully repaid, new construction, and new loans to support construction, abruptly halted. As lenders curtailed their lending activity, private debt as a percentage of GDP began to decline. And once the loan faucet was shut off, land prices dropped accordingly – and precipitously. Lenders who had made loans at peak land prices for now-empty buildings found themselves heavily saddled with bad debt. The total of loans outstanding declined slowly because, although few new loans were being made, borrowers were struggling to repay existing loans, so those loan balances remained high until they were later written off as losses. The government and financial institution regulators in Japan scrambled to whitewash the problems for much of the 1990s, then capitulated to reality with a recapitalization of banks that began in earnest in 1998, and which took fifteen years. Though private debt fell, the government responded with such large increases in spending that the ratio of total debt to GDP declined only for a few years.

That is the basic plot of a banking crisis.

OUR MOST RECENT GREAT FINANCIAL CRISIS

The Global Financial Crisis of 2008 also arose from unchecked, irresponsible private debt growth – in this case, in household mortgages. These mortgages doubled in the US, from $5.3 trillion in 2001 to $10.6 trillion in 2007, bringing a short-term boom but silently and perniciously piling up the unpayable loans that would wreck the economy.

In terms of sheer volume, the largest share of the problem were actually 'prime' mortgage loans – theoretically, the better loans – but where credit criteria used by mortgage lenders had been compromised. 'Cash-out' refinancings – loans where the borrower received cash for an increased value of their home – were also an issue, and perhaps the worst-performing loans of all. 'Subprime' loans – industry jargon for loans to the least creditworthy borrowers – were also extended under liberal or nonexistent credit criteria; these accounted for $1.7 trillion of total loans.

The bulk of this mortgage overlending happened rapidly, between 2002 and 2006. Billions of loans were made to unqualified or under-qualified buyers, with far too many new houses getting built to meet demand that was high only because it was credit-fueled.

While it lasted, this lending boom brought economic euphoria to the US, just as it had in Japan. Mortgage brokers who had been making $100,000 a year were now making $1 million. Swanky restaurants were full. Luxury cars were flying off dealer lots.

In late summer 2007, just before everything began to unravel, the stock market and overall household wealth were nearing all-time highs. The unemployment rate was at a five-year low. Consumer and business confidence were both strong. Banks – the very institutions whose ostensible expertise was to assess lending risk – were so confident in their economic outlook that they were setting aside historically small reserves for future loan losses. Most bankers, investors, economists, businesspeople, and politicians and government officials were not viewing the high levels of mortgage lending with any alarm.

Within weeks, the largest financial crisis to hit the US since the Great Depression shook the economy's foundations. In October, the stock market began a drop of nearly 50 percent, banks and corporations started to fail, and unemployment was on a trajectory to double to 10 percent.

Most economic observers and policymakers were unaware that, by 2005 – almost two years before – the financial crisis was already inevitable. By then, over $1 trillion in bad loans had been made in a lending industry with roughly $1.5 trillion in capital. Mortgage lenders had employed battalions of telemarketers, paid on commission, to foist these loans onto households, including people not looking for a new mortgage or home. This is a key characteristic of all booms: lenders are highly aggressive in seeking out borrowers and promoting loans.

These mortgage lenders enticed borrowers by reducing down payments to little or nothing. By 2006, 43 percent of all new loans went to borrowers making no down payment whatsoever. Lenders also offered temptingly low initial interest rates which, after one or two years, ratcheted to much higher rates. Many borrowers understood that they would then face far higher payments, but homes were appreciating by 10 percent to 15 percent annually, so they reasoned that, in the worst-case scenario, they would simply sell their house at a profit.

At the same time, the volume of commercial real estate loans was also growing. Between 2002 and 2007, commercial real estate loans went up by 74 percent, to a total of $3.4 trillion. As with residential mortgages, many of these loans were written using lax credit criteria. This, too, would exact extensive damage, though comparatively less compared to residential mortgages.

As is typical during a boom, margin loans for stocks vaulted upwards by 120 percent over five years. This helped power the Dow Jones Industrial Average to a record high, at the time, of 14,165 on October 9, 2007.

After the crash in real estate prices and stock markets, 9 million Americans lost their homes. Many of them never recovered their previous income level or financial status. This wreckage was wrought all because too many lenders made trillions of dollars in ill-advised mortgage loans over a short period of time, many under misleading or unsustainable terms. The vast overcapacity of homes that was created would take years for the economy to absorb. Few of the executives and board members of those lenders lost their jobs or saw any adverse consequence.

Congress and the Federal Reserve responded quickly and forcefully with spending and monetary support to ameliorate the effects of the financial crisis. The private debt to GDP ratio contracted, but higher government spending and debt meant that total debt levels never declined.

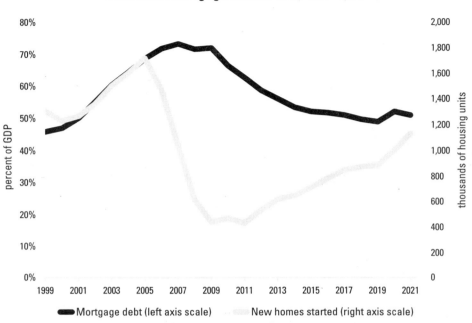

FIGURE 7.2. US new single-family homes, residential mortgage debt to GDP, 1999–2021

Figure 7.2 tells the underlying story. The number of new homes built annually went up from 1.2 million in 2000 to 1.7 million in 2005, the peak year. That was hundreds of thousands of homes above demand, made possible with hundreds of billions of dollars in loans that would never get fully repaid. Mortgage loans by themselves vaulted from 47 percent to 74 percent of GDP.

Figure 7.2 also illustrates exactly why it takes so long for an economy to rebound after a banking crisis. There are two forces at work – one is the surplus of houses built during a boom that largely sit empty for years, as it takes a long time for demand to catch up to (over)supply. A second force, and one just as powerful, is that so many builders and their lenders are so badly burned in a crisis that they are highly cautious about the amount of new building they are willing to undertake for many years afterwards. This is especially the case with speculative development, where homes are built without a commitment in hand from a buyer. In ordinary times, a builder and their lender might be willing to build an entire neighborhood 'on spec', trusting that there will be sufficient demand for the houses to be bought in a reasonable time frame to recoup outlays. But that confidence takes years to return after the trauma of a crisis. In combination, those two factors explain the tentative, sluggish upwards slope of new home starts in the first years after the 2008 crisis, as shown in Figure 7.2. By 2019, new starts had still not regained their 2000 level, a benchmark well before the excess lending that created the crisis had started.

Economists at the Federal Reserve missed predicting the 2008 crisis because they largely ignored the most relevant and prophetically telling data needed to do so: trends in US private sector loan volumes or, in other words, debt. The Fed's model for economic forecasting assigned no role to loans. Yet, runaway mortgage and commercial real estate debt had the leading role in this great financial crisis and the recession that followed it. The overall ratio of private loans to GDP had increased by a very high 18 percent in the previous five years, and in 2007 this ratio exceeded 171 percent of GDP.

Based on analysis conducted with my colleagues, I have observed that when the ratio of private debt to GDP in a major, developed country increases by at least 15 percent to 20 percent in five years or less, then a financial crisis or some other economic calamity is likely, especially if the overall private debt ratio is at 150 percent or higher. This increase of 15 percent to 20 percent or more measures the rate of *acceleration* in lending; it is a measure of how rapidly capacity – or better yet, *over*capacity – is being created. Note that a private debt to GDP ratio of 150 percent or more does not foretell a crisis, at least not on its own. There are a lot of countries with over 150 percent private debt to GDP that are not on the precipice of a financial crisis. The key is the acceleration in the rate of loan growth, which, especially if the overall private debt ratio is at least 150 percent, signals that new homes or new buildings are being built and added to the supply far too rapidly, often beyond demand. That means those homes and buildings will not be sold or leased, and the loans that enabled them will therefore not be paid.

Nor do I mean here that government debt of over 150 percent will bring a crisis. Financial crises come when borrowers cannot repay debts, and this only happens within the domain of private debt. Governments in major countries can easily pay their debt by issuing more debt – or, to use that misleading colloquialism, they can 'print' more money. Private sector borrowers do not have that luxury.

Another, more direct, way to detect if purchases of existing assets are high enough to threaten overvaluation of those assets is simply to measure the ratio of Type 2 debt to GDP. As shown in Figure 7.3, Type 2 debt to GDP grew by 20 percentage points, or 35 percent, between 2002 and 2007. That is simply excessive. An increase of such scale most often assures that asset prices will be pushed to unsustainable levels, if they are not already there. In fact, the Case–Schiller home price index, calculated by the credit rating agency Standard & Poor's, went from 128 in 2002 to 204 in 2007 – an increase of 60 percent. Yearly growth was 5 percent or more from 2001 through 2006, at which point we now know most of the bad loans had been made. In almost the same window of time, household capital investment increased 30 percent relative to GDP, peaking in 2006, which proved that too many new houses were being built; this added to the disaster. While helpful, this second metric, also shown in Figure 7.3, is not as powerful as those tied directly to debt, since it is high levels of problem debt which bring financial crisis.

Around 2006, some astute investors who were carefully tracking the extraordinary growth in lending became convinced it would turn disastrous and began making very large bets against the credit quality of residential mortgages. To do this, they used an investment vehicle called a credit default swap.

FIGURE 7.3. US Type 2 debt and capital expenditures, 2001–2012

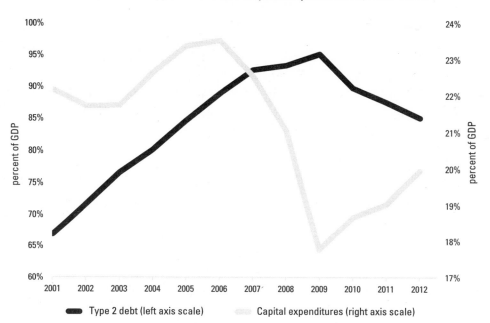

Type 2 debt (left axis scale)   Capital expenditures (right axis scale)

Credit default swaps are a kind of insurance policy, or hedge. Buyers bet against the quality of associated loans while sellers bet that those loans are good.

So naively confident were the sellers of credit default swaps in 2006 and 2007 that these investments were priced such that if the underlying loans went bad, the sellers would have to pay out a huge amount of money and the buyers would reap a huge windfall.

Over $61 trillion in credit default swaps were sold in 2007 alone. This had the effect of greatly amplifying the crisis. Without these investments, there still would have been a financial crisis, but a smaller one. The lure of easy profits from selling credit default swaps simply made the crisis much larger and longer than it would have been otherwise, because this lure expanded the net of financial institutions which were caught in the crisis's net. Some major financial institutions, such as insurer AIG, which would not otherwise have been affected by the 2008 financial crisis, were ensnared by credit default swaps and got grievously hurt.

THE CATCH-22 OF OVERLENDING

The banking crises in Japan in the 1990s and in the US in 2008, like essentially all banking crises, have in common irresponsible, runaway private lending, used primarily for asset purchase and creation. Both banking crises were preceded by a boom in private debt. They stand in stark contrast to periods of low growth in the ratio of private debt to GDP, which rarely if ever culminate in calamity.

Without doubt, a lending boom brings good – and all but irresistible – news while it is happening. The economy gets better because bank lending creates new money and thus creates more demand. Businesses that obtain loans expand spending and hiring, and consumer borrowers increase their spending. Government receipts go up because businesses and individuals are making more money and therefore paying more taxes. The benefits of excess lending cascade as new jobs proliferate, unemployment declines, incomes rise, housing and other asset values go up, and the government debt profile improves.

Booms do not just arise from banks. They often come from a secondary type of financial institution that is subject to less regulatory scrutiny, which makes it easier for management to relax credit criteria and cut corners. For example, in the US, trust banks played the leading role in the Panic of 1907 and savings and loan entities played the leading role in the 1980s crisis; in Germany a special type of lender called Baubanken were central to the 1873 crisis in that country.

In 2008, too much mortgage and other lending was extended from an area of the financial industry often referred to as *shadow banking*. Although this term might suggest an obscure subsection of the industry, it includes major lenders such as the Federal National Mortgage Association (Fannie Mae) and the Government National Mortgage Association (Ginnie Mae), insurance companies, hedge funds, and private equity funds. It is called 'shadow banking' in some respects *because* these organizations are not subject to the same regulatory oversight as banks.

In a dangerously accelerated lending boom, such as the ones which concern us here, lenders rarely resist the siren song of increased loan growth. It begins as some lenders gingerly depart from their conservative lending practices to make loans that have somewhat, but not inordinately, greater risk. As they take these initial steps into more aggressive lending, the economy gets better, employment and growth trends improve, and asset values rise. If lending in a given sector increases, the value of that sector's assets goes up, because the lending increases demand. This is especially true in real estate. Lenders believe they are following a trend of improved real estate valuations when, in fact, their loans are driving that trend. It is a seductive feedback loop: because more lending qualifies and enables more borrowers, it also provokes higher real estate prices. If you are selling a house and you have ten qualified buyers with loans, you will command a higher price than if you have just two qualified buyers, or only one.

In turn, increasing real estate prices increase lenders' confidence that they have lent sagely, which translates into yet more lending. Unbeknownst to them, this confidence is a self-fulfilling prophecy – or, more aptly, a self-fulfilling illusion. But while it lasts, the earnings of these lenders, and their company stock valuation, go up. Other lenders take notice and are criticized if their lending trends fall behind the market leaders, and most respond by accelerating their own lending growth. Soon enough, much of the lending industry is unwittingly locked in a competition to make riskier and riskier loans. Borrowers are all too often happily complicit. Many borrow solely because loans are so readily available. They believe that the time to borrow is when lenders are lending.

As overcapacity becomes clear, lenders find themselves in a catch-22. The only way to maintain prices is to continue to make real estate loans using high valuations, but that very lending creates even more overcapacity and bad debt. Yet if lending abates, then values decline, which exposes problem loans like a low tide exposes debris. The good times that lending booms bring are so very good, and the bad times that a reversal will bring are so very bad, that those who benefited most from rising prices are highly reluctant to accept the troubling news of declining prices.

These crises are pivotal examples of how debt distorts the economy. Excessive debt pushes valuations to unsustainable levels, because that debt serves as a form of demand that is well beyond both need and economic justification.

The overcapacity in a financial crisis is never just a matter of a few degrees or percentage points. There have to be far, far too many new houses or office buildings, or some other real asset, being built for a crisis to result. Building one new high-rise condominium in a given neighborhood in a single year is not a problem; building five, ten, or twenty is, because there are not enough buyers or renters to support the excess in such a short time period. This is how overlending curdles good loans into bad.

When far too many loans have been made by a given bank and those loans start to sour, the bank starts to lose its own funding, perhaps through a run on the bank's deposits. Losing funding is tantamount to failure for a bank, so typically a regulator steps in and the bank is closed or rescued by the government. To reach the threshold of a financial crisis, failures must be so pervasive that they involve large numbers of lenders and thus threaten the country's economic growth and stability.

Importantly, the government debt of major, developed economies has not been a factor in the lead-up to any of the financial crises in the database analyzed with my colleagues. Rapid growth in government debt typically only comes *after* the moment of crisis, as tax revenues decline and governments spend more to repair the economic wreckage. And it takes time to absorb the overcapacity and create the new capital necessary to repair damaged lenders and companies.

FINANCIAL CRISIS IS FORESEEABLE

To our detriment, regulators, policymakers, and even many economists often assert that financial crises like the ones that afflicted Japan in the 1990s and the US in 2008 could not have been predicted. Crises are often described with labels that convey this inherent unpredictability – a 'black swan' event or a 'perfect storm'. Some insist, with what amounts to fatalistic if not cheerful nihilism, that the crisis was created by things simply too complex for anyone to explain. Such thinking casts us all as victims of forces we can neither foresee nor prevent. Far from it.

The importance of private debt is minimized by some, who reason that for every borrower there is a lender, and thus it all nets to zero. But that logic does not capture the duress of borrowers forced to constrain their economic activity and their lives because they are overleveraged – the person who took out a mortgage loan to buy a house for $400,000 only to find its value has dropped to $300,000 at the same moment that they have lost their job. Nor does it capture the crippling impairment to lenders when too many loans are not repaid.

Where pundits have been willing to put forward an explanation for a crisis, they tend to point the finger at many other factors, separately or in combination, which may indeed contribute to a crisis but are not the fundamental cause of calamity. Popular among these red herrings are declining interest rates, trade, and global savings gluts, to name just a few. By my analysis, all are misleading. They focus policymakers on ancillary issues, and so we are left ill-equipped to prevent the next crisis when it comes. In the largest sense, false narratives of financial crises betray the many millions who did not contribute to a crisis but are badly hurt by it nonetheless.

Financial crises can be foreseen, and prevented, once we start paying attention to the factor at the heart of them: excessive lending and debt. In large part, we have not learned the dangers of overlending for a simple reason: banks, bankers, and other lenders make money through growing loans. That is what garners promotions, industry accolades, high stock prices, and large bonuses. Rapid lending growth brings good times and increased wealth to the cadre of actors who make the decision to lend more. Ambition leads to excess – a bank's desire to grow loans is no different than a car company's desire to sell more cars, a coach's desire to win more games, or, for that matter, an emperor's desire to conquer more realms. In the most elegant terms, lending booms are driven by ambition and competition, abetted by the fear of falling behind or missing out.

A lending boom is optimism on steroids. It shows up in rosy earnings projections and more accommodating lending credit criteria, both of which are fed by that deeply human characteristic of willing delusion and, particularly, self-delusion. Euphoria is the hardest habit to quit. Lenders convince themselves that property values will continue to rise rapidly, housing demand will continue to increase, and corporate earnings will continue to improve. Borrowers convince themselves that property values will continue to rise long enough that they can sell at a profit if they ever start to feel too stretched. Lending and debt are the agents and catalysts of that euphoric delusion. To seek to explain booms solely through impersonal, technical factors is to miss the fact that economics is a behavioral and not a physical science. It is to miss the essence of financial crises.

Rather than ask why lending booms happen, we should invert the question and ask why they do not happen more frequently. Given that there is almost always the drive to grow loans aggressively, and that the initial phase of a lending boom brings good news, why are there periods when loan growth does not run too hot?

One answer is that lending booms do not occur when regulators or risk managers have the upper hand. This is most typically the case when lenders are chastened in the years following a crisis. In fact, some countries have gone so far as to put some form of limits on post-crisis credit growth. Comparative lending quietude can also occur when businesses and other borrowers have a residual level of overleverage and thus are not in a position to rapidly increase their borrowing.

Apart from those post-crisis periods, the bias is always towards higher lending growth. Memories of even the worst crises fade, and lenders can point to a lengthening accumulation of years in which problems have not emerged, and so they begin to escalate lending and slacken lending standards once again. 'This time is different' justifications – or amnesia – set in. Before too long, a new lending boom begins.

Financial crises do not generally erupt at a single moment in time. Instead, they tend to unfold over years. We call it the 'Global Financial Crisis of 2008' for convenience, but housing construction peaked in 2005, housing prices tumbled in 2006, the stock market started to fall in 2007, and the epoch-defining Lehman Brothers failure came in 2008. In Japan, overbuilding came in the late 1980s, stocks plummeted in 1990, real estate values tanked in 1991, and the government widely recapitalized banks in 1998.

BOOM AND BUST TOWNS

In reviewing all of the major banking crises of the past two hundred years, I have observed, to paraphrase Leo Tolstoy, that lending booms are all alike, but every bust (and recovery) is a bust in its own way. Recoveries, in particular, can vary widely in duration and severity, depending on the policies employed to combat them. Government response can range from passive and hands-off to active and interventionist. Institutions can be allowed to fail or they can be rescued.

Active government intervention to help troubled institutions, businesses, and households can significantly mitigate a crisis's severity. Typically, active intervention means a softer, shorter-term impact on the economy but a high level of residual, longer-term debt. That certainly was the case after the Global Financial Crisis of 2008. Conversely, less intervention can mean significantly more short-term distress but greater deleveraging and a cleaner debt slate after the anguish, as was the case in the Great Depression.

This boom-and-bust thesis is not entirely new, but it has been widely glossed over in the economic literature and its implications underappreciated. My colleagues and I have done extensive research on the history of banking and come to believe that there was a much more direct understanding of the boom-and-bust dynamic in the 1700s and early 1800s than there is today. Take the story of the Second Bank of the United States and Thomas Mellon.

In its second year of operations, 1818, the Second Bank, led initially by a grossly incompetent president, grew loans from $13 million to $41 million – 14 percent of all US bank loans at the time – flooding money into the fledgling economy. Settlers and entrepreneurs in newly developing towns of the 'Far West' – places like Cincinnati, Ohio – got too many of these loans and suddenly had more buildings and houses than they could use or support in the foreseeable future. This lending boom came crashing down in the Panic of 1819, and the Second Bank ended up repossessing a huge amount of property, including much of the town of Cincinnati.

In western Pennsylvania, a six-year-old Thomas – who would later found one of the great US banking dynasties – had to spend the remaining years of his youth working every night after school to help his struggling family repay the debt on the house they had grossly overpaid for during the boom. Mellon never forgot. He and his contemporaries clearly made the connection between bank overlending and financial crisis, often employing the term 'speculation', which they most definitely used as a pejorative. The lessons of the Second Bank lived large in the American imagination for a generation or two. It took modern economists to overcomplicate the story and lose the trail of that hard-won wisdom.

More recently, the American economist Hyman Minsky (1919–1996) picked up that trail again. He directly attributed banking crises to overlending, outlining details of the life cycle of overlending where, during prolonged periods of prosperity, lenders, businesses, and households take on more risk until they are spellbound by a speculative euphoria. He argued that lenders begin with 'hedge' loans – loans where interest and principal can be repaid from cash flow. Next, they move to speculative loans – loans where cash flow can service interest, but not principal. Last, they move to so-called Ponzi loans – loans where cash flow can repay neither interest nor principal, and the asset or business must be sold to repay the debt. When a large percentage of the loans in a sector fall into the Ponzi category, a crash becomes highly likely. This movement of the financial system from stability to fragility, followed by a sudden collapse that heralds a crisis, has come to be known as the 'Minsky moment'.

To this I would add that lenders do not have to believe that they are making a speculative or Ponzi-type loan for it to end up as one. They may truly think they are making one of Minsky's hedge loans if, swept up by the mania of a boom, their projections for a borrower's future revenues are too optimistic, or if competitive circumstances or other things change for the worse after the loan is made.

Because this chapter has portrayed private debt as the villainous character – the economic malefactor in financial crisis – I hasten to remind readers that private debt is a necessary and positive element of an economy. It is one of the fundamental ingredients of growth, trade, profit, and investment. Debt is the creator and the destroyer, the hero and anti-hero.

Remove private debt and economic activity as we know it would collapse. The US suffered a series of financial crises in the 1800s, but, according to analyses by British economist Angus Maddison (1926–2010), per capita GDP increased 275 percent in that century, and private debt was indispensable to that growth. Many of that century's crises stemmed from the overexpansion of railroads but they left behind a railroad network and infrastructure that enabled American progress and growth. China's meteoric rise since 1980 has been largely built using the equivalent of private (non-government) debt. This rise would have been impossible without debt, even after reckoning for the impact of crises like the Evergrande implosion in 2022 and whatever might come next.

Life goes on after a crisis. An economy that had been growing will typically resume its course after a period of recovery, and periods of growth are more frequent than periods of bust. Understanding the profile of financial crises can help economists, bankers, lenders, regulators, policymakers, politicians, and business leaders to better predict and deflect crisis, or at least mitigate the worst-case impact. This should be seen as a critical obligation and duty to those millions who will not cause the crisis but will be badly hurt by it, and to the governments and political systems that are disrupted.

THE SPECIAL PROPERTY OF PROPERTY DEBT

In both Japan in the 1990s and the US in the 2000s, overlending was concentrated in real estate. But what if the overlending occurs in a non-real estate sector of the economy? Recall from Chapter 2 that, in 2021, the combination of both household and real estate lending totaled $18 trillion, roughly half of all private sector lending. All other sectors had far lower debt.

The size of the sector makes a huge difference. A very large bout of overlending occurred in the US energy sector from 2011 to 2015, with energy loans rising by 42 percent as a percentage of GDP, culminating in a credit crisis in that sector. So much lending occurred that debt-financed overcapacity in drilling and extraction ensued. Just as in 1986, too much capacity meant a drop in the price of oil, in this case from $106 per barrel in 2014 to $30 per barrel in 2016. With that sharp drop in price, many loans could not be repaid. Loan defaults in the energy sector went from 0.1 percent in 2011 to 16 percent in 2016. Banks and other lenders stopped lending to energy companies and energy companies had to curtail their activities. A large number failed or had to be recapitalized. For the energy sector and its lenders, this was a full-blown crisis. But energy sector loans totaled only $1.3 trillion at the time – a proverbial drop in the bucket of $29 trillion in total private debt and $49 trillion in total debt in the US – so these credit problems could not achieve a magnitude that would damage the entire economy. People whose businesses and livelihoods were not tied to the industry barely noticed, if they noticed at all.

Tracking credit growth within a sector, especially credit growth for capital formation, is a useful way to predict credit problems within that sector. In the national or global context, tracking credit growth for the real estate sector as a whole, or for the economy as a whole, is a useful way of predicting a banking crisis for the entire economy.

Just as the size of a sector matters so too does the rate of growth in private debt levels – a point worth reiterating. Let's consider data for the US from 2012 to 2019. The ratio of private debt to GDP was very high, at over 150 percent, throughout these years, but it barely budged from year to year, growing only from 154 percent to 157 percent of GDP between 2012 and 2019. While that slight debt growth would not portend a banking crisis, it did mean that businesses and households were lugging around too much debt, which curtailed their ability to spend and invest, and this stultified GDP growth. It was a big part of what made the post-2008 recovery so frustratingly tepid. If a person or business has to spend a big part of their income on interest and principal on a loan, then they have less income available for spending and investing, which are the things that power an economy forwards. Private sector debt is now three times what it was in the 1950s (see Figure 2.8), and carrying that debt requires a bigger chunk of household pay packets. As discussed in Chapter 2, the problem reveals itself in the debt service ratio, which in recent years has been 30 percent higher than it was in the 1950s and 1960s – the two highest growth decades after the Second World War. The lower debt service ratio and historic GDP growth in those decades is not a coincidence.

This chapter has focused on the worst species of banking crisis, which sometimes include a rare and painful decline in the ratio of total debt to GDP like the one that metastasized across economies during the Great Depression. The other type of calamity that can affect a painful decline in the ratio of total debt to GDP is *very* high inflation or *hyperinflation*. 'Very high' is something of a term of art, but it typically hovers in the low double digits. Hyperinflation is defined as 50 percent inflation per month. That may sound practically impossible but, unfortunately for some developing economies, inflation at very high or hyperinflation levels has been a fact of life for months or even years. From 1994 to 1996 Brazil's total debt fell from 125 percent to 92 percent of GDP while annual inflation averaged 39 percent and peaked at 66 percent. From 1998 to 2010, Indonesia's total debt went from 135 percent to 55 percent of GDP while annual inflation averaged 9 percent and peaked at 20 percent. And from 1995 to 2001, Mexico's total debt went from 82 percent to 63 percent of GDP while annual inflation averaged 17 percent and peaked at 34 percent. The fall in debt as a percentage of GDP occurred in each of these cases because inflation was out of control. Comparatively lower, but still painful, inflation, has sometimes not even done the job. For example, in the US in the inflationary years from 1973 to 1982, total debt levels actually *increased*, from 128 percent to 136 percent of GDP.

Total debt grows as fast or faster than GDP – except in periods of calamity. By focusing on lending and private debt, and recognizing and responding decisively to debt's warning signals, we shall be better positioned to avert much of the damage wrought by financial crises.

8

THE LIMITS OF DEBT

We often hear about 'financial cycles' or 'debt cycles', and in a sense this concept of GDP growth and debt growth occurring and re-occurring in patterns over periods of time is accurate. But in another sense the economic activity we are observing is not properly speaking cyclical, because debt does not arrive back at the same starting point after each bout. Instead, debt levels measured in ratio to GDP go up a lot, come down a little – if at all – and then go up a lot, once again. So, over time, debt levels end at a point higher than their prior baseline. Perhaps we should call this process a *debt staircase*, with each 'cycle' ending with a country's households and businesses one step higher in debt.[40]

These processes, or cycles, have recurred four major times in US history. In one, starting in 1950 until 1980, total US debt plateaued in the range of 130 percent of GDP. Then it quickly shot up to around 180 percent, slowed for a bit, then again quickly shot up to around 250 percent during the Global Financial Crisis of 2008. In the aftermath of that crisis, debt growth slowed. Then it shot up to just over 300 percent of GDP during the pandemic, when a market bubble was created by massive government spending on pandemic relief.

Figure 8.1 charts the progression of government debt, private debt, and the sum of the two – total debt – over the course of US history. Across the entire 240-year span, declines in the ratio were infrequent

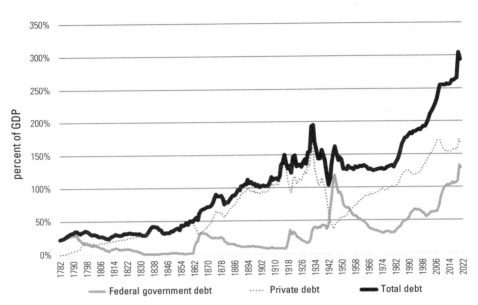

FIGURE 8.1. US private, government, and total debt, 1782–2021

and generally moderate, even in periods of extraordinary calamity, such as the Great Depression. From 1950 onwards, the total debt line always steps up, like a staircase, never coming down.

Taking steps up the debt staircase is the norm in modern, developed economies.

BIRTH OF THE MODERN DEBT AGE

Debt has been fundamental to economies since the beginning of civilization. The modern age of debt is distinguished by two things: the emergence of very large-scale government debt to finance wars, coupled with the proliferation of banks – a proliferation that first happened in Britain and the US.

In Britain, the modern age of debt dates back to 1694 and the chartering of the Bank of England, an institution whose initial and principal purpose was to help finance England's ongoing war with France. It began in America with the financing of the Revolutionary War in 1775, including the chartering of the Bank of North America in Philadelphia in 1781, whose purpose then was to help finance the waning years of the war against Britain.

It is no accident that the emergence of large-scale government debt and the proliferation of banks happened in rough tandem. While in these earliest years, government bonds could be purchased, they were purchased with gold, so the amount of gold limited the issuance of government debt. In no small part, it was banks that made it possible for governments to issue large amounts of debt: banks bought the debt themselves, financed the purchase of that debt by others, and, through lending, created the money that indirectly purchased the debt. We saw this phenomenon in LoanLand in Chapter 1, where the issuance of government debt depended on the existence of deposits, and deposits are created largely by bank lending.

At the inception of the modern era of debt, the primary purchaser of British government debt was the Bank of England. This debt climbed as a percentage of GDP from 1694 to 1815, in line with the Second Hundred Years' War (1689–1815) with France. Over the same period, the number of British banks climbed from less than one hundred in number to 1,092.

In the US, the Bank of North America was quickly augmented by the First Bank of the United States, which was established in 1791. Like the Bank of North America, the First Bank served as a key lender to the government through the form of purchased debt. The number of US banks proliferated in the early years of the republic, from one bank in 1781 to 212 by the end of the War of 1812. After the War of 1812, up until the Civil War, US government spending dropped to almost nothing and bank lending was largely to the private sector; it was not until the twentieth century that US government debt joined private sector debt in the journey up the debt staircase (see Figure 8.1).

It is also no accident that the modern age of debt emerged roughly coincident with the emergence of the era of trans-Atlantic trade and the Industrial Revolution. Banks helped to finance these epochal surges in trade and industry and thus were a necessary character in these stories. But without the initial government need for large-scale lending and debt, the financial sector may very well have developed more slowly or more sporadically.

THE STAGES OF DEBT GROWTH

Looking at the journey of government debt to GDP over the long course of history is revealing. Patterns emerge that can be hard to spot in ten years, twenty years, or fifty years of data. On closer examination, the pattern of modern debt growth can be seen to follow four stages.

STAGE ONE – WAR DEBT. War is that unwelcome booster that takes government debt (and total debt) to onerous new heights.

As noted above, the first great accumulation of government debt for Britain came as a result of the Second Hundred Years' War, which consumed most of the years from 1689 to 1815 and included the French and Indian War, the American War of Independence (which, for England, morphed into a global war with France), and the Napoleonic Wars (with government debt peaking around 1816); England and France were at war for an estimated 80 of the 126 years in this period. The other great peaks in UK government debt correspond to the First World War (peaking in 1923) and the Second World War (peaking in 1945). For the US, surges in government debt occurred with the American Revolution (peaking in the 1780s), the Civil War (peaking in 1866), the First World War (peaking in 1919) and the Second World War (peaking in 1945). Figure 8.2 shows government debt for the US and the UK from 1700 onwards.

The peaks in the government debt ratio followed truly major wars, not more contained and limited conflicts such as the war in Vietnam, during which the US government debt ratio actually improved. The ratio of private debt to total debt tended to decline during these wars for two reasons: the government provided the private sector with much of the financing for the manufacture of war matériel, and so GDP grew primarily through government war spending, not private sector spending. This is usually the case. After all, governments declare wars, not businesses or households, in major, modern economies. Note, also, that the US government debt peak after the First World War is less than we might expect, and much less than the corresponding UK government debt peak. This is because the US private sector financed much of the war-related matériel, as the US government did not enter the war until 1917 and, before then, US lenders were providing financing for European combatants and for the US arms buildup, with US private sector debt reaching a peak in 1916.

FIGURE 8.2. US and UK government debt, 1700–2021

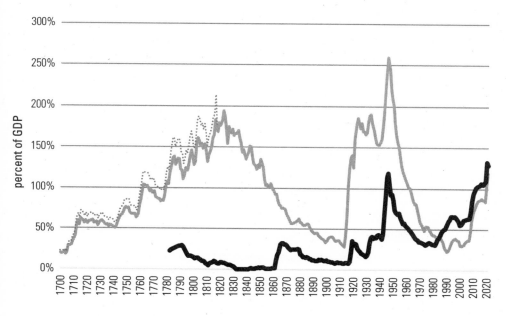

STAGE TWO – DEBT SWITCH. In the aftermath of war, total debt starts to build as a function of a debt-led private sector resurgence. The amount of government debt might not decline, or decline only modestly, but the government debt to GDP ratio does, because private debt growth is powering GDP growth and this makes the government debt smaller by comparison. I call this stage the 'debt switch' or 'great debt switch' because the rising private debt ratio and falling government debt ratio are so fundamental to the total debt staircase.

STAGE THREE – DEBT EXCESS. Almost inevitably, after years of brisk post-war growth, private debt growth (as a percentage of GDP) gets supercharged, reaching new heights and creating excess capacity. This stage is characterized by too much of an otherwise good thing: strong private sector debt growth turns to wild excess in a key area of the economy – usually in some aspect of the real estate sector, or railroads, which involved significant real estate acquisition, in the 1800s. As we saw in Chapter 7, human nature conspires with this stage, as it reliably spurs the lending industry to excess. This precipitates financial difficulty, crisis, or calamity, and growth in private debt either plateaus or declines to some extent. GDP growth flattens or contracts, causing a slowdown, recession, or depression. Invariably, these crises have outsized political and social consequences that shape countries for years afterwards.

STAGE FOUR – GOVERNMENT RESCUE. Government debt quickly rises as a percentage of GDP in the aftermath of the private debt crisis, either involuntarily – as tax revenues shrink in the ensuing slowdown or recession – or intentionally – as the government buttresses the economy through spending programs. This stage is characteristic only of late twentieth century and twenty-first century crises. In the 1800s, governments did not act to offset crises in this way. (The idea was suggested but dismissed.)

Stages three and four usually repeat at least once or twice in the interlude between major wars. With each repetition, private debt and government debt each move a step up the debt staircase. Then another war starts and the whole process begins again, but with the ratio of debt to GDP starting at a new, higher plateau.

THE LIVED EXPERIENCE OF DEBT CYCLES

The UK has excellent government debt data but its private debt data is largely missing for the 1700s and the early 1800s. My colleagues and I have scoured primary and secondary sources to fill these gaps, and will continue to do so, but for now it is impossible to confidently map the stages of debt for the early part of the UK's modern debt history. So let's instead focus on the debt cycles and stages for the US, which has more complete and accessible (though still lacking) private lending data, extending back to the start of its modern debt age in 1781.

FIGURE 8.3. US debt, financial crises, and wars, 1782–2021

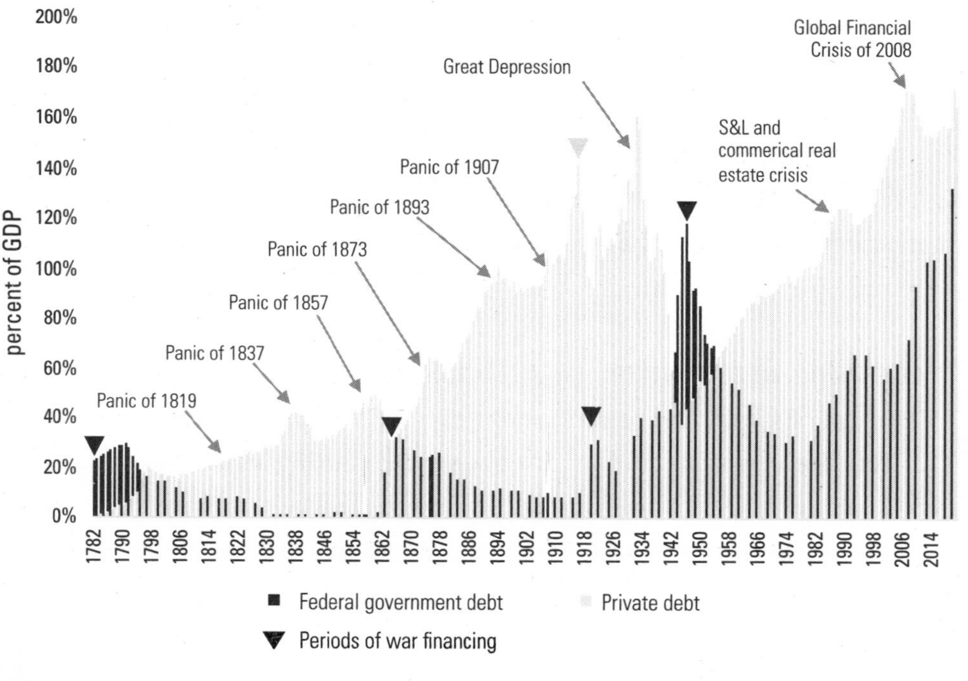

Figure 8.3 shows year by year US private sector debt and government debt as a percentage of GDP. The arrows indicate private debt peaks that correspond to a period of overlending ending in crisis. Periods of major war financing – peaking in the 1780s, 1866, 1919, and 1946 – are also marked. In three of these four war-financing periods, private debt is low or declines in the war. The First World War is an anomaly, because of the reliance on private sector debt before the US entered the war, so there is a marker on both the typical government debt peak and the atypical private debt war peak.

This figure has all the data I refer to below when examining each of the four US debt cycles, stage by stage.

CYCLE ONE – THE AMERICAN WAR OF INDEPENDENCE

STAGE ONE – WAR DEBT. In 1783, the last year of the Revolutionary War, the nascent US was struggling under debt accrued in the fight for independence. Its debt, which was the debt of Congress, is estimated to have been around $45 million. The only chartered bank in the country – the Bank of North America – had less than $1 million in loans and total GDP was around $200 million, so the ratio of government debt to GDP was likely around 25 percent, and bank loans less than 1 percent. This level of government debt was extraordinarily high and punishing for the brand-new nation, whose capital markets were only just being born.

STAGE TWO – DEBT SWITCH. By 1810, US private debt had grown to 18 percent of GDP, and government debt had declined to 6 percent. This was the country's first great debt switch, during which private debt took the lead in powering GDP growth. This allowed the government debt ratio to steadily improve, though government debt did increase briefly when hostilities with the British broke out again in the War of 1812.[41]

STAGE THREE – DEBT EXCESS. In the lengthy interlude between the Revolutionary War and the Civil War, which erupted in April 1861, private debt growth powered huge gains in US GDP, financing the canal era and the beginning of the railroad era. Time and again, private debt growth raced out ahead of itself, bringing erratic booms and busts in the panics of 1819, 1837, and 1857. The ratio of private debt to GDP peaked at 23 percent during the Panic of 1819, 42 percent during the Panic of 1837, and 47 percent during the Panic of 1857.

STAGE FOUR – GOVERNMENT RESCUE. There was no stage four at this early point in America's debt history. During the busts of the antebellum 1800s, there was little appetite for government intervention, even to fortify a broken economy, and so the federal government remained inert. Still, the damage had clear political consequences. The Panic of 1819, caused in large measure by the profligate overlending of the Second Bank of the United States, scarred Andrew Jackson's finances, which fueled his enmity towards the bank in its epic but ultimately unsuccessful battle to renew its charter in 1832, when he was the US president. The Panic of 1837 led to a depression in the 1840s – known as the 'Hung Forties' – that ruined the once-promising presidency of Martin Van Buren. The Panic of 1857, the first in a series of railroad-related financial crises in the US, fed the dour mood that ushered in the Civil War.

CYCLE TWO – THE US CIVIL WAR

STAGE ONE – WAR DEBT. To fund the Union Army's fight against the Southern rebellion in the Civil War, federal government debt grew from 2 percent to 32 percent of GDP. The ratio of private debt to GDP dropped as Congress provided much of the financing of manufacturing and agriculture during the war. Nevertheless, given the degree of wartime spending, total debt reached a new, all-time high: 66 percent of GDP.

STAGE TWO – DEBT SWITCH. After the war, between 1866 and 1873, private debt galloped ahead, rising from 34 percent to 54 percent of GDP, while government debt dropped to 24 percent. This was the second great debt switch.

STAGE THREE – DEBT EXCESS. Imprudent growth in private debt provoked the panics of 1873, 1893, and 1907.

STAGE FOUR – GOVERNMENT RESCUE. Once again, there was no stage four in this cycle, because few contemplated providing governmental support for the slumping economy during each of the debt excess crises. And also, once again, there were high-profile political consequences for the lack of government intervention. The Panic of 1873 brought a long and foul depression in which the federal government's will to carry on with Reconstruction faltered and then disappeared. A backroom deal reportedly handed Republican Rutherford B. Hayes the presidency over Democrat Samuel Tilden in exchange for the Republican Party's agreement to end federal control of Southern state governments.

The economic tribulation of the early 1890s, especially the Panic of 1893, stoked a surge of populism and the rise of the Populist Party. Unemployment soared to over 10 percent and stayed there for half a decade. The homeless were thrown into workhouses for the crime of vagrancy and punished with thirty days of hard labor. In 1894, an Ohio businessman named Jacob Coxey spearheaded one of the first initiatives to get the government to enact post-crisis financial support. His aim was to march on the US Capitol and present a proposal for a $500 million federal jobs plan, called the Good Roads Bill, to give the poor and unemployed the work they needed while also helping to improve the country's infrastructure – an idea that predated FDR's New Deal by four decades. The rallying cry of Coxey's Rebellion was that 'Congress takes two years to vote on anything. Twenty-million people are hungry and cannot wait two years to eat.' He and other leaders of the protest were arrested when they arrived at the Capitol, however, and the movement for government crisis support dissipated.

The Panic of 1907 exposed and exacerbated Americans' disgust with recurring banking crises, as well as their unease with the government's dependence on J. P. Morgan. Morgan had served as the 'lender of last resort' to help save the economy in both the 1890s and again here, organizing stronger lenders to provide lifeline loans to more troubled lenders in the middle of the financial maelstrom. Discomfort with the country's economic reliance on Morgan was part of what led to the law establishing the US Federal Reserve system, whose original purpose was to serve as a new, government-sponsored lender of last resort in a crisis. With the Federal Reserve set up, the government and the banking industry persuaded themselves – incorrectly – that they had vanquished financial panics and crises.

CYCLE THREE – THE FIRST WORLD WAR

STAGE ONE – WAR DEBT. As noted earlier, the First World War was an exception to other US debt cycles, because financing for war matériel was provided by both the government and the private sector. The order of magnitude and the global span of this war, along with the advent of tanks, planes, and long-range artillery, meant that it was more expensive than any previous conflict. The sum of private and public war financing took the US to another new, all-time total debt high of 150 percent of GDP.

STAGE TWO – DEBT SWITCH. After private war financing ended, the private sector went on a debt growth rampage. Between 1919 and 1923, private debt climbed from 97 percent to 106 percent of GDP, pushing the ratio of government debt to GDP down from 36 percent to 26 percent in the third great switch.

STAGE THREE – DEBT EXCESS. Then came a burst of lending that, according to the US Bureau of Economic Analysis, saw private debt rise from $116 billion in 1923 to $156 billion in 1928, a debt frenzy like few others in American history. It led to an exorbitant oversupply of both residential and commercial real estate, along with a monu- mental stock market bubble. Margin debt hit an all-time high of 10 percent of overall stock market value. This debt-financed house of cards began to collapse in the late 1920s, as there were nowhere near enough home buyers or building tenants to fill all the new construc- tion. This was punctuated by the stock market crash on October 28, 1929, with stocks of overleveraged utility companies leading a down- wards plunge of nearly 13 percent on this single day. The Treasury and the Federal Reserve's mishandling of the collapse was so monumental that the damage from this stock market tumble stretched through the dark decade of the Great Depression.

As mentioned above, in the 1890s and again in 1907, J. P. Morgan had stepped in to organize funding support for troubled banks. The new Federal Reserve had been created specifically to assume this responsibility but now neglected to act decisively, at least in the moments that mattered. Worse, the highly influential Treasury secre- tary, Andrew Mellon, was intentionally neglectful, reportedly saying: 'Liquidate labor, liquidate stocks, liquidate the farmers, liquidate real estate. It will purge the rottenness out of the system. High costs of living and high living will come down. People will work harder, live a more moral life. Values will be adjusted, and enterprising people will pick up the wrecks from less competent people.' The combined neglect of the Fed and the Treasury transformed the crash into a depression every bit as bad, if not worse, as those of the 1840s and 1870s, in part because many Americans were now in urban manufacturing and, as compared to those earlier crises, did not have the nearby farms of relatives and neighbors to fall back on.

STAGE FOUR – GOVERNMENT RESCUE. For the first time, the government interceded to support the economy. This was the landmark New Deal – the first great government intervention in the aftermath of a financial crisis. The New Deal changed the federal government's relationship to the people. Though timid by later standards, New Deal spending took the government debt ratio from 16 percent to 41 percent of GDP.

CYCLE FOUR – THE SECOND WORLD WAR

STAGE ONE – WAR DEBT. The ratio of total debt to GDP during the Second World War rose to 162 percent of GDP, higher than it had during the previous global conflict. This debt was primarily government debt, which climbed from a Depression-era high of 42 percent of GDP to 118 percent.

It's worth noting that the total debt ratio of 162 percent was not quite a record. Total debt had touched 195 percent of GDP in 1933, not so much because debt had grown but because GDP collapsed by 45 percent from its 1929 peak.

STAGE TWO – DEBT SWITCH. The greatest great debt switch of them all took off with the end of the war. Private debt had tumbled down to 37 percent of GDP during the conflict, so the private sector was blissfully deleveraged and extremely well positioned to power post-war debt and GDP growth. Capacity in the US was also low, due both to wartime deprivation and baby boom population growth, so there were decades of room for this stretch of robust private debt growth to create more capacity without listing into overcapacity. The Second World War debt switch extended all the way from 1945 until 1980, during which time private debt climbed from 37 percent to 101 percent of GDP, while government debt fell from 118 percent to 31 percent.

STAGE THREE – DEBT EXCESS. It was only after this lengthy debt switch that the banking crises of this cycle emerged, and those crises were enormous and extravagant ones: the savings and loan (S&L) and commercial real estate crises of the late 1980s and the Global Financial Crisis of 2008. The lending booms associated with these crises saw private debt peak at 125 percent of GDP in 1990 and 171 percent of GDP in 2007.

STAGE FOUR – GOVERNMENT RESCUE. In the 1980s crash, the US government, through monetary policy spearheaded by Federal Reserve Chairman Alan Greenspan, stepped in assertively to prop up the stock market. After the 1987 stock market crash, Greenspan flooded the market with new money, and stocks rebounded quickly. This became known as the 'Greenspan put' – creating the belief that the Fed would no longer allow stock markets to tank without moving to rescue them with a fast infusion of liquidity.

There was much less aggressive support on the fiscal side. The poorly funded Resolution Trust Corporation was left, essentially on its own, to clean up the savings and loan mess. Government debt still rose from 50 percent to 66 percent of GDP, due to falling tax receipts during the recession of the early 1990s.

The lending excesses of the Reagan era forged a path directly to this recession. And the pain of that recession was the key reason Reagan's successor, George H. W. Bush, did not earn a second term, echoing the failed first term of President Martin Van Buren 150 years earlier.

By 2008, the lessons of governmental neglect in the Great Depression were finally being internalized. The Obama administration boldly offered stimulus support to combat the effects of the financial crisis with an unprecedented $1 trillion in stimulus. This raised government debt from 64 percent to 103 percent of GDP, an unprecedented level of assistance dictated by the depth of the crisis. The government stimulus pulled the country out of recession, but a residual overhang of private debt continued to burden households and businesses, and the extensive oversupply of homes and buildings kept the real estate industry in the doldrums for years. Nine million Americans lost their homes, millions more had mortgages underwater, and no one stepped up to help them. Many believe this engendered a deep, pervasive discontent that was a key factor in the electoral success of candidate Trump in 2016.

Each of the four debt cycles in US history landed the country on a higher plateau of debt in relation to GDP, so that each subsequent cycle began at a higher step on the debt staircase. Then came the pandemic, with government stimulus and relief support topping $4 trillion in 2020 and 2021, a new peak in government debt (see Figure 8.1). It was a level of government debt and spending that made the extraordinary support of the 2008 financial crisis seem modest, and in fact, it was a level of spending previously only seen in America's major wars. Government debt rose to 130 percent of GDP, and total debt to 300 percent of GDP – a new record.

In many respects, Congress approached the pandemic with an urgency, and a willingness to defeat its economic casualties, equivalent to full mobilization in war. And if the pandemic effectively amounted to a war of a different kind, then it is not unreasonable to speculate that government and total debt levels in the pandemic have initiated the fifth debt cycle in US economic history.

We can look at Japan's debt profile (Figure 4.12) for hints as to what this next cycle might look like. They are not encouraging. In the aftermath of Japan's 1990s crisis, the government has had to prop up the economy for a generation. The government rescue was prolonged by the impact of the 2008 financial crisis, and only in very recent years has private debt begun to grow as a percentage of GDP, with the possibility that a debt switch might be realized so that private debt growth takes the place of government debt growth to shoulder GDP growth going forwards.

If the US has entered a fifth US debt cycle, there will be less opportunity for strong GDP growth fueled by private debt growth, given the already high level of private sector debt. It may take years of reliance on government debt.

DELEVERAGING IS DIFFICULT

Although we have much less complete private debt data for Britain, especially for the 1700s and 1800s, we do have adequate data to see the outlines of the economy's private debt booms and busts in the 1860s and 1920s, as well as good data for the booms and busts of 1974, the early 1990s, and the Global Financial Crisis of 2008. Both Margaret Thatcher and Ronald Reagan benefited reputationally from huge private debt booms, and the associated increase in wealth, in the 1980s, but these booms led to overlending, and their reversals brought economic woes that adversely impacted the administrations and reputations of their successors, John Major and George H. W. Bush, respectively.

Figure 8.4 adds the available UK private debt data to the government debt shown in Figure 8.2. It turns out that the UK boom in the 1980s well exceeded the one in the US in the acceleration of private

FIGURE 8.4. UK debt components, 1700–2020

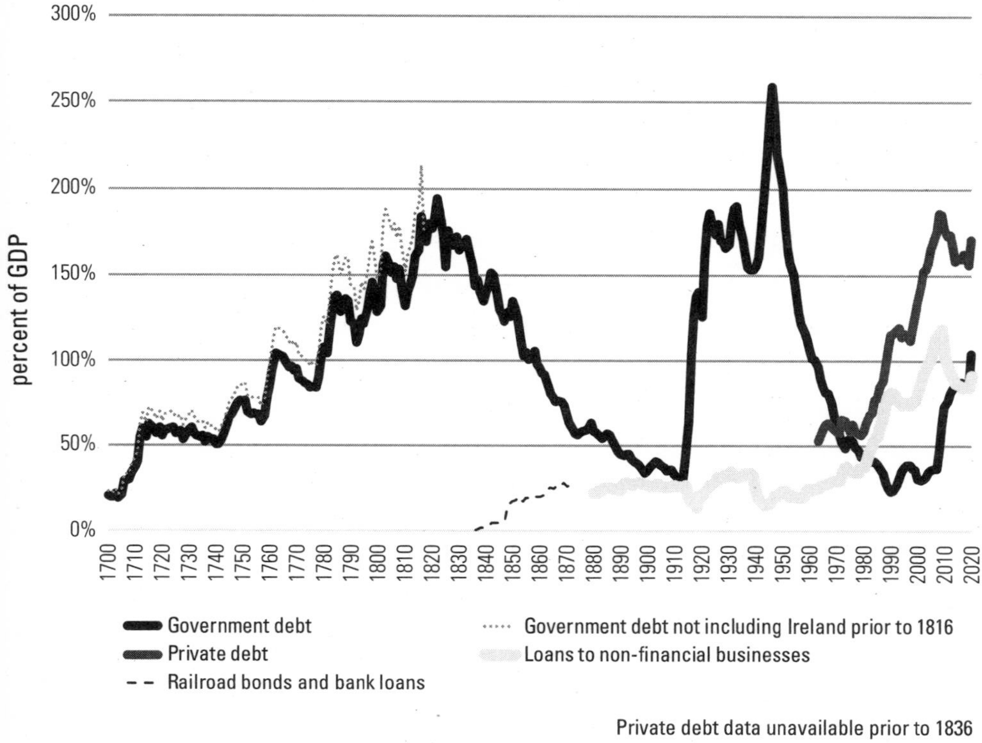

Government debt

Private debt

- - Railroad bonds and bank loans

····· Government debt not including Ireland prior to 1816

Loans to non-financial businesses

Private debt data unavailable prior to 1836

debt growth, with private debt exploding from 58 percent of GDP in 1980 to 107 percent of GDP in 1990, compared with 100 percent in 1980 and 125 percent in 1990 for the US.

The basic debt cycle and its four stages are also visible in the data covering the period after the Second World War: massive war debt, switching to a surge in private debt that eventually leads to excess, followed by government spending coming to the rescue. There is, however, very limited private debt data available for the period following the Napoleonic Wars, when Britain so famously deleveraged from a government debt to GDP ratio of over 200 percent. From what data is available, it seems reasonable and likely that economic growth from private sector debt enabled that deleveraging.

If a high level of private debt – the burdensome legacy of an expired lending boom – stultifies growth, then decreasing that level of debt should be part of any successful effort to reinvigorate GDP growth. Only when households and businesses are freed from excessive debt can they contribute vigorously to economic growth. Even if they cannot reduce the absolute amount of debt, we want them to be able to reduce the level of debt in relation to their income – in other words, we want income to grow faster than debt. We want to support opportunities for deleveraging.

Some may assume that such deleveraging is easy. Economists, policymakers, and politicians often seem to talk this way, suggesting that debt woes might be quickly resolved through individual or collective willpower, belt tightening, and other moral correctives. But it is actually very challenging to lower debt. The vestiges of high debt are like a tree stump that is all but impossible to uproot.

It is worth examining the merits of some of the solutions regularly proposed for reducing debt burdens. Among the most popular are:

- growth – the idea that an economy can grow its way out of a debt burden;
- inflation – the idea that an economy can inflate its way out of a debt burden; and
- payment – the idea that an economy can simply pay down a debt burden.

Can we grow our way out of debt?

The first of these propositions – growing our way out of debt burden – is most frequently put forward by politicians and economists, especially in relation to public debt. Superficially, it is a highly appealing approach, but deleveraging to a level low enough to meaningfully improve growth rates is truly rare in economic history. The Great Deleveraging that occurred after the Second World War was possible only because private debt grew very rapidly in its place. Between 1950 and 1980, US government debt fell from 86 percent to 32 percent of GDP *because*, in the very kind of debt switch we have discussed, private debt simultaneously vaulted from 56 percent to 101 percent of GDP. The actual dollar total of government debt did not decline at all; it was only the *ratio* that improved. Absent that strong private sector debt growth, US GDP growth would have been tepid or nonexistent, and the government debt ratio would have remained high.

The converse is also true: private debt deleveraging has generally only occurred when accompanied by very high public debt growth. During Japan's 1990s financial crisis, private debt was a startling 219 percent of GDP. It was deleveraged, down to 153 percent of GDP, over the next two decades, and this very deleveraging contributed to Japan's low economic growth during the period. At the same time, government debt rose from 80 percent to 230 percent of GDP. If not for government spending and debt growth, the Japanese economy would have contracted severely.

When the public debt ratio declines, it is generally because the private debt ratio has increased, and when the private debt ratio declines, it is generally because the public debt ratio has increased. This great debt switch has happened many times.

In dissecting the data, my colleagues and I found no instances among the top ten economies in the world where private and public debt in relation to GDP have declined in tandem at least 10 percent within five years since 1950. Looking at the next ten economies in size, we found only three instances where this happened: Saudi Arabia in 2012, due to its very high net export surplus from oil; the Netherlands in 2019, because of its high net export surplus in agricultural products, manufactured goods, and more; and Mexico in 1988, due to very high inflation. That is three cases among the top twenty economies over the last seventy years.

It comes down to a simple axiom: you cannot deleverage *total* debt through growth because you need increased debt to grow.

Can we inflate our way out of debt?

Inflation is also proposed frequently as a lifeline out of a growth-impeding debt ratio. Although deleveraging through very high inflation is rare in developed economies, it does sometimes work in less developed countries. With high inflation, especially where inflation exceeds the effective interest rate on debt, prices and incomes will grow faster than the principal balance of debt, and this can be used to improve the ratio of debt to income.

We considered this, to some extent, in Chapter 7, as we looked at the causes and consequences of economic calamities. But I would like to underscore here, as I did in the previous chapter, that inflation is a cure worse than the disease – and likely an ineffective cure at that. Inflation in the US in the 1970s did not improve the ratio of debt to GDP. It would take inflation in the range of 10 percent for several years in a row to make a substantial dent in either the private debt or government debt ratio in the US and other Big 7 economies.

Can we simply pay off our debt?

So why not take the most obvious route, and deleverage by having businesses and households simply pay down their debt? Asking private sector borrowers to pay down debt en masse would not work.

First, most borrowers do not have the resources and capacity to pay down debt immediately (although I would always encourage an individual to pay down debt where possible, as would most economists). If indeed borrowers had these resources, they likely would not have incurred the excess debt to begin with.

Second, if consumers and businesses paid down debt all at once, it would crush the economy. We saw why in our visit to LoanLand. A dollar used to pay down debt would come from a reduction in spending, and because GDP is a measure of spending, this would result in a net contraction in GDP – a recession or depression. As of 2021, US households had $17.9 trillion in debt. An aggregate paydown of 5 percent of that debt would total $895 billion, which would almost certainly come from an $895 billion reduction in spending. Because GDP is, by definition, a measure of spending, this paydown would exact a 4 percent collapse in US GDP. Mass debt paydowns, whether voluntary or forced, result in economic contraction.

In contrast, a *debt jubilee*, a concept discussed in greater depth in the next chapter, offers a way to reduce debt without contracting GDP, because borrowers are not required to reduce spending. In fact, it would likely increase GDP, because funds used to pay debt would become available for spending.

DELEVERAGING IS DOABLE

While the three options described above range from problematic to impossible, there are two approaches that can be used to improve debt ratios: high net exports and moderating debt growth.

High net exports, although rare, actually do lead to national private debt reduction. We saw this in the net income analysis in Chapter 4 for China and Germany, to name just two examples. High net exports make trading partners unhappy, but even taking this drawback into account, if the US could create an export surplus of just 10 percent of GDP, or thereabouts, for about a decade or so, the economy's ratio of debt to GDP would improve significantly. And it would grow GDP without growing debt, because the growth in GDP would be coming from high exports – in other words, growth in debt from the ROW.

The US and some other Big 7 economies would struggle to do this, however. For its part, the US has never shown such a pronounced surplus, and since 1975, it has not had a surplus of any kind. In fact, since 1975, the US has had a trade deficit, which at times has reached as high as 5.6 percent. President Trump tried hard to reduce that deficit, but it only worsened during his presidency. And even if the US could muster a large trade surplus, then by definition other countries would have to be large net importers – a status they would not acquiesce to gently.

There is that second way to reduce an economy's total debt ratio, and though it is rare, it is important to understand: the debt to GDP ratio will improve if we simply do not let debt outgrow GDP by *too much* – in other words, we just need to have less growth in Type 2 debt than Type 1 debt, or GDP. If a given economy's total debt ratio is above 100 percent of GDP, especially if it is far above that figure, and debt growth exceeds GDP growth by just a bit, then the mathematical ratio will improve over time. For example, total debt in the UK declined from 265 percent of GDP in 2012 to 239 percent in 2019, even though the UK's total debt outgrew GDP by £346 billion, or 70 percent.

But there is a major obstacle here: in the world's largest economies, debt is not just slightly outgrowing GDP, but enormously doing so – by as much as 300 percent to 600 percent. Even in export-advantaged Germany, debt has outgrown GDP by over 100 percent.

So it would take heroic restraint in debt growth by the government and private sector of a given economy for this path to work – restraint that would itself diminish asset acquisition. In the data across forty-seven countries and half a century that my colleagues and I reviewed, we found only five cases where growth restraint was used to improve an economy's total debt ratio (as opposed to inflation or high net exports). The private sector in developed countries is rarely this self-restrained.

While there are a few effective maneuvers to enact deleveraging, high debt to GDP ratios are very stubborn.

THE HIGHEST HEIGHTS OF DEBT

If, as I argue based on the data, the progression within each debt cycle is a staircase, always taking us to a higher, more debt-burdened level, then the natural question becomes: is there any limit on how high debt might climb?

Private sector debt definitely has a limit, and most likely it is not a great deal higher than the 200 percent to 250 percent of GDP where the economies with the very highest level of private debt to GDP currently reside. Households and businesses not only have to pay the interest on their debt but also the principal. So even if interest rates were zero, a person with $50,000 income could not buy a $1.5 million dollar house, because they would have to use all of their pretax income each year just to pay down the principal, even if the loan amortized over thirty years. While it is true that, for all intents and purposes, China's lenders largely no longer require non-financial businesses to repay principal, and so borrowers in China do not have to pay either interest or principal, and private debt there could in theory climb infinitely high, this is an unsustainable position – not dissimilar to the one China began to face in 2022 after the Evergrande debacle.

In 2022, the large, developed economies with the highest private debt in the world – Sweden and Switzerland – had private debt of 271 percent and 270 percent of GDP, respectively. Both of these countries also had very large current account and trade surpluses. Without such a net trade benefit, I believe a debt to GDP ratio in the range of 200 percent to 250 percent is at the upper end of sustainability.

Given the practical limits on trade surpluses – namely, the objections of other countries – once economies reach the top limit of private debt growth, their only alternatives will be to suffer slower or negative GDP growth, or shift to heavier reliance on government spending and debt growth. The latter is, in essence, Japan's strategy.

This is because there *are* limits on private debt growth but, for developed economies, there are no limits on government debt growth, or at least not limits that would become salient anywhere near as quickly as for private debt. These two facts eventually and inevitably push every economy towards greater reliance on government debt and seem to point to a continued broad transition of developed economies towards the government debt and spending model.

So the question then shifts to the limits, if any, on government debt growth.

As of the end of 2022, Japan was at the high end of all countries on this measure, with government debt at 245 percent of GDP. The government uses about 90 percentage points of this debt to fund asset purchases, so the net government debt to GDP ratio is 155 percent. By contrast, US government debt was 129 percent of GDP.

As an aside, because deposits are required for the private sector to buy new government securities, and these deposits then remain in the system, it is reasonable to expect that total US Treasury debt, very roughly speaking, would be less than or equal to M2 (deposits) plus foreign-owned Treasury securities (because, for foreign-owned US Treasury securities, foreign deposits or reserves are used to make the purchases). This is an oversimplification, of course, but it is roughly what can be seen in the economy. Notably, in periods in which private sector debt significantly exceeds US Treasury debt, the sum of M2 plus foreign-owned US Treasury securities well exceeds total

Treasury securities. More recently, as US Treasury debt has increased to be closer in size to total US private sector debt, the sum of M2 plus foreign-owned US Treasury securities has been close in volume to total Treasury securities. As a practical matter, if total US Treasury debt grows to exceed private sector debt, it follows that a larger and larger percentage of that Treasury debt will be purchased by the Fed.

More fundamentally, the recent experience of Japan does indeed suggest that there may be a law of diminishing returns when it comes to the creation of wealth through debt. Growth in debt in Japan is no longer a sure route to increasing asset values. This would signal a major breakdown of the debt economics paradigm that has fueled GDP growth for at least the past hundred years. It would usher in a world where rising debt brings only more burden and little reward.

But the more concerning limit on the efficacy of government debt in the operation of economies is linked to the impact debt growth has on inequality. Our reliance on debt growth for GDP growth comes with profound societal consequences. Already we are seeing these consequences manifested through increasingly polarized politics across the Big 7 economies.

Whatever the reason, growth in government debt cannot be sustained forever. The perpetual rise in debt must be a concern.

Because essentially all of the conventional remedies to slow, stall, or stop the rise in debt are unrealistic, by process of elimination, we are left with only one path: debt forgiveness and restructuring. We turn to this concept, along with other potential policies for addressing the issues of debt and growth, in the next chapter.

9

POLICY THOUGHTS AND PROVOCATIONS

In this final chapter, I offer a suite of policy ideas regarding the issues surrounding debt that have been raised in this book. Each of these ideas deserve book-length treatment of their own, so I do not presume to suggest that what follows is anything more than thoughts and provocations for consideration.

Nor do I wish to suggest that any of these ideas, alone or in combination, is a panacea. The paradox of debt is deeply embedded in the structure of the economy of the US and other Big 7 countries, as well as many other countries around the world. It will take much more to deal with these issues than can be contained within the scope of these pages. So I do not delve into certain subjects, such as taxation and the minimum wage, that have garnered much attention from others. This does not mean they are not of great importance to the economic health of a nation, or play no role in debt and GDP growth. Instead, I focus here on approaches to big questions that have largely been overlooked or willfully avoided:

- how to moderate the inexorable rise in total debt;
- how to reverse a large trade and current account deficit;

- how to tame inflation and encourage inflation reduction;
- how to build the incomes and relative net worth of the bottom 60 percent of households, and thus reduce inequality; and
- how to grow an economy without creating more debt.

My goal is more to redefine and understand these problems and potential solutions than to outline a comprehensive package of policies.

MODERATING THE RISE IN TOTAL DEBT

Throughout the previous chapters, we have seen that when total debt rises too rapidly, it usually leads to financial calamity. This is worrying in the context of the ever-rising levels of debt as Big 7 economies make their way up the debt staircase. Rising levels of debt are, however, necessary for economic growth. The paradox of debt is that, at some point in a debt cycle, debt levels will get too high and strangle this economic growth, at great personal cost to many households and businesses.

For this reason, the first and most basic policy intervention to support debt growth moderation is simply to monitor aggregate private debt levels, to better detect when a problematic level of excess is emerging.

It is abundantly clear that runaway lending has, again and again in history, led to credit problems for lenders in the US. It might be tempting to embrace a laissez-faire stance and argue that the lenders caused the problem, and thus the lenders should suffer the results. But if we have learned anything from the Global Financial Crisis of 2008 and similar events, it's that the consequences of lender misbehavior are not easily quarantined, and typically extend well beyond the subset of lenders whose errors directly kicked the economy off on the road to crisis. Millions become collateral damage in a disaster not of their own making.

As made clear in Chapter 7, the 2008 financial crisis was no black swan or storm of the century phenomenon; instead, it would have been easy to spot, and might have been foretold years, not months, in advance, if analysts had been looking in the right direction and at the right things. Like most financial calamities, the 2008 crisis was born from the unbridled growth in private sector debt – a key trend that is straightforward to track.

To ensure such a crisis does not take the world by surprise again in the future, we should institute a regulatory practice of monitoring the pace of growth in loan balance totals, both for total private debt and also for each major private debt sector – real estate debt, energy sector debt, student debt, automobile lending debt, and so on (in short, the categories listed in Figure 2.1). The simplest and best way to do this is to look at each category of debt as a percentage of GDP and monitor rate of growth through time.

For each category, a threshold of growth should be established, such that growth in excess of that threshold would trigger increased regulatory scrutiny. The key is to look at *acceleration* in lending. For the national economy of a large, developed country, an overall threshold of growth acceleration in the range of 15 percent to 20 percent within five years is a reasonable benchmark; for a single sector of the economy as opposed to the whole, a threshold of 50 percent growth to GDP is a reasonable benchmark. These benchmarks would translate to annual total debt growth of 3 percent to 4 percent, as a percentage of GDP, and annual single sector debt growth of 5 percent to 10 percent, or more, of GDP, and growth of that magnitude for two to three years in a row would suggest potential for concern and warrant deeper scrutiny. Such levels of debt growth are a signal that an economy or sector is on the verge of entering the third stage of a debt cycle – debt excess. Alongside these data on lending acceleration, overly rapid real estate capital formation would be another useful warning metric, based on the trends observed in Chapter 7.

When an economy or sector is at or above these thresholds, regulators would know to look more closely at credit policies, and rein them in where necessary. In my investigations of banking crises, it became painfully clear that a harmful level of overlending simply cannot occur unless credit criteria have been loosened significantly if not excessively. At this trigger point, analysis should move beyond an understanding of loosened lending criteria and become multidimensional. If the potential danger involves the housing sector, it would include things such as an analysis of unsold housing inventories. If the issues are in the energy sector, it would include things such as an analysis of rig count and drilling capacity.

In my experience, the level of overcapacity that signals an impending crisis is never hard to spot, when you go looking for it; there is always an *egregious* overcreation of capacity. For example, in 2006, there were 3.7 million unsold houses in the US, whereas in the year 2000 that number was 1.7 million, nearly a threefold increase. What lenders, I would ask, were lending to build new houses with that level of unsold inventory? What lenders made the loans in 2004 and 2005 that contributed to such rampant overbuilding? Similarly, in 1982, the number of oil and gas drilling rigs was 4,521 – 202 percent higher than five years earlier. The price of oil was over $30 per barrel, and this surfeit of drilling capacity drove prices down to $12 per barrel. Within a few years almost every major Texas bank – the primary lenders to the oil and gas industry – had failed. The analysis to detect overcapacity of the magnitude sufficient to create a national or sector-level crisis is not complex or subtle.

As the real estate and energy sector crises were fulminating, participants in these industries generally did not self-curb or self-police.

Instead, they kept waiting for other companies in their sector to curb their excesses. This is why regulatory scrutiny is key.

If, in any sector, lending exceeds the early warning thresholds but a regulator investigates further and finds credit policy stable and the relevant inventories reasonable, then so be it. Further, if debt growth begins to moderate organically, then regulatory scrutiny would diminish accordingly. However, if there is clear evidence of compromised credit standards and egregious overcapacity, then regulators should at the very least have the authority to increase capital and reserve requirements for lenders, short of exercising a more explicit cease and desist authority.

In other words, I am not suggesting hard and fast rules that would in turn dictate mandated actions. These metrics, benchmarks, and tools would merely comprise a set of guidelines for heightened regulatory attention, and potentially for regulatory admonition. Often, attention and admonition alone are sufficient to heighten prudence among lenders. They reduce the perceived costs of being a 'first mover' to adopt – or reaffirm – more conservative and cautious credit policies.

Critically, however, this regulatory scrutiny cannot occur only within the banking sector. Regulation must extend to debt markets in their entirety, including shadow banking entities. That has been one of the fundamental flaws in the regulatory process over the past fifty years: bank lending may be contained well enough while dangerous overlending is originating from another type of institution. It matters not where the overlending originates; the risks and consequences to the economy are the same. So monitoring of overlending signals and analysis of overlending trends must cover private sector debt as a whole and regulators should have the needed authority over all material sectors of the lending industry.

Such policy and practice, had they been in place, would have alerted regulators as early as the mid-2000s that mortgage lending merited increased scrutiny. Indeed, the importance of this scrutiny is retrospectively illustrated by its absence in the years before the 2008 financial crisis. Beginning in 2001, mortgage loans grew 7 percent annually as a percentage of GDP, a level far in excess of my recommended threshold. At that point, if regulators had investigated credit criteria and capacity, they would have found an appalling abandonment of sound lending policies – including a reduction of down payments, eventually to zero, and a relaxation of income requirements, eventually to the point where lenders did not check or confirm incomes at all – and a million or more excess new home starts. They would have found the makings of a financial crisis before it was too late to unwind its causes.

The level of credit and capacity in key sectors cannot be left solely to the discretion of lenders. By the mid-2000s, rapid mortgage lending was creating a boom that was making lenders so rich that at least some meaningful portion of them were highly unlikely to self-restrain. Further, when the savings and loan industry was irresponsibly lending in the 1980s and the regulator Edwin J. Gray tried to corral it, the industry used its political clout – derived largely from political contributions – to have him removed as chair of the Federal Home Loan Bank Board and the more compliant M. Danny Wall appointed in his place. The savings and loan crisis followed.

The idea of regulators intervening on credit matters can undoubtedly provoke an energetic backlash from the industry, but this sort of intervention is important for two reasons. First, the Federal Deposit Insurance Corporation (FDIC) insures US bank deposits, so it has a fiduciary responsibility to ensure the safety and soundness of these lenders, and lending policy is at the heart of a bank's financial soundness – or lack thereof. Second, and much more importantly, widespread bank failures can hurt thousands or even millions of individuals who have nothing to do with the excessive lending activity. In the lead-up to the 2008 crisis, millions of individuals bought homes – not as speculators but in the ordinary course of their lives – and millions ended up losing those homes or holding large, underwater mortgages. Of course, there were plenty who applied for mortgages knowing they were not reporting their income accurately, and abetted the problem when they bought a property they knew was above their income level – especially when their intention was to flip the house to make fast money. But this accounted for a minority of overall mortgage activity.

One of the objections I often hear when I raise the idea of more oversight is that markets manage themselves better than does the government. But, over the course of history, we have seen multiple, repeated episodes where lending markets self-manage poorly, *if at all*, and, when they do self-manage, it is only after their overlending has set a crisis in motion.

Another objection I hear is that interfering with debt growth impedes GDP growth – an objection with which I have sympathy, given the structures of debt economics that I've laid out in the previous chapters. Yes, but it is Type 2 debt that is the issue, and by definition it has lesser adverse GDP impact. And the monitoring parameters I've suggested are sufficiently loose, and the regulatory responses sufficiently reasonable, that any growth curbed would be from the toxic levels that create harmful excess.

Still another objection is that this is just one more example of government trying to pick winners and losers, and only the wisdom of markets can do that. Well, in 2007, the market was picking no-down-payment mortgage loans as winners and how did that work out? Similarly, in 1982, the market was picking more drilling rigs as winners and forecasting perpetually rising oil prices, and that did not work out, either. The equity and debt markets are strewn with examples of the missed calls and botched wisdom of the marketplace. For lending, it turns out, markets are not the efficient, self-correcting mechanism that Adam Smith and his acolytes envisioned.

In stark contrast to the mythical notion of some laissez-faire path of business achievement, the government has never been at arm's length from the economy or economic activity. It has been the driving – and absolutely necessary – force in many of the most important trends in US economic history, starting with its forceful intervention to jumpstart America's manufacturing industry during the Revolutionary War and the decades immediately thereafter. The government helped finance the building of the Erie Canal and the Transcontinental Railroad, and the invention of the internet.

Economist Mariana Mazzucato at University College London has observed that, without the substantial amount of US public investment behind the Information Age, cutting-edge products such as the iPhone, which have changed the way people around the world work and communicate, would have been impossible. Apple surfed a wave of major US government investments in twelve 'revolutionary' technologies that enabled the breakthrough features of smartphones. These twelve technologies include the internet, GPS, touchscreen displays and communication technologies, microprocessors and central processing units, and dynamic random-access memory.

Those who assert the government cannot pick winners but the marketplace can are making an argument not well supported by history. It takes a lot of spending, support, and intelligence, from both the government and the marketplace, to move an economy forwards – especially with an increasingly capable global competitor, like China, where the government is making ever larger investments to propel certain business sectors ahead.

DEBT JUBILEES

It's well enough to talk about policies to help prevent high debt in the future, but what about the high debt that already burdens growth today? Here, I argue that we need to develop some form of debt relief. This relief might be called debt amnesty, debt cancellation, debt forgiveness, debt restructuring, or the increasingly preferred term, *debt jubilee* – the word used in Ancient Israel to describe a series of events centered on debt cancellation.[42]

Examples throughout this book demonstrate how the debt to income ratio of the private sector in the US and other Big 7 economies appears to increase inexorably. The consequences of that inexorable rise are profound and need attention. If the engine of your car continually overheated, you would get it fixed, knowing that, if you did not, at some point the engine would falter or break down entirely. The fix would be to install a cooling system or find some way to let the heat escape, say, by allowing it to 'vent' through valves or an exhaust system, so as to restore and maintain a temperature equilibrium. A debt jubilee would serve as a key part of such a cooling system or heat escape valve for the economy as a whole.

Debt forgiveness is actually an ancient idea. Kings of Ancient Egypt and Babylon routinely proclaimed an amnesty from debt when debt levels began to crush the population, which provides surprising attestation to the universality of the problems of debt overaccumulation. We need modern-day private debt jubilees to be a component of our economic system if we are to reduce accumulated debt sufficiently to meaningfully improve both lives and economic growth, and to do so without damaging the economy.

Among contemporary lenders, debt restructuring occurs every day. It is employed for individual borrowers if, after a job loss or medical emergency, the loan balance owed far exceeds the borrower's resources. In such a case, the lender might 'settle' for partial repayment if it believes the alternative might be no repayment at all. Debt restructuring or renegotiation also occurs every day for business loans where the ability to pay has been compromised. Indeed, many lenders have departments dedicated exclusively to these restructurings.

However, to significantly impact an economy's overall debt numbers, debt forgiveness or restructuring would need to be implemented on a much larger scale. It would also need to be structurally embedded, as an ongoing feature of the economy, rather than occurring on an ad hoc basis. This is one of the reasons I like the term 'debt jubilee': in Ancient Israel, debt cancellation happened every fifty years, in the year after each seventh sabbath year.

Proposals for debt jubilees have generally been resisted and dismissed on the principle that debt is not only a contract but also a moral obligation of the borrower. But, as noted above, debt contracts are often restructured, and that should happen without an overlay of moral judgment, as most credit problems stem from things such as a job loss, medical problem, or family breakup. The vital thing to bear in mind is that the payment of debt is a civil, not a criminal, matter. If someone finds that they cannot repay a debt because of a health crisis or business failure, this is neither a moral nor a criminal failing. As the late, brilliant anthropologist David Graeber reminded us: debt is a contract, and contracts get modified all the time. Lenders charge interest in part as a recognition of risk – which implies that every act of lending is by its nature risky, and therefore creditors can hardly be surprised if that risk does not pay off, or not to the extent that they had hoped.

In addition to inappropriate moral judgment, debt jubilee programs have engendered uneasiness and even opposition, usually based on one of three main objections: 1) issues of fairness, 2) issues of cost, and 3) the moral hazard that debt forgiveness might create.

On fairness, the argument goes, how can we forgive one person's student debt, when another, under similar circumstances, has fully paid theirs?

On cost, the sticking points tend to be around who bears the cost as much as how expensive debt forgiveness might be. In the desperate years just after the 2008 financial crisis, there were so many troubled loans requiring relief that forgiving all of them would have caused many lenders to fail. But if instead the government steps in to bear the cost, then many would reasonably question why taxpayers should bear this cost, which could run to tens or hundreds of billions of dollars, or more. Even those who acknowledge that the government has the capacity to take such a step may still justifiably question why public funds should go to a debt jubilee rather than to other programs.

On the moral hazard, the contention is that people who get bailed out when they are struggling with a debt burden will be more imprudent in their future borrowing; their experience of debt forgiveness will make them feel confident and emboldened that they will get bailed out if they fall onto hard times again.

All are good points. Any debt jubilee proposal needs to take these objections into account, even if they do not fully resolve them.

Each of the programs I outline below is an attempt to introduce a more structural, and structured, form of debt jubilee that – consistent with the perspectives of debt economics laid out in this book – will reduce inequality and make the nation's economic engine run better. These proposals are attempts to describe what is possible, rather than more quixotic ideas of debt relief that are unlikely to be embraced by politicians, policymakers, and lenders. In my view, the downside of policy conservatism is more than offset by the upside of policy feasibility.

The areas of private debt most in need of relief are student loans, mortgage debt, healthcare debt, and small business loans. I also touch on policies to reform bankruptcy, which is a crucial kind of debt jubilee that already exists, but which needs improvement.

Student debt relief

Student debt is a scourge, weighing down the financial lives of millions of Americans, young and old, for years after they have left university.

Carrying this burden results in deferred home buying, delayed household formation, and other trends that impact people's long-term financial, physical, and mental health.

The problem has been simmering for more than a generation but has truly tipped into dangerous territory over the past ten years. In 2012, US student loan totals were $1 trillion, or 6 percent of GDP. By 2020, they had shot up to $1.7 trillion, or 8 percent of GDP. As recently as 2003, student loans totaled $250 billion, or 2 percent of GDP.

In August 2022, President Biden announced a broad student debt amnesty program, canceling $10,000 in debt on student loans extended by the Department of Education for borrowers who earn less than $125,000 a year, or married couples who earn less than $250,000 a year. According to the White House press release, the move would help more than 43 million people who owed a combined $1.6 trillion in federal student debt; about 14 million people who owed less than $10,000 in federal student loans would see their debt fully canceled. Under the program, borrowers who have received a Pell Grant, which are reserved for students with the greatest financial need, will be eligible for up to $20,000 in student loan debt cancellations. This was estimated to be about 60 percent of all federal student debt holders, about 27 million people. These debt cancellations were accompanied by a repayment restructuring plan that would substantially reduce future monthly payments for middle- and lower-income borrowers.

The program was entirely in line with the spirit of debt jubilee advocated in this book, though it left the question of fairness unaddressed – an issue raised by a number of detractors. Surprisingly, objections were also raised about the risk of provoking higher inflation as those freed from student debt will presumably increase their spending on other things. However, given the monthly amounts involved, impact on inflation is unlikely to be an issue. More problematically, the student debt amnesty program was set to be argued before the US Supreme Court on the grounds that the power to cancel these debts should, under the Constitution, be reserved for Congress.

As bold as it is, Biden's program also leaves open the question of debt cancellation for future borrowers. It is a one-time deal. I believe the economy would be best served by structural, ongoing forms of debt relief, in addition to ad hoc dispensations like this. What would such a program look like for student debt?

Under the Department of Education's existing Public Service Loan Forgiveness program, individuals who serve in the government or not-for-profit sector, and who have also made 120 consecutive monthly payments on their student debt, qualify to have the remainder of that debt forgiven. I would propose that the government introduce a program for student debt forgiveness outside of public employment, based on applicants performing substantial volunteer work for a qualified not-for-profit institution. The parameters would be that if a student debt holder who is employed outside the government and not-for-profit sectors has done volunteer community service for an approved government or not-for-profit organization for at least 800 hours, and has also made payments for 90 consecutive months, then the remaining balance of that person's student debt would be forgiven. I also suggest changing the Public Service Loan Forgiveness program to require only 90 consecutive payments on the student debt to make it more feasible. These programs should also be oriented to clearly include debt to study at a trade or technical school as well as debt carried by university graduates.

A policy along these lines would address the moral hazard and fairness issues by requiring a commitment from the borrower to make a meaningful, sustained contribution of their time and labor in civic or charitable work – something like an in-kind paydown of some of the loan – in addition to making a significant number of payments towards their debt before qualifying for forgiveness. In effect, it's a step beyond the current system, which crushes too many borrowers, but remains short of a full-fledged student debt jubilee, in order to assuage concerns about fairness. As an added benefit, the option of community service could help to create a new era of volunteerism, rekindling the spirit of connection that comes from doing purposeful civic and community work.

A student debt jubilee, in whatever form it takes, would be a tangible recognition that education is critical to the continued evolution of the economy, especially in a world where other nations, including China, have narrowed the gap or surpassed the West in higher education attainment.

Mortgage debt relief

In the aftermath of the 2008 financial crisis, home values plunged, causing over 10 million of the nation's 52 million mortgages to go underwater, so that the value of their home was at least 10 percent lower than the amount of their remaining mortgage. That 10 million compares to just 1 million mortgages today.

In the throes of that recession, I envisioned a program through which lenders would forgive the underwater portion of mortgages on primary residences. Lenders are loath to write down a mortgage, because they normally have to take the entire write-down as a loss at the moment they take this step. For this reason, I suggested that lenders would stagger or spread the write-down of the underwater portion over thirty years, instead of all at once, in cases where the lender immediately and proportionately reduced the principal on the borrower's mortgage and monthly payment. The lender would still be able to take the tax benefit of the loss in the current period, and the deferred amount would not be subtracted from the lender's capital or reserves. Notably, there was precedent in US regulatory history for mortgage write-down deferrals – the deeply discounted savings and loan mortgage values, and losses upon sale, structured in the early 1980s. To address the fairness issue, I proposed that, in exchange for this restructuring, the borrower would have to give the lender some portion of the gain on the eventual sale of the home, based on a negotiated percentage. If the percentage negotiated were 30 percent, then when the home was sold down the road, the lender would get 30 percent of any gain. This would all be done at the option of the borrower, who would be choosing between a lower payment today but less upside in the future versus the same payment today but full upside in the future.

Clearly, this idea was more suited to the aftermath of the 2008 crisis than to the 2022 context of the pandemic and the war in Ukraine, but something in the same spirit could be customized to pandemic relief.

At the end of 2021, pandemic mortgage payment forbearance programs ended in the US, and deferred mortgage payments had to be paid or otherwise dealt with. Often lenders arranged to tack the deferred amount to the end of the loan. In place of this approach, I would propose a debt jubilee – a program offered, in this case, for a limited and defined period, say, through the end of 2025 – that would allow missed payments and interest, plus up to an additional 20 percent of the principal balance, to be written down at the borrower's option. This would provide significantly lower payments – and thus substantial relief – to borrowers who took advantage of the program. The lender would amortize the write-down over thirty years, get a current tax benefit, and receive equity upside on any sale, with the equity share and lower mortgage payment both negotiated with the borrower.

Healthcare debt relief

Healthcare costs are a bane to US households and the economy. Recent reports suggest that half of all overdue debt on credit reports in the US is tied to medical debt. From high monthly premiums to high deductibles on health insurance, from unexpected healthcare problems to surprise medical bills, healthcare costs and healthcare debt too often descend into a nightmare.

As previously noted, the Fed reported that roughly half of all American adults would have difficulty covering an unexpected $400 expense before the start of the pandemic. It's not surprising, then, that unplanned medical expenses can quickly put a household in arrears on all other debt. The costs can grow so great that some postpone needed medical procedures, which only compounds their future medical problems and costs.

A means-tested program should be introduced whereby individuals with less than a certain level of income, say $85,000, could apply for government reimbursement for any debt incurred for a select number of critical healthcare expenses, including vital procedures to treat diabetes, cancer, and heart disease.

This would benefit households, healthcare providers, lenders, and the economy as a whole, because healthier citizens and diminished bad debt have broad positive effect. A policy like this could deliver some of the core benefits of a national health insurance program without turning the government into the primary, or single, negotiator or payer of healthcare bills.

Small business debt relief

The debt of smaller businesses – those employing perhaps one hundred or fewer employees – more closely resembles personal household debt than the debt of major corporations, because most small businesses are owned by individuals or families. There are at least 10 million such businesses in the US. This kind of debt deserves consideration for jubilee as well.

I would propose debt relief for smaller businesses similar to the mortgage program proposed above – specifically, a temporary and voluntary program of small business debt relief for loans where the enterprise or collateral value has fallen 10 percent or more below the loan value. At the borrower's option, the lender would write down all or part of the difference over a span of thirty years, so long as the terms ensured that the debt was restructured to reduce the principal to the borrower by the same amount. In exchange, the borrower would give the lender a negotiated portion of the gain on any future sale of the business or its key assets.

Reforming bankruptcy law

The US bankruptcy laws function as a structural form of debt forgiveness. In a sense, an individual who files for Chapter 11 bankruptcy is getting a jubilee in the form of a debt reset, or clean slate, albeit with penalties to their credit rating, and thus to their subsequent access to credit. But US bankruptcy laws are in dire need of revision. As currently written, they are clumsy, counterproductive, and, in some respects, defeat the purported objective of restoring the individual to healthy participation in the economy.

In my view, stricter bankruptcy laws have neither reduced credit losses for lenders nor improved the financial health of households. In fact, the tightening of bankruptcy laws in the US over the past twenty years has actually accelerated losses, and may be exacerbating credit losses on an ongoing basis because the stricter laws have made borrowers' struggles all the more harrowing and damaging. Bankruptcy laws that provide balanced, thoughtful relief would result in more measured, prudent, and healthier lending practices and financially healthier households. We need to recognize that bankruptcy serves two purposes: it is a way to cope with untenable financial circumstances as well as a check on the system – a safety valve for households that curbs overly aggressive lending practices.

Nearly 90 percent of families declare bankruptcy for one of three reasons that are in many respects beyond their control: a job loss, a medical problem, or a family breakup. For these reasons, bankruptcy laws should be designed to repair rather than to punish, and should help household borrowers retain their jobs and keep their families together in the future.

Much of the most constructive thinking in this area has been led by Massachusetts Senator Elizabeth Warren, whose area of expertise as a law professor was bankruptcy. Any recommendations for bankruptcy law reform should reflect her research and ideas. Healthy bankruptcy reform should allow:

- borrowers to modify their mortgages in bankruptcy, which is generally prohibited by current law, just like they can negotiate other debts;
- renters in bankruptcy to continue paying their rent if this would avert eviction;
- debtors who are no longer in residence at a home to be released from future liability for taxes and code violations;
- debtors to keep their cars by paying the lender the fair market value of the car over a reasonable time, thus making it easier for them to have transportation to get to their work and care for other members of their household;
- student loans to be discharged in bankruptcy, just like other consumer debts; and

- accumulated local fines and fees to be discharged in bankruptcy, just like consumer debts.

This set of reforms, in full or in large part, would help to truly give families a new start after bankruptcy. Getting households to a place where they can genuinely rebuild their financial lives should be the objective of the law, in recognition of the reality that most individuals enter bankruptcy because of a crisis outside their control.

There should also be more stringent consequences for acts by creditors that are already prohibited, including attempting to collect debts during bankruptcy proceedings and attempting to collect discharged debts after the proceedings have been completed. We should have zero tolerance of harassment for payment of debt that may be or has been discharged. It only puts families into further distress.

All together, these bankruptcy reforms would benefit households, the nation's household debt burden levels, and the health of financial institutions. Everyone benefits – lenders, borrowers, and the economy as a whole, as financial lives are rebuilt.

Moderating the debt bias in tax law

No list of remedies for the rapid rise in debt would be complete without a comment on the disparate tax treatment of debt and equity. Stated simply, under US law, debt gets a tax benefit and equity gets a tax penalty. This is a rather stunning inversion of what an economic system should desire and incent. The inexorable rise in levels of debt could be muted at least somewhat if this were modified or changed.

A curbing of the interest deductions for large businesses and the wealthiest individuals would change the tax advantages of debt and thus the use of debt in the economy in aggregate. For example, all interest deductions for businesses with over a certain level in assets, say $50 million, could be lessened or eliminated. All mortgage interest deductions for loans of over $1 million could be struck from the tax code.

At the same time, the tax disadvantages of stock ownership should be curbed. Eliminating tax on dividends for the bottom 60 percent of households – which is a form of double taxation – would help to encourage stock accumulation among these households.

Debt jubilee programs would provide much-needed boosts to the economy and beneficially reduce the never-ending climb of the economy up the debt staircase.

Reducing household debt, by whatever means, will allow households to more vibrantly participate in the economy. It will revive people's optimism about their economic prospects and give them well-founded hope that they will be able to keep their homes, pay for necessary healthcare, and afford to invest in education for themselves and their children.

Debt jubilees hold the promise of reduced household debt with little or no harm to GDP growth – and likely, instead, a boon to growth in the economy.

REVERSING A LARGE TRADE DEFICIT

On the campaign trail and while he held the presidency, Donald Trump thundered against the evils of the US trade deficit and proclaimed that it would be easy to fix, if only the people in power cared to address it. Yet his tough talk and tariffs did little to change the balance of the equation. When he left the Oval Office in 2021, the US had a *larger* net deficit than when he entered it in 2017.

As we saw in Chapter 2, a trade deficit exists when, on balance, the country as a whole purchases more products and services made in other countries than foreign countries purchase from it. Essentially, that deficit speaks to the relative appeal and desirability of each country's products and services. Viewed this way, the solution to a trade deficit is simple to conceptualize: make more and better products and services that more people in other countries want to buy. Admittedly, this solution is easier to conceptualize than it is to realize.

In his landmark 1990 book *The Competitive Advantage of Nations*, Harvard Business School professor Michael E. Porter observed that the surest signal of a country's competitive advantage relative to others was a high level of exports. It follows that an aggregate net import position would suggest a decline in competitive advantage. For much of the past 150 years, ever since the US seized the mantle of invention and productivity which the UK firmly held during the Industrial Revolution, the US offered superior products and services compared to the rest of the world. But over the past few decades, much of the world has caught up, and then some.

The exports of a country can be measured according to their complexity. Complex products might include such items as robots, high-end computers and telecommunications equipment, high-end medical and surgical devices, specialized industrial equipment, and even genetically engineered biological materials. The Observatory of Economic Complexity, once part of MIT, publishes something called the Export Complexity Index (ECI) which, as its name suggests, measures this. Export powerhouses such as Germany, Japan, and South Korea rank among the highest on the ECI index, with 2020 ratings of 1.88, 2.19, and 1.88, respectively, and rising. The US ranks ninth, with a 2020 index of 1.56, and has declined from a 2011 rating of 1.61. China has risen from 0.78 in 2011 to 0.96 in 2020, which puts it in thirtieth place, but it is rising.

The US average net export surplus has been negative 3.7 percent over the last twenty years, while China's has been a positive 3.3 percent. In fairness, much of China's surplus has historically come from its wage advantage. However, for at least the past decade, China has been shifting from having a wage advantage to having an advantage based on manufacturing prowess. A group of researchers affiliated with the University of California at Berkeley, MIT, and other universities have created a modified version of the ECI adjusted for factors such as overall export volume and the difficulty of exporting certain products, to better understand China's trade advantage. This index, called the ECI+, shows that China is already *first* in the world's trade league charts, and trending *upwards*. The US is fourth and trending down.

The ECI+ analysis speaks directly to the trade deficit dilemma facing the US: given that the most complex and advanced products are likely most in demand and best positioned to command price premiums, countries that manufacture complex products, such as computers, have a decided competitive advantage, and China dominates the manufacture of complex products. Today, even cars and household appliances are computers, so complexity now applies across an ever broader range of products.

In healthcare, certain products are now exponentially more complex, such as manufactured biological and genetically reengineered materials. This is the best area of opportunity for the US and other major, developed economies with a trade deficit problem, such as the UK, to regain ground on the ECI+. For example, Dr. Carl H. June of the University of Pennsylvania opened a new chapter in genetic engineering through a new treatment for cancer called chimeric antigen receptor (CAR) T-cell therapy. Dr. June's first patient was Emily Whitehead, a seven-year-old girl who was fighting the most common childhood cancer, acute lymphoblastic leukemia (ALL), which can be terminal. In 2012, she was treated with CAR T-cell therapy. This required collecting T cells, a type of white blood cell central to immune responses, from Emily's blood and sending them to a lab where they were reprogrammed to attack her cancer tumors.

She then received an infusion with her altered T cells. Within days she was cancer free. Since her treatment, hundreds of patients with ALL have become cancer free, and trials using June's approach have been initiated for dozens of other types of cancer.

In another major genetic engineering breakthrough, in 2012 Jennifer Doudna of the University of California at Berkeley and her colleagues debuted the CRISPR/Cas9 gene editing system. CRISPR technology allows researchers to precisely target, cleave, activate, or silence specific genes – in other words, to genetically edit cells, including human cells. In addition to having many applications in agriculture and food manufacturing, CRISPR offers the prospect of groundbreaking innovation in medical treatments for an unimaginably wide range of maladies (as well as sobering thoughts about the potential for ethically dubious or adverse uses of this new gene-editing power).

Similarly, important mRNA vaccine research that led to the rapid creation of the Covid-19 vaccines was conducted by Drew Weissman and Katalin Karikó of the University of Pennsylvania. The work on mRNA-based vaccines has wide applications; labs are developing approaches to prevent sickle cell anemia, malaria, and a roster of other maladies using them. A more effective vaccine for the flu, which costs the US economy about $10 billion each year, is also in scientists' sights.

Complex biological and healthcare technology products such as CAR T-cell therapy, CRISPR gene editing, and mRNA vaccines demonstrate the vast potential for improving the trade equation without reshoring significant conventional manufacturing from China. If academics and businesses in the US and the UK can invent, manufacture, and own more of these extraordinary things, it will help both economies progress towards trade equilibrium, and perhaps even return to the days of trade surplus. The investment in these areas must be ongoing, however, given that the pace of change in the world is only accelerating.

The US held an outsized lead in global trade beginning in the late 1800s through to the early 1970s, and then it faded. The story of this shift from a trade surplus to a trade deficit originated decades ago, but escalated in the 1990s, particularly with the enactment of the North American Free Trade Agreement (NAFTA) in 1994 and the creation of the World Trade Organization (WTO) in 1995. Many companies presumed that they would be offshoring rote, meaningless manufacturing work and keeping the work of innovation in the US, ensuring that they would continue to reap all the benefits of intellectual property and its worth.

But as manufacturing has become increasingly more complex, manufacturing itself has required innovation and thus generated its own intellectual property, so a major element of China's manufacturing advantage is the intellectual property inherent to building sophisticated things. Because so much electronics manufacturing was offshored, the US now finds, to its chagrin, that it can seemingly no longer muster the skills and knowledge to build things like iPhones – not simply because domestic wages are too high, as some allege, but because of lost manufacturing prowess. In other words, the intellectual property advantage of product development, as compared to 'mindless' manufacturing, has been partially ceded to the manufacturing side for higher-end, higher-priced complex products.

In 1900, 25 percent of US workers were in manufacturing and 25 percent in service. In 1950, 35 percent were in manufacturing and 50 percent in service. Indifference and disregard to the downsides of offshoring, plus acquiescence to legislation like NAFTA, ended in 63,000 American factories closing between 2001 and 2013, taking 5 million jobs with them. Ouch. By 2010, 15 percent of US workers were in manufacturing and 80 percent in service. A similar trajectory can be seen in UK labor statistics, with the manufacturing workforce falling by nearly 40 percent between 1998 and 2010 as the UK offshored jobs and took advantage of the open borders of the EU to find cost-savings in the supply chain. China added 14.1 million jobs over roughly the same period. Thomas Friedman, in his 2005 book, *The World Is Flat*, celebrated the globalization of manufacturing – at the very moment that manufacturing wherewithal was slipping perilously away from the US and the UK. Friedman's widely read paean elided the dark side – some might say, the ravages – of the transformations being wrought by globalization in national economies.

And of course, while the US was progressively offshoring large sections of its supply chain, China was gaining the sophistication in manufacturing intellectual property and skills that are the main drivers of its trade advantage today. That prowess has allowed China to develop extraordinary capabilities in a number of areas, including advanced cellular network technology (5G and 6G), electric vehicles, supercomputers, artificial intelligence, and genetic technology. China has begun to vie with the US for market supremacy in all of these areas.

Historically, the US economy's competitive advantage was tied to sophisticated, complex products and services. It needs to regain that edge. There is no surer path to better and more advanced products than increased levels of basic research and development. But US investment in basic research has declined significantly; funding for the US National Institutes of Health (NIH), the National Science Foundation (NSF), and other government research organizations has declined by more than 60 percent in relation to GDP since the 1960s. The 2022 CHIPS and Science Act should help, by providing $280 billion in funding to boost domestic research and manufacturing, especially in the field of semiconductors. But the work to increase government investment has barely begun.

The innovation to fuel big breakthrough products – products with the sort of widespread benefit, application, and appeal of the iPhone, CAR T-cell therapy, and CRISPR/Cas9 technology – arises out of core research and development typically funded by the NIH, the NSF, and other government research programs. This is because it can take decades of research, with many false starts and dead ends, before a vital new innovation is identified and transformed into a marketable product. The private sector does not have the appetite to take on all of the necessary cost of long-term investment. The government provides the bedrock, and prerequisite, investment for truly radical innovations. If the US wants to close the trade gap, it should double or triple government investment in research and development, well beyond the provisions of the CHIPS Act.

But to reiterate, it is not just investing in and developing new products that is critical to the trade equation. The US also needs to recapture manufacturing prowess, especially as it is now so clear that the triumphalist premise of offshoring was wrong.

In the past decades some analysts have emphasized the labor cost differences between the US and the UK, on the one side, and China and other offshoring destinations, on the other. However, advances in robotics and software have minimized such wage disadvantages, and technological prowess has become the chief consideration when businesses decide where to locate manufacturing in the industries with the most complex, and thus economically desirable, products. The US and the UK have the opportunity to compete for the most coveted and cutting-edge forms of manufacturing, including the manufacture of genetically engineered materials, although much work will need to be done to seize even a share of this potential.

Regardless, any attempted renaissance in research and development must aim to address, and redress, the loss of manufacturing prowess relative to China. Let's say a small start-up has made a discovery about how to build an electrical component so that it delivers revolutionary improvements in cost and efficiency and has decided to get these components manufactured offshore to be competitive, because domestic manufacturing costs twice as much. If the company could also develop automated processes for making the components, then the manufacturing cost disadvantage would decline, but the start-up is unlikely to have the funds to do this, because it requires a daunting and prohibitively expensive investment in engineering and equipment beyond the company's core business. There is some NSF grant funding available for developing automated manufacturing processes like this, but it is not nearly enough. This too needs to be doubled or tripled to propel a rebound in US manufacturing.

It is worth noting that there is a link going forward between a trade surplus and higher wages, especially where that trade surplus is built on more complex products that require high-skilled employees. A trade surplus is evidence of strong demand. It implies a country is making products that people are willing to buy at a higher price. And higher prices are generally a platform for higher wages.

One final note: for lower-end products, the wage difference will always make it more difficult for US and UK manufacturers to compete against offshore alternatives. Success in reshoring should be focused on complex products.

TAMING HIGH INFLATION

Debate and analysis about inflation could fill volumes, and this topic has been covered, in at least some detail, in Chapter 6. So I focus the comments in this section on addressing the energy-related component of inflation.

This makes sense for a variety of reasons, most of all that there is, in fact, a very short list of commodities which have an outsized impact on economic activity, and thus have an outsized impact on inflation. This short list is comprised of oil, natural gas, iron, steel, wheat, and corn. A key historical cause of inflation has been the supply disruption and depletion of these commodities, so understanding their price dynamics can tell us much of what we need to understand the direction of inflation.

Oil and natural gas have played the biggest role in the most recent episodes of inflation – both the inflation of the 1970s and the bout of pandemic inflation that was exacerbated by the war in Ukraine. The price of oil and natural gas impacts the prices we pay for a large number of items and also distorts geopolitics. To be sure, neither Russia's President Vladimir Putin nor the Crown Prince of Saudi Arabia, Mohammed bin Salman, would command anywhere near their current level of global attention were it not for their grip on major parts of oil and gas supply.

The things that could free us from this ugly source of inflation and geopolitical instability are at hand: solar power, wind power, and technologies, such as electric vehicles, which open the way for products previously powered by fossil fuels to be powered by 'green energy' sources instead. The economics of solar power, wind power, batteries, and other green energy technologies has improved markedly over recent decades, making green energy competitive with oil and gas. We are now at a point where a major investment in green energy could radically decrease global dependence on hydrocarbon-based power. In fact, the economics of green energy have improved so much that many such investments now make economic sense.

These investments, if made at a large scale, would liberate economies from a key source of inflation and a major cause of occasional geopolitical risk and enfeeblement – and, as a bonus, they would positively impact the environment. Alternative energy development needs to be near the top of the national to-do list.

BUILDING THE INCOMES AND NET WORTH OF THE BOTTOM 60 PERCENT

Much of this book has focused on the rise in wealth inequality, and, more pointedly, the inevitability of that rise. Wealth inequality has produced an atrophying middle class, with the bottom 60 percent seeing far less of the benefits of GDP growth and carrying a disproportionate share of the debt wealth used to create it, and if wealth inequality is allowed to continue to grow, that proportion will get larger.

I assert that devising policies to buttress the economic position of average working citizens and provide them with a better path for advancement should be the centerpiece of policies to address the problems of debt. At the heart of this would be policies and programs to advance incomes and spread the opportunity for wealth accumulation across more households.

This is a daunting challenge. As others have underscored, the most reliable, time-tested path for someone to be in the top 10 percent of households by income is to be born into the top 10 or 15 percent. The other route is to start a business that becomes an oligopoly or an effective monopoly, with overbearing market power, in some sector of the economy, but most entrepreneurs will not follow in Jeff Bezos's footsteps. By far, most business start-ups fail, and so most working Americans would be better off working for a medium-sized to large corporation with good income growth prospects and good benefits to help offset healthcare costs.

If we want to further boost the net worth of the bottom 60 percent, we therefore need to focus on programs that facilitate and incent the purchase of stock and real estate. Ownership of those two assets, as I demonstrated in Chapter 3, has been key to truly building significant net worth on the household level.

To start with, the US could improve the parameters of the venerable and time-tested individual retirement accounts (IRA) and 401(k) employment-based retirement accounts on a means-tested basis. For examples, limitations on contributions per year and penalties for withdrawals from IRAs could be lifted for those in households with less than $125,000 in annual income. This would give these individuals a chance to accumulate far more in pretax wealth (and entrust them with managing it appropriately). In addition, I would propose offering a further boost by giving a 10 percent tax credit for any stock purchased in an IRA account, subject to a holding period. These changes would facilitate significantly higher family savings and support more rapid accumulation of, and access to, funds for things like a down payment on a home.

For many, net worth tied to real estate will continue to largely be tied to their primary home. Existing programs could be improved to allow for means-tested purchase of homes. More favorable interest rates on home mortgages – for example, an interest rate 1 percent or 2 percent below prevailing rates – could be introduced.

Some might balk at the potential cost of such changes. However, by definition, these policies and programs would not – and could not – be prohibitively expensive in relation to the economy's total GDP, because those households with less than $125,000 in income currently hold only 14 percent of the stocks and real estate in the US. In fact, the collective ownership of stocks and real estate in this group is so modest that, even if the changes I am proposing were much larger, they would not materially alter the revenue or debts of the US, except to the good over the long run.

With these two changes, the stock and real estate ownership percentage for the bottom 60 percent would steadily climb, both in relation to income and to higher income groups. This lower income group's share of ownership in stocks and real estate could grow to 25 percent within a generation. The total value of the net worth of this group has been 60 percent of GDP, but we could expect that it could grow to 80 percent to 100 percent of GDP within a generation or two. That is still modest in comparison to the net worth of the top ten percent, which is 288 percent of GDP, but it would moderate the present trend towards greater inequality, and so, on its own terms, it would be an extraordinarily positive achievement.

Conventional thinking holds that we can build the net worth of the bottom 60 percent and reverse some of the trends towards worsening inequality by expanding welfare, expanding and extending healthcare cost insurance through the Medicare and Medicaid programs, providing a universal basic income (UBI), or dispensing $1,400 checks when events call for it, as during the pandemic. In short, the US government could augment the role, scope, and disbursements of its social safety net. I am in favor of many of these types of efforts. But although social safety net programs prevent individuals from falling further behind, they do not achieve much in terms of increasing their earning power or their net worth. That is in no way intended to discredit the value of these programs, but merely to clarify their purpose and effect. Social safety net programs are crucial to recipients' survival and a minimum quality of life – collectively they are, truly, a *safety net*. They are not primarily designed to help people *advance* financially.

The programs I have put forward would provide means-tested ways to wealth-building asset ownership among lower-income and middle-class households. But what if an individual or family has little or no extra cash? How can we boost their income and help them start to accumulate assets, even if simply in the form of cash? The first, most obvious path – and the most urgent need – is to boost the marketable skills of the millions of people who are currently *under*employed in the economy. Much of this effort needs to be directed towards the segment of the population who, in the past, could have relied on the sorts of well-paying jobs that have been lost to automation, artificial intelligence, new technologies, or offshoring. Many people, aged in their twenties through their sixties, find themselves in jobs that pay half or less of what they or their parents previously made. Much of this underemployment trend in the US correlates with the adverse trend in the US trade deficit.

Automation has steadily replaced jobs that involve rote or repetitive skills in the US since as far back as the nation's founding in 1776, and yet for most of economic history, this has not prevented the upwards march in overall real household incomes. But recent, exponential advancements in software, robotics, and artificial intelligence make this challenge more daunting, and the need to train underemployed individuals in new skills all the more urgent. As but one example, a very large number of Americans work in two occupations – trucking and cashiering – both of which are likely to be heavily if not entirely automated in the coming decades.

The extraordinary irony is that, in 2022, unemployment in the US was low. As the economy recovered from the worst of the pandemic, businesses were unable to fill millions of jobs because they could not find people to fill roles in good-paying fields such as computer programming and technology, electronics, high-skilled healthcare, high-tech construction, building trades, and more. Too many Americans simply lack the appropriate skills to apply for these better jobs, and do not have the time or funding to acquire the skills required to compete for them. Yet, the so-called Great Resignation has made clear that many people are in no hurry to return to low-paying, low-skill jobs post-pandemic.

More people need to have the opportunity to do well on their own. At heart, this is a logistical challenge. As much as we need improvements in the educational system, from the level of pre-school through university, to benefit the economy tomorrow, we have a problem *today*. There is an urgent need to train adults – the wide swaths of workers who hold jobs that are not only inadequately compensated but also hold no potential for income or skills advancement.

The ideal approach would involve a new national skills program. Although there are already scores of government-led, small-scale job training programs in the US, many of which are effective, few are as effective as hoped – and even when considered together, the scale of the training efforts is small relative to the need. Some of these programs date back to the 1990s, when the Clinton administration introduced welfare-to-work reforms; they were effectively faux training programs, designed to give the appearance of training so that welfare recipients could continue to get desperately needed payments, and most of these programs have not been closely tied to the real-time needs of employers.

Only through a large-scale endeavor that leverages the strengths and capacities of vocational and technical schools, private training firms, and other organizations will it be possible to upskill a significant number of individuals in the immediate future. There are already local programs that regularly increase participants' salaries by anywhere from 50 percent to 200 percent upon graduation. In one such course in computer programming, which lasts for less than six months, graduates receive on average two to three times their former salary after the training. This type of training needs to be delivered en masse.

The key is to have the entities who are looking for workers involved in designing the training, so that the training matches their recruitment needs. Employers would need to commit to hiring a specified number of individuals who enter the program, to avoid the all-too-common situation of participants receiving training and then being unable to find a job because the program was not adequately in sync with employers' openings. To support that end, funding for these training programs could go from the government to employers, after an employer makes bona fide job offers to upskilled graduates.

One concern often aired in responses to these types of training schemes is from employers considering the prospect of paying to train a potential employee only to have them leave their company for a competitor's higher wage. This issue has been addressed in other countries through the creation of cooperative intra-industry training programs, where employers pool training resources and collectively commit to hiring graduates.

The typical training program would last six to twelve months. Participants would have all of their training expenses paid for and receive a living wage during the training. To cover situations where people engaged in training happen to live some distance from the need for workers, funding should be made available for both relocation and the establishment of remote working facilities. A successful effort will take advantage of all the pandemic has taught us about remote training and remote work. Through diligent participation in such training, many individuals will earn – and get – a better job, without having to accumulate debt. Yet the payback to the economy promises to be swift and transformative.

The scorecard – the measure of success – would be simple and contain just one figure: how many upskilled individuals land jobs that pay significantly more than their current job after they complete the training.

We should aim high. In the US, a million people should be trained for better jobs a year. And not a million for one year, but a million every year for ten years. This would fundamentally transform the economy, especially if it is coupled with improvements in the education of young people and an investment in lifelong learning and re-learning programs for everyone. Over time, this would build an efficient machine for lifting lower-income households into the middle class, and lifting the incomes of all households in the bottom 60 percent. By my calculations, it should all cost less than $100 billion to $200 billion per year – a bargain considering its potential to transform the lives of a vital part of the US workforce and address social fissures.

The population of the US and other major, developed economies is aging. Lifelong education is not a temporary challenge, nor is this solution meant to be a stopgap for a few years while we wait for well-trained young people to fill the ranks. We have to learn how to train, re-train, and properly utilize the full complement of an aging workforce.

GROWING THE ECONOMY WITHOUT CREATING
MORE DEBT

The last item on my list of policy recommendations is more abstract than the others. I have shown throughout the pages of this book that it takes money to grow an economy, and money is created by debt. I've further demonstrated how, as a consequence of this, debt grows faster than GDP. However, ever-growing debt stultifies economic growth, exacerbates inequality, and brings the risk of financial crisis. All of this provokes an audacious question, or hypothesis: is there a way to grow without debt?

Axiomatically, in contemporary history, money only comes from more debt, but this has not always been the case. In the past, one form of non-debt-based money was the actual printing of new currency; for example, when the Lincoln administration helped to finance the Civil War by printing greenbacks. Greenbacks were not debt in the strict sense because they had no maturity and no convertibility to another form of money, such as gold. Yet, when the US spent that new money, it brought GDP growth. We should not forget, of course, that the Confederacy also printed new currency and had a disastrous experience, with the collapse in the value of Confederate dollars making it impossible for the South to fund its rebellion, primarily because they vastly overprinted this currency, whereas the printing of greenbacks was comparatively moderate. There are other, similar high-profile disasters of this sort. But in spite of the reputation for disaster, economic historians such as Edwin J. Perkins in his magisterial history, *American Public Finance and Financial Services, 1700–1815*, have shown that much of the use of *de novo* currency served its purpose responsibly.

Alternative forms of money and currency creation may be unfamiliar to most today but from the adoption of the US Constitution until well into the nineteenth century, money in the US could be created through many different methods. In fact, in the periods of its greatest growth, the US did not even have a national currency, let alone a monopoly on printing the money circulated in the economy.

Reflexive aversion to different forms of money betrays a lack of knowledge about monetary history. In the earliest decades of the US – a flourishing, high-growth period for the country – banks created most of the currency used in the economy, dispensing it as the proceeds of loans. The US Treasury occasionally issued small-denomination debt that was used explicitly as currency, though the government was loath to call it that. (This sort of Treasury debt was how the government funded part of the War of 1812.)

I submit that an economy where all money is created by debt is structurally unstable, and inherently prone to the very problems this book has described. Figuring out a way to spend without creating debt, or at least debt as we know it, would bring growth that is less inherently unstable.

In particular, the growth that comes from government spending could come instead from a non-debt-based source. All it takes is for the Treasury to sell a non-interest-bearing instrument with no maturity to the Federal Reserve. The Fed would pay for it with a deposit to the Treasury General Account, the operating account of the US government. An instrument that pays no interest and has no maturity is, in essence, not debt; instead, it can be viewed as pure currency or even a type of equity. The US government could then spend the proceeds in exactly the same way that it spends the proceeds of conventional Treasury bond sales. This would be money created without debt.

Let's call this instrument *perpetual money*. It may well be that a balance between debt-based money and perpetual money is a healthier and more technically sound way of managing monetary policy.

The problem with perpetual money is that, unlike government debt, if you create too much of it, it is indeed inflationary. So a government – and a nation – would have to be disciplined in its use. Perpetuals, unlike debt, do not have the accountability mechanism of a maturity and interest payment.

But to address this risk of inflation, the government could simply set parameters on the use of perpetuals, with the key to avoiding inflation caused by perpetuals coming down to their volume. As perpetuals are used, we may very well observe a linear relationship: the more non-debt-based growth, the more inflation. The correct titration of perpetuals into the money stream would limit the threat of inflation. Perpetuals would always need to be used judiciously.

There is nothing stopping a government from creating non-debt-based money if it wants to. This book has shown that having an economic system where growth solely comes from debt is fundamentally problematic, and is part of the inexorable buildup in debt worldwide. This is argument enough for spurring the thoughtful consideration of how perpetuals might be introduced.

This chapter's provocations are intended to spark new policy thinking around the core problems inherent in the paradox of debt – the inexorable rise of debt to income, inflation, the widening inequality gap, and, for some countries, unfavorable trade deficits. There are promising policies to pursue – if we are willing to think beyond the current strictures surrounding money and debt.

EPILOGUE

Debt is the creator and the destroyer.

Debt is often vilified or ignored by politicians and financial media and by politicians – or, to be more specific, government debt tends to be treated as a villain while private sector debt is taken for granted, or treated as an untouchable component of the laissez-faire economy, or worse yet overlooked altogether. Indeed, the Global Financial Crisis of 2008 took most by calamitous surprise because private debt had been overlooked by so many for so long. It was just assumed that the machine would keep going without breaking down.

As we have seen, the role of debt in a modern economy is much more multifaceted and complex than this dichotomy. By using the tools of a debt profile, coupled with other conventional financial tools such as income statements and balance sheets, we can gather a much better understanding of how debt works in an economy and how to address its worse consequences. Taking this approach country by country, macrosector by macrosector, and, where possible, household income strata by strata, it has become clear that debt will always grow in relation to income. This has revealed the paradox of debt: debt builds household net worth while also increasing inequality; it is essential for economic growth and yet, in excess, leads all but inevitably to periodic economic calamity and stagnation. As a result, the paradox of debt portends the certainty of economic challenges and difficulties going forward, unless we are willing to get creative – and ambitious.

Any new set of government policies and programs to address increasing debt must, first and foremost, understand debt's paradoxes. Only by focusing on mitigating the negative dimensions of debt and seizing on debt's positive attributes can we hope to put the economy on the path to better equilibrium in the twenty-first century.

The current context – recovery from the pandemic and the war in Ukraine – makes the need for new ways of thinking all the more urgent. I believe a brighter future awaits, if we leverage our understanding of the paradox of debt to better serve all participants in the economy.

ACKNOWLEDGMENTS

I would like to express my deepest thanks to Dan McShane and his team of analysts and researchers – Michael Grady, Menachem Hauser, and Gary Jarvis. They have worked tirelessly on this and many other of my books and articles, and have developed a profound familiarity and proficiency in US and global macroeconomic data, both in current and historical periods, along with an ever-deepening knowledge of the workings of economic history. This book is the culmination of over a decade of very intense work that we have done in those areas, and their knowledge and insights have made a huge difference in collective progress on the theories and observations herein.

It goes without saying that I have been dependent on the fearless support and guidance of George Owers and his colleagues at Forum Press, as well as the long-standing support of Mary Francis and Penn Press.

I also benefited greatly from discussions with and comments from Michael Lind, François-René Burnod, Andrew Dittmer, Moritz Schularick, and Matthew Baron. In some cases, that took the form of strenuous critique and pushback; in others, extensive review and correction of portions of the manuscript. They are each far more knowledgeable and accomplished than I am, and I learned a great deal from all of them. In all cases, their involvement made me think more deeply about this work and was of enormous help. All errors are of course my own.

I would like to thank Steve Clemons, who has long been my guiding light on all matters national and global, and his husband Andrew Oros, another leading intellectual light, for their guidance on this and so many other things, and for the friendship extended to my wife, Laura, and me.

Most of all, I would like to thank my beloved wife, Laura, and our six children, all now adults – Lauren, Victoria, Sophia, Eric, Davis, and Mikael. Laura is my biggest fan and constant companion, and our kids a source of continual pride and joy.

Appendix A

NOTES ON DATA

HOW WE GOT OUR DATA

Generally, the central government debt information analyzed for this book was readily available. This data about debt is carefully documented by governments and central banks as part of their processes for making and monitoring monetary and economic policy.

In contrast, private sector debt totals, despite usually being appreciably larger, are often much harder to obtain. In many countries, as well as in many earlier periods, there was no imperative to document the total private sector debt in economies. The further back in time you go, the more elusive and sparse the data on private debt becomes. As a good measure of private debt, I have used nonconsolidated, gross debt securities plus loans.

To add to these data woes, the private sector debt data that is available varies from one country to another. Often little or no information on the specific category of private debt is included, so that commercial real estate debt and energy sector debt, healthcare sector debt and technology sector debt, student loan debt and auto loan debt – all are wrapped up together. Where categories of private debt are differentiated, this data can often only be obtained by purchase from a proprietary commercial database. These commercial sources often categorize types of debt differently, or are otherwise misaligned.

The timing of data releases is also a challenge. Analysts can get some government data within a few days of the end of a given month, but key parts of the balance sheet and income data are not available for months, or even a year or more, later.

DATA SOURCES FOR FIGURES

Below I have listed the organizations whose data were used or analyzed to create the figures. Additional detail about these data and data used in other analyses in this book can be found at paradoxofdebt.org.

INTRODUCTION
Figure 0.1. Federal Reserve (Z.1); Organization for Economic Cooperation and Development (OECD); CEIC Data
Figure 0.2. Federal Reserve (Z.1); Bank for International Settlements (BIS); OECD

CHAPTER 1
Figure 1.1. Federal Reserve (Z.1)
Figure 1.2, n/a
Figures 1.3 to 1.5. Federal Reserve (Z.1); Bureau of Economic Analysis (BEA); author's calculations

CHAPTER 2
Figure 2.1. Federal Reserve (Z.1); Standard & Poor's Capital IQ database (S&P); Treasury Direct; New York Fed
Figures 2.2 and 2.3, N/A
Figures 2.4, 2.5, and 2.6. Federal Reserve (Z.1)

Figure 2.7. OECD
Figure 2.8. OECD; Federal Reserve (Z.1)
Figure 2.9. New York Fed; Federal Reserve (Z.1)
Figure 2.10. Federal Reserve (Z.1); S&P

CHAPTER 3

Figure 3.1. Federal Reserve (Z.1); OECD; New York Fed
Figures 3.2 and 3.3. OECD
Figure 3.4. Federal Reserve (Distributional Financial Accounts)
Figure 3.5. Survey of Consumer Finances (SCF); BEA
Figure 3.6. Survey of Consumer Finances (SCF)
Figure 3.7. Congressional Budget Office (CBO)
Figure 3.8. Federal Reserve (Z.1); S&P Dow Jones Indices LLC
Figure 3.9. Federal Reserve (Z.1); Bureau of Economic Analysis (BEA); CEIC Data
Figure 3.10. Bloomberg; Financial Industry Regulatory Authority (FINRA)
Figure 3.11. S&P; Federal Reserve (Z.1)

CHAPTER 4

Figure 4.1. World Bank
Figures 4.2 and 4.3. OECD; CEIC
Figure 4.4. World Inequality Database
Figure 4.5. OECD; CEIC
Figure 4.6. OECD; BIS; CEIC
Figures 4.7 and 4.8. OECD; CEIC
Figure 4.9. OECD; BIS; CEIC
Figures 4.10 and 4.11. Ministry of Statistics and Programme Implementation (MOSPI); CEIC Data
Figure 4.12. BIS; CEIC Data
Figures 4.13, 4.14, and 4.15. OECD; BIS; CEIC
Figures 4.16, 4.17, and 4.18. CEIC Data; OECD

Appendix B
GLOSSARY

BALANCE SHEET

A balance sheet, or statement of condition, is a document that summarizes the overall financial condition of a business, person, or other entity at a given point in time, usually at a year's end, though it could be at any date. The statement is usually divided into three sections – assets, liabilities, and net worth. Net worth is the difference left after subtracting liabilities from assets.

BANK

A bank is a financial institution licensed by the government to take current checking and savings deposits as well as make loans. Banks also provide related services such as individual retirement accounts (IRAs).

Banks can create money by lending, with the proceeds of the loan deposited in the borrower's account or conveyed as a payment to an entity designated by the borrower.

Banks may be regulated by the government (national or local) or by non-governmental regulators that are appointed by the government.

There are several types of banks, including retail banks and commercial or corporate banks, but typically licensure and regulation by the government is required to qualify as a 'bank' as compared to being a non-bank lending institution – the so-called shadow banking sector.

BANKING CRISIS

See 'Financial crisis'.

BIG 7

My term for the seven largest economies in the world – the US, the UK, China, France, Germany, Japan, and India.

CAPITAL

Capital means a variety of things. It is often used today to describe both debt and equity, which are two very different things. In this book, however, I use the term 'capital' in a very specific way. It refers to the financial value of a person, business, government, or country after liabilities are subtracted from assets. Thus, for our purposes, it is effectively synonymous with net worth. (See also 'Net worth'.)

Capital has a variety of other valid but less specific meanings that are not encompassed by its use in this book, including:

- wealth in the form of assets, especially money, that is owned by a person or organization, or available for a specific purpose, such as starting a company;
- anything that confers value or benefit to its owners, such as a factory and its machinery, intellectual property such as patents, or the financial assets of a business or an individual;
- business capital derived from debt; or
- specialized terms that are nevertheless different than the meaning we intend, including working capital, debt capital, and trading capital.

CAPITAL FORMATION

Technically, 'capital formation, gross fixed' is also known as 'gross fixed investment'. As defined by the Organisation for Economic Cooperation and Development (OECD): 'Gross fixed capital formation (GFCF), also called "investment", is the acquisition of produced assets (including secondhand assets), including the production of such assets by producers for their own use, minus disposals. The relevant assets are those that are intended for use in the production of other goods and services for a period of more than a year, such as equipment, tools, transportation assets, and real estate, during an accounting period for a particular country. The term "produced assets" means that only those assets that come into existence as a result of a production process are included. It therefore does not include, for example, the purchase of land and natural resources. This indicator is available in different measures: GFCF at current prices and current PPPs [see below] in US dollars, and annual growth rates of GFCF at constant prices, as well as quarterly data for percentage change over previous period and percentage change over the same period the year before. All OECD countries compile their data according to the 2008 System of National Accounts (SNA). The indicator at current prices and current PPPs is less suited for comparisons over time, as developments are not only caused by real growth, but also by changes in prices and PPPs.'

The majority of capital formation is financed by debt. Too much capital formation in a short period can lead to oversupply and the inability of borrowers to repay debt they have used to finance investment.

Producing more goods and services can lead to an increase in national income levels. Too much capital formation can lead to temporary excess and economic difficulty, because the majority of capital formation occurs through the use of debt.

CURRENT ACCOUNT BALANCE

See 'Trade balance'.

DEBT

Something, typically money, that is owed or due, and governed by a contract, explicit or implicit. At a conceptual level, debt – which is another word for a loan – brings money from the future into the present, in essence by providing the borrower with their future projected income or revenue today, in exchange for a time-based contractual obligation to pay for the associated time value and risk. Debt is the primary mechanism for accessing that future income.

DEPOSITS

A sum of money put in a bank account, to be used to make payments or to receive interest. See also 'Money'.

EQUITIES

See 'Stocks'.

FINANCIAL CRISIS, ALSO CALLED A BANKING CRISIS

A systemic financial crisis occurs when many banks in a country have serious solvency or liquidity problems at the same time – usually due to high levels of bad debt. More specifically, a systemic banking crisis is when a country's non-financial businesses, households, or financial institutions face great difficulties repaying debt contracts on time and, as a result, loan losses increase sharply and a high percentage of the aggregate banking system capital is exhausted. This situation may be accompanied by depressed prices for assets such as common stock and real estate, often after steep run-ups in those prices before the crisis. In some cases, the crisis is triggered by depositor runs on banks, though in most cases the crisis begins with a general realization that systemically important financial institutions are in distress.

Banks are susceptible to a range of risks. These include credit risk (loans and other assets turn bad and cease to perform) and liquidity risk (withdrawals exceed the available funds).

In a financial crisis, banks either fail or have to be rescued, generally by the government. These crises can extend to include other types of lenders, including non-bank mortgage lending companies.

GDP, OR NATIONAL INCOME

For our purposes, it is useful to think of GDP as the aggregate income in an economy, or the aggregate spending in an economy – two totals that are normally very close to each other in almost all countries. There is more to it than that, but not a lot more, and conceiving of it in this way is useful in thinking through the issues presented in this book.

GDP provides an economic picture of the size and growth rate of a country's economy, generally measured in three ways, by using expenditures, production, or incomes, and then often adjusted for inflation and population to provide additional insights. Real GDP takes account of the effect of inflation while nominal GDP does not.

Not all productive activity is included in GDP, such as unpaid or illicit work. These are difficult to measure and value.

GDP does not take into account the depreciation on the machinery, buildings, and other capital stock used in production. Net domestic product is gross domestic product less depreciation.

GDP calculations in most countries follow the established international standards in the System of National Accounts (1993) compiled by the European Commission, the International Monetary Fund (IMF), the OECD, the UN, and the World Bank.

GOVERNMENT DEBT

Government, or public, debt is the total outstanding debt – bonds and other securities – of a country's central government. For our purposes, it also includes the debts of state, regional, and local governments.

Central government debt for the US and certain other major, developed countries is different from state and local debt in that the central government is not mandated to balance its budget, whereas most state and local governments are. Further, central governments issue the currency and effectively control the central bank, and thus have the privilege of paying debt by issuing currency, having debt financed by purchases from the central bank, and generally having more credit to refinance existing debt.

INCOME STATEMENT

An income statement, also known as a 'profit and loss (P&L) statement' or 'statement of revenue and expense', is one of the three important financial statements used for reporting a company or individual's financial performance over a specific accounting period, the other two statements being the balance sheet and the statement of cash flows.

As calculated in this book the income statement is prepared on a cash basis, so any receipt is income and any disbursement, including a paid dividend, is an expense. So the purchase of a house would be a deduction from income for the buyer and an increase in income for the seller (but it is not a cash flow statement!).

An income statement can also be prepared on an accrual basis, in accordance with generally accepted accounting principles (GAAP). On an accrual basis, the purchase of a house would be recorded as an asset and added to the balance sheet but not subtracted from income. The items subtracted from income related to the purchase of a house would be things such as interest expense on any associated mortgage loan.

INVESTMENT

In economic analysis, investment is typically looked at on a grossed fixed basis, also called 'gross fixed capital formation'. For this more technical meaning, see 'Capital formation'.

LENDERS

Generally, the term 'lender' refers to an entity whose primary function is to lend money to households, businesses, or other institutions. The term encompasses banks but also non-banks such as mortgage companies, student lenders, business development companies, and a host of other companies.

LEVERAGE

Leverage is the use of borrowed money. Increased leverage means the increased use of borrowed money. Deleveraging means either the reduction of borrowed money or the increase in revenue and income relative to the amount of borrowed money. Releveraging means increasing the relative level of debt in a country or for an individual, business or other entity from a lower level to a higher level previously recorded.

LIABILITIES

A liability is something owed or borrowed, usually but not always money, by a person, company, or other entity. Liabilities are the opposite of assets, which are things owned. Liabilities can include such things as loans, accounts payable, warranties or guarantees, and can also mean a legal or regulatory risk or obligation.

Debt is one type of liability. The main difference between liability and debt is that liabilities encompass all of an entity's financial obligations, while debt is only those obligations associated with outstanding loans. Thus, debt is a subset of liabilities.

MACROSECTOR

One of the five key subsegments of an economy, namely households, non-financial businesses, financial institutions, government (including national, state, local, and national governments), and the 'rest of the world' (ROW), which is the sum of financial activity between a given country and all other countries.

MARGIN DEBT

Margin debt is the debt of a brokerage customer. When buying securities through a broker, investors can use a cash account and cover the entire cost of the investment, or use a margin account, with which they borrow part of the initial capital from their broker. The part the investors borrow is known as margin debt, while the portion they pay for themselves is the equity or margin.

US Federal Regulation T sets the initial margin at a minimum of 50 percent, which means an investor can only take on margin debt of 50 percent of the account balance. Meanwhile, the typical margin requirement is 25 percent, meaning that customers' equity must be above that ratio in margin accounts to prevent a margin call. The use of margin debt, a form of leverage, can increase returns, but also increase losses.

MONEY

Money is another term that has a wide variety of definitions. Generally, money is a system of value that facilitates the exchange of goods and services. Most money systems are controlled by central banks which use standardized currencies.

For the purposes of this book, I use the Federal Reserve's definition of M2, the most commonly used measure of the money supply: M2 is a measure of the US money stock that includes M1 (currency and coins held by the non-bank public, checkable deposits, and travelers' checks) plus savings deposits (including money market deposit accounts), small-time deposits under $100,000, and shares in retail money market mutual funds. See also 'Deposits'.

NET INCOME

Net income, also called 'net earnings', for a business is calculated as sales minus cost of goods sold, selling, general and administrative expenses, operating expenses, depreciation, interest, taxes, and other expenses. This number appears on a company's income statement. It is a useful number for investors to assess how much the revenue of an organization exceeds its expenses, and thus indicates a company's profitability.

For an individual, net income is income from all sources minus all expenses.

NET WORTH

Net worth is assets minus liabilities. It is in a sense a current expression of the future income from the assets owned by a person, business, or other entity, after deducting for debt obligations. It is, in some sense, the present value of future income of things owned, net of future obligations due to be paid on those things. See also 'Capital'.

NOMINAL VALUE, VERSUS REAL VALUE

The nominal value of any economic statistic means the actual prices that exist at a given time. The real value is the nominal value adjusted for inflation.

NON-FINANCIAL BUSINESSES

Non-financial businesses are entities which are *not* primarily in the business of lending money to, or investing money for, others. (Lending activity is primarily the purview of banks, other lenders, and certain investment management firms.) Non-financial businesses include businesses in the legal form of a corporation as well as non-corporate businesses such as partnerships and sole proprietorships.

A non-financial corporation is an entity whose principal activity is the production of market goods or non-financial services. Non-financial corporations include the following entities: legally constituted corporations, branches of non-resident enterprises, quasi-corporations, notional resident units owning land, and resident non-profit institutions that are market producers of goods or non-financial services.

PRICE-TO-EARNINGS RATIO (P/E RATIO)

The price-to-earnings ratio is the ratio of a company's current share price relative to its earnings per share. It is also known as the price multiple or the earnings multiple. P/E ratios may be estimated on immediate past or future earnings.

P/E ratios are used to determine the relative value of a company's shares to the shares of other companies or to its own past or projected performance. The P/E ratio of an entire market can be used to compare it to other markets or to performance over time.

PRIVATE SECTOR DEBT

Private sector debt, often shortened to 'private debt', is the aggregate debt of businesses and households, including business inventory loans, commercial real estate loans, household mortgages, credit card debt, student loans, auto loans, and much more. That is the functional definition I use in this book. In a more expanded sense, however, it also includes financial debt and accounts receivable and payable.

Technically, it is misleading to label the debt of businesses and individuals in China as private sector debt. You might more accurately call it 'non-central and non-local government debt'. I use the term 'private sector debt' with respect to this category of debt in China for convenience, because it is conceptually equivalent to private sector debt in the other countries of the Big 7.

PURCHASING POWER PARITY (PPP)

One popular way of conducting macroeconomic analysis is to compare measures such as GDP and debt between countries by converting currencies using the purchasing power parity method. This is an alternative to the currency exchange method, which simply converts values at the rate that the countries' currencies can be commercially exchanged.

The purchasing power parity method compares different countries' economic statistics by developing a select list of goods in specified quantities – called a 'basket of goods' – that is used as a metric for how much can be purchased with each currency.

The two methods yield similar values among developed Western economies but yield fairly different values in the case of China and less developed countries. Using the currency exchange method, the US has a larger GDP than China. Using the PPP method, China's GDP is larger.

REAL VALUE

See 'Nominal value versus real value'.

REST OF THE WORLD (ROW)

The rest of the world sector is a grouping of entities without any characteristic functions and resources other than that they are engaged in financial transactions with the domestic entities of a specific country. It represents the sum of transactions of all foreign entities with all entities in a country.

STATEMENT OF CONDITION

See 'Balance sheet'.

STOCKS

A stock, also known as 'equity', represents the ownership of a fraction of the issuing corporation. Stocks are also called 'shares' because ownership of them entitles you to a proportion of the corporation's net worth. The current value of a stock can vary widely, is subject to many variables, and is one of the most important factors in regards to a given company. It can reflect the straightforward equation of assets minus liabilities, and thus be the effective equivalent of net worth, or it can be the present value of all the future projected earnings of that company, and therefore a reflection of current beliefs in the projection of that company's earnings and of future interest rates, which discount those earnings to the present.

Stocks are largely bought and sold on stock exchanges, though they can also be privately held by a single investor or very small group of investors. They are a widely owned investment.

Stock trades have to abide by government regulations meant to protect investors from fraud.

TRADE BALANCE

A country's trade balance is a subset of its current account balance. A country has a trade deficit when the entities within it spend more on imports than they sell as exports. It has a trade surplus when the entities within it spend less on imports than they sell as exports. A trade balance is the general term, encompassing both deficits and surpluses.

The current account balance is a broader measure than the trade balance. A national current account deficit is when a country sends more money abroad than it receives from abroad, and a surplus is when it receives more money from abroad than it sends abroad. The current account balance includes numbers such as income, transfers, foreign remittances, foreign aid, and international investment.

The trade balance is usually the largest component of the current account balance, but not always. It is also possible for a country to have a current account deficit when it has a trade surplus, but that is highly unusual.

At the end of 2020, the US had the world's largest current account deficit while China had the world's largest current account surplus.

Appendix C

LIST OF SUPPLEMENTAL APPENDICES ONLINE

Appendices D through J can be found at paradoxofdebt.org.

NOTES

1 To make these comparisons, currencies of other countries were converted to US dollars on an exchange-rate basis.

2 I have used select terms of economics and finance in very specific ways in this book. Among these terms are 'money', 'capital', 'debt', and 'balance sheet'. Effort has been made to explain uses of terms when they are introduced in the text. Readers may also consult the glossary in Appendix B.

3 My colleagues and I have most frequently used data from the OECD to compare balance sheets and income statements for the Big 7 economies. The OECD gathers data from each country's central bank and presents financial accounts data using the System of National Accounts 2008 accounting standard published by the UN, European Commission, the International Monetary Fund (IMF), and the World Bank. I have also used data from Eurostat, the UK Office for National Statistics (ONS), select commercial databases, and other sources. Readers should treat statistics from the People's Bank of China and the Reserve Bank of India with caution, as their central banks are not independent of political authorities. More information on data sources can be found in Appendix A. Supplemental data analyses available online are listed in Appendix C.

4 Because LoanLand has ten people in it rather than a single person, it is a group and thus avoids the 'fallacy of composition' issue, where it is mistakenly assumed that beneficial behavior for an individual is also beneficial for a group.

5 If John Doe repays the $100,000 loan, whether voluntarily or because his lenders called the loan, deposits in the system will be reduced by that amount, meaning that the money supply will fall by that amount. Loans will also be reduced by that amount. If, for example, a store relies on a loan for inventory to stock its shelves, or an individual relies on a mortgage loan to own their home, and the lender forces repayment of that loan, that store will likely have to close and the individual will likely have to sell their home. That was a major factor in the Great Depression.

6   A key adjustment to Figure 1.3 is a timing adjustment for the fact that much of the huge amount of the debt issued for Covid relief programs was raised a year before it was spent. The data used in this figure and others in the book can be found in Appendix A and the supplemental appendices available online are listed in Appendix C.

7   Banks can also sell Treasury securities to the Fed, but that creates new bank reserves instead of new deposits.

8   The money 'raised' by the US government in this way goes into the Treasury's account at the Federal Reserve, and this account is not counted in the M2 total.

9   I might better say, 'Government spending creates money, but Treasury debt issuance drains money.' That is, if debt is issued first, money is drained from the economy and is then replenished by government spending. The US Treasury is required by law to pre-fund spending, but this is not true of all the countries under discussion. For example, the UK's Treasury has a contingent overdraft facility at the Bank of England, known as the 'ways and means' overdraft, which has the effect of combining Treasury debt issuance with central bank purchase, in effect an OMO, which creates money as all OMOs do. This is called *debt monetization*. It is arguably what central banks did during the pandemic, and what the Bank of Japan has been doing for years, whereby the government issues debt and the central bank immediately buys it, creating money immediately.

10   A complete reconciliation of the year-to-year creation of deposits from 1972 to 2020 can be found in supplemental Appendix E. Deposit Creation, available online at paradoxofdebt.org.

11   The non-financial business macrosector includes corporations and other businesses, such as, for example, incorporated energy and resource firms, agriculture, forestry and fishing businesses, manufacturers, companies engaged in distribution of products (wholesalers and retailers), entities engaged in construction and real estate, transportation services, and other non-financial services (professional, scientific and technical services), as well as information and cultural services.

12   Unlike the US, LoanLand has no margin requirement for buying stock. In the US, a stock buyer must pay for half of a stock purchase out of their own cash – that is, only half of a purchase can be funded by loans.

13   Using our method for calculating country net worth, this scenario would also increase total country net worth by $20,000. Using a different method (which subtracts stock valuations from the net worth of non-financial businesses as a liability), there would instead be no change in total country net worth. See Note 24 for a comparison of net worth calculations.

14 All methods would count the $5,000 in total country net worth. See the country net worth discussion in Note 24.

15 Farmer Jack's travails underscore a technical point regarding the difference between the *financial economy* and the *real economy*. Many economists would note that some of the debt-based wealth creation mentioned here is solely financial and not matched by an increase in the real economy. They argue that there is a real economy that reflects the actual production of an economy and the actual standard of living of its people as apart from the financial recording of that production and standard of living. Jack's farm shows this because he *did* produce more. These economists would further note that there are production limits in the real economy which come into consideration and which may not exist in the financial economy. This does not change my basic observation and conclusions because my primary focus is the financial dimension of money and debt.

16 These global and country debt totals do not include accounts receivable, which can be considerable in amount. Further, they do not include financial services debt, because that would 'double count' debt. However, Appendix G. Income Statements and Statements of Condition for the Big 7, by Macrosector, Including Accounts Receivable and Payable and Financial Company Debt, available online at paradoxofdebt.org, includes both accounts receivable and financial services debt for a number of these countries. The debt of the financial institutions macrosector was $18.1 trillion in 2021. Debt growth in this macrosector largely comes from funding of private sector loan growth – the other side of the balance sheet, if you will, since financial companies make most of the loans to the household and business sectors.

17 This is a cash income statement, as will be explained more fully in Chapter 4.

18 Some economists further argue that because household saving finances government debt, there is some 'crowding out' of household consumption, or of non-financial business investment. But as I see it, government debt in essence finances itself. The private sector has to write checks to buy government bonds, but the government spending enabled by the bonds usually occurs almost immediately afterward and, dollar for dollar, replaces the deposit used to buy the bond. Consumption in the private sector is largely funded by the creation of new money through bank lending. After forty years of high growth in both government and private sector debt, I think we can safely observe that neither crowds out the other.

19 These income statements are prepared on a cash basis, so the purchase of a new home is counted as an expense in the year it was built, as discussed more fully in Chapter 4.

20 It is worth noting that income received by households is first deposited in a bank account but then can be used for other things, such as buying stock, so an exact reconciliation of income and expenditures requires more detailed information.

21 I use the terms 'stocks', 'company shares', 'equities', 'equity assets', 'ownership', and 'equity ownership' interchangeably in these pages. All refer to ownership of shares of stock in companies.

22 Incidentally, there are at least two major asset types that are not individually accounted for in my data and which may not be fully captured: gold and cryptocurrency. However, my colleagues and I do not believe their inclusion would materially affect our analysis or my arguments in this book.

In 2022 gold's global value was estimated to be $12.5 trillion. The data used for this book directly accounts for only $500 billion in household ownership of gold, mostly in the form of jewelry. It is assumed that the remaining global gold assets are partially captured and included in various kinds of investments.

In 2022 global cryptocurrency holdings were estimated to be $1 trillion, with less than $50 billion owned by US residents. The Federal Reserve financial accounts data used for this book currently does not capture household cryptocurrency wealth.

In the accounts of both non-financial businesses and financial institutions, both gold and cryptocurrency assets would be categorized as 'miscellaneous assets'.

23 Even with its negative net worth, the US federal government has certain financial and non-financial assets, mostly consisting of its operating account, a sort of 'checking account', at the Federal Reserve, called the Treasury General Account; student loans it has made; and buildings and lands it owns. The Fed does not capture or report some portion of the government's land holdings, which, if taken into account, would reduce the size of its negative net worth, at least to some extent.

24 There are at least three different ways to combine the balance sheets and net worth of the domestic macrosectors to derive a total country net worth. This is a challenging equation, notably from the complexities of the financial institutions macrosector, which contains not only lenders but also investment companies whose balance sheets are intertwined with households and public corporations. There are a few methods which can be used to avoid double-counting equities and other assets and liabilities in a total net worth calculation.

First, the Federal Reserve's B.1 table 'Derivation of net wealth' derives total US net worth by adding all of the sectors' non-financial assets together, along with the market value of public corporations, and net financial position with the ROW. The Fed's table does not add in any domestic financial assets or liabilities and assumes they net to zero, which just leaves the value of non-financial assets and of equities.

Another, different method adds together the household macrosector and the government macrosector but does not add in the non-financial business and financial institution macrosectors, with the assumption that their entire value resides in the common stock held by the household sector. This is a reasonable and defendable approach.

The OECD uses a third method, adding all domestic macrosectors together, which includes all equity value of non-financial businesses and financial institutions as a liability for those macrosectors, because the asset value is captured in the stocks held by households and others. This method could inflate the asset and liability totals as a whole, but the entries will net out in the net worth calculation. This is also a reasonable and defendable approach, and is the one I use in the analysis in this book. It explains the low or negative net worth of the non-financial business macrosector, since it results in a situation where the higher the value of stocks held, the greater the amount that needs to be subtracted from non-financial business net worth.

These three approaches are different but lead in a similar direction as regards overall trends and conclusions.

25 The current account deficit primarily refers to the trade deficit plus net international transfers of capital.

26 This includes partnerships, limited liability companies, sole proprietorships, and non-corporate farms.

27 These warnings have included fears of crowding out – the view that there is a limited amount of money to lend, and the more people who seek to borrow, the higher rates will go and the less money will be available to lend to others. But as we have seen, lending creates money.

28 Because the original scenario in Chapter 1 had only ten people living in LoanLand, Laura by herself represents the top 10 percent. However, the example would work just as well if LoanLand's population grew and any other owners of shares in Laura's Supermarket were also members of the top 10 percent. If LoanLand is like the US and most other countries, the odds are very high that they would be.

29 Unfortunately, while India merits close attention, there is a paucity of macroeconomic data available for the country, as we shall see later in this chapter.

30 A more complete set of income and balance sheet statements for each country can be found in Appendix G. Income Statements and Statements of Condition for the Big 7, by Macrosector, Including Accounts Receivable and Payable and Financial Company Debt, available online at paradoxofdebt.org.

31 Population growth is favorable in the sense of its impact on GDP growth. There are other issues to consider, notably environmental impact.

32 Data for China is not as current as for the other countries in the Big 7 because it is slower in releasing it.

33 Note that the term 'private debt' is a misnomer when used in the context of China, since much of the debt is state-owned. For our purposes, it means debt tied to the balance sheets of households, non-profit institutions serving households, and non-financial businesses including state-owned enterprises.

34 Comparisons also raise questions as to whether to use a currency exchange method or a purchasing power parity method, how to properly account for inequity in wealth distribution, whether valuations of privately held stocks are comparable to publicly traded stocks, and this list goes on. Fortunately, there has been much noteworthy scholarship where revised valuations have been established for many of these issues. Such debates will long continue, with the outcome of better data and more instructive and useful analysis.

35 More complete comparative data of total country net worth and other line items is available in supplemental Appendix H. Comparison of Big 7 Net Worth, available online at paradoxofdebt.org.

36 Both approaches can be seen in supplemental Appendix I. Big 7 Charts by Purchasing Power Parity and Currency Exchange, available online at paradoxofdebt.org.

37 Insurance and pension assets are shown in Appendix G online at paradoxofdebt.org.

38 As of this writing, the US balance sheet and income statement for the fourth quarter of 2022 and full year-end figures were not yet available. Stocks for the full year were down 8.8 percent.

39 It should be noted that this ratio went haywire in 1931, 1932, and 1933, due to the collapse of the denominator, GDP.

40 Despite my misgivings, I use the term 'cycle' in this chapter to describe the general, recurring processes of GDP growth and debt growth. The term is too well established in the economic literature to discard it altogether.

41 The War of 1812 cost the US between $90 and $160 million – a lot, but less than the cost of the Revolutionary War. US GDP had increased sixfold between the end of the Revolution and the War of 1812, so the costs of this war were also much more manageable to bear.

42 Readers interested in a more extensive discussion of debt relief and forgiveness may refer to my 2021 book, *The Case for a Debt Jubilee.*

INDEX

Great Depression, 18, 30, 54, 174,
178, 190, 194, 196, 206, 209
Great Resignation, 251
Greece, 114
Greenspan, Alan, 208
Gross Domestic Product (GDP),
definition of, 12–13, 269

H

Hawaii, 175
Hayes, Rutherford B., 204
healthcare debt relief, 235
"Hung Forties," 203
hyperinflation. *see* inflation

I

income statement, definition of, 270
incremental transaction model, 14
India, 87–88, 92, 98, 103–105, 133,
135, 140, 170, 266
Indonesia, 194
Industrial Revolution, 198, 240
inflation, 8, 25, 55–56, 64, 66, 83,
151–152, 156, 157, 174, 194,
212–214, 217, 221, 269, 273
1970s energy crisis, 156
causes of, 169
and commodities, 246–247
fear of, 159–162
frequency of, in the United States,
162–165
hyperinflation, 194
and interest rates, 153
measures against, 246–247
and OMOs, 164–167
during pandemic, 101
and perpetual money, 256–257

relationship to debt, 130
relationship to GSCPI, 171
relationship to student debt, 231
Ukraine war, 169–170
Inflation Reduction Act, 159
initial public offerings (IPOs), 77
Institutes of Health (NIH), 244
Iranian Revolution, 163
Israel, 163, 228
Italy, 87

J

Jackson, Andrew, 203
Japan, 24, 88, 106–110, 136, 139,
140, 145, 169, 175–177, 213,
218–219, 240
1990s financial crisis, 175–177
government debt, 108–109,
218–219
Lost Decade. *see* Lost Decade
stimulus, 166
total debt, 106–108, 210
June, Carl H., 241–242

K

Karikó, Katalin, 242

L

lenders, definition of, 271
leverage, definition of, 271
liabilities, definition of, 271
Lincoln, Abraham, 254
local government financing vehicles
(LGFVs), 117, 124
Lost Decade, 24, 60, 107
Lost Generation. *see* Lost Decade